Green Gone Wild

Green Gone Wild

Elevating Nature
Above Human Rights

M. David Stirling

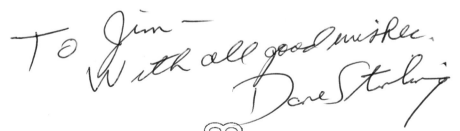

MERRIL PRESS
BELLEVUE, WA 98005

Green Gone Wild © 2008

By M. David Stirling

All Rights Reserved.

Green Gone Wild

is published by

Merril Press, P.O. Box 1682, Bellevue, WA 98009.

Web: www.merrilpress.com

Phone: 425-454-7008

Distributed to the book trade by

Midpoint Trade Books, 27 W. 20th Street, New York, N.Y. 10011

Web: www.midpointtradebooks.com

Phone: 212-727-0190

FIRST EDITION

LIBRARY OF CONGRESS CATALOGING-IN-PUBLICATION DATA
STIRLING, M. DAVID, 1940-
  GREEN GONE WILD : ELEVATING NATURE ABOVE HUMAN RIGHTS / M. DAVID
STIRLING.
    P. CM.
  INCLUDES INDEX.
  ISBN 978-0-936783-53-6 (PBK.)
  1. DEEP ECOLOGY. 2. GREEN MOVEMENT. 3. ENVIRONMENTALISM. 4. POLITICAL
ECOLOGY. I. TITLE.
GE195.S75 2008
333.72--DC22

                    2008002063

PRINTED IN THE UNITED STATES OF AMERICA

Table of Contents

PREFACE

THE REAL-LIFE STORIES that gave rise to this book became familiar to me only after I joined Pacific Legal Foundation in 1999. For as long as I can remember, incidents of people being unjustifiably pushed around or mistreated by government have troubled me. My concern was not for people who committed crimes or knowingly engaged in serious violations of the civil laws, but for those who were confronted with, or may have run afoul of, questionable, ill-founded, or unfair laws, where government's enforcement practices were selective, unnecessarily excessive, and imposed onerous financial burdens.

During my 20 years of working in various positions of authority in government – two of them with supervisory oversight responsibilities for attorneys and other regulatory personnel with power to bring the weight of the government down on those they suspected or charged with violations of law – I had the daily opportunity to observe how formidable that power could be. While I regularly tried to temper their activist inclinations where I believed it excessive, unreasonable, or counterproductive, it was a daunting and ongoing task and one that ran contrary to the institutional mind-set of government and how it perceived its role. It is what Thomas Jefferson had in mind when he warned that "[t]he natural progress of things is for liberty to yield and government to gain ground."

For several years I had been familiar with the good work of Pacific Legal Foundation in defending private property rights and advocating for balanced and commonsense environmentalism in the courts. But it wasn't until I joined the Foundation and got close to the legal cases the attorneys were working and arguing in the courts that I recognized how well-founded my earlier concerns about government heavy-handedness had been. In fact, it was worse than I had realized. From the beginning, one federal law and its enforcement in particular stood out to me as most representative of my earlier concerns about harsh and overreaching government. It was the Endangered Species Act of 1973 (ESA).

Because the ESA and its widening impact on people intrigued me, I began to collect PLF's ESA case reports, newspaper and magazine articles on the subject, and other real-life accounts of people losing their lives, their jobs and businesses, and the reasonable use of their property in order to save a so-called endangered or threatened plant or wildlife species. I also read several books on biological science from different perspectives to try to understand whether, or to what extent, the science on which the ESA is based and implemented is well-founded.

One day not long after an ESA article I wrote was published, I received a letter written in the elderly hand of Dr. J. Gordon Edwards, Ph.D., Professor Emeritus of Entomology, San Jose State University. He enclosed one of his many earlier written articles on biological subjects – this one about the politicalization of the modern environmental movement. He asked if I might like to receive other articles he had written on biological subjects, including the Endangered Species Act. And so, every couple months over the next year I received another of Dr. Edwards' articles, including the chapter he authored for a major textbook publisher, describing the lack of good science behind the ESA. There was always an explanatory cover letter which closed with an encouraging note about the good work PLF was doing in court by trying to limit the reach of the scientifically flawed ESA. As I came to appreciate the value of Dr. Edwards' expertise and special insights into this subject that I found so compelling, the idea of this book was conceived. I soon recognized that it was a book that needed to be written.

I am grateful to Dr. Edwards who never wavered in his commitment to the true biological definition of "species." Although he is gone now, I like to think that through his handwritten letters and copies of his articles, he was encouraging me to tell the whole story. I believe he would have had a good chuckle over the title.

My thanks to Lloyd Billingsley who performed the substantive editing of my manuscript with great skill and creativity. His efforts vastly enhanced my presentation and made it more powerful.

I am most appreciative to Donna Greene of the PLF staff for her keen knowledge and skills in the writing of the English language. She was my technical editor extraordinaire.

My thanks also to Catharina Gonzales of the PLF staff for her many quick responses to my urgent calls for help over the strange and frequent tricks my computer meanly played on me during the writing.

My thanks also to PLF legal secretary Tawnda Elling who converted most of the nearly 500 footnotes appearing in the manuscript text into endnotes.

I especially would like to thank the PLF attorneys for their tireless dedication to the ideas of limited government, private property rights, and environmental balance and common sense. Their effective efforts to establish legal precedent in the federal and state courts that recognizes and protects those critical undergirdings of freedom not only served to inform many of the stories related in this book, but are daily an inspiration to thousands of others in America who are the victims and potential victims of government's ever-increasing intrusiveness into our lives, livelihoods, and property.

Finally, it is with continued sadness that I remember our friend and PLF Star attorney, Russ Brooks, who passed away of a sudden heart attack on February 25, 2007, at the age of 41. "Arguably the best-known public interest lawyer in the Pacific Northwest, Russ used his legal skills to help average citizens oppressed by big government. He fiercely resented arbitrary regulations that cost people jobs and freedoms without accomplishing anything of substance for society or the environment," said PLF President Rob Rivett. In addition to his extraordinary legal skills, Russ had the natural talent to coin a phrase for the media that was unsurpassable in its clarity, brevity, and imagery, and – as delivered in his mild Texas accent – in its humor. Russ is sorely missed, but fondly remembered.

OF MICE AND RATS

RESIDENTS OF THE southeastern United States, particularly Florida, know what to expect from the Atlantic hurricane season, but in 2004 it arrived with particular ferocity. In mid-August, Hurricane Charley made landfall on the western side of Florida, near Fort Myers, causing over $14 billion in damage. In early September, Hurricane Frances knocked out power to more than a million homes in Florida. Governor Jeb Bush declared a state of emergency, prompting the largest evacuation order in Florida history – for nearly three million residents. The Sunshine State is no stranger to such actions, but the worst was yet to come.

Hurricane Ivan, at one point wielding Category-5 strength, proved the heavyweight champ of the 2004 season. At peak power Ivan ripped up virtually every house on the island of Grenada and even destroyed a prison built of stone. Jamaicans dubbed the storm "Ivan the Terrible," with good reason. It was the worst natural disaster there in half a century. After causing 60 deaths and massive property destruction across the Caribbean, Ivan reserved a Category-3 punch for Florida. Its impending landfall led officials to order evacuation of the Florida Keys. Ivan struck Florida's Gulf coast, near Pensacola, with winds of 130 mph and a storm surge of 12-14 feet.

That spelled trouble for Paul and Gail Fisher and other residents of Perdido Key, a barrier island situated equally below Florida and Alabama. A few hundred yards wide in most places and some 16-miles long, on September 16, 2004, as the Fishers were expecting to celebrate their anniversary, Ivan struck Perdido Key. The hurricane destroyed their home and, as on Grenada, most of the other homes and business structures on the island, while rendering many of the roadways impassable. The Fishers were fortunate to survive. All told, the storm killed 25 people in the United States, eight in the Florida panhandle.[1] Many survivors faced a grim situation.

The destruction of one's home, along with family heirlooms and irreplaceable items of family history, is one of the most devastating losses anyone can suffer. Even in a tropical climate, shelter is a basic human need. On Grenada and Jamaica, those Ivan had left homeless set out to rebuild and repair their homes, as they had for generations, in the wake of many a storm. Likewise Paul and Gail Fisher, and other victims on Perdido Key, sought to rebuild their homes and businesses and return their lives to normal. Unlike their fellow victims on Grenada and Jamaica, however, they found themselves barred from doing so. The problem was not any lack of willingness, nor any damage to the land caused by Hurricane Ivan. It was the federal government of the United States, the same one that sends in the Federal Emergency Management Agency (FEMA) in the wake of disasters, including this one. This time it was different. An agency of the federal government was acting not on behalf of people, but for a mouse.

In 1985, the U.S. Fish and Wildlife Service (FWS), a large agency within the federal Department of the Interior, listed the Perdido Key beach mouse as an endangered species under the Endangered Species Act (ESA.) For many years, a full 60 percent of the island, situated on the public lands of federal and state parks, has been designated critical habitat for the beach mouse. Nevertheless, three months after Ivan struck, the FWS indicated its intention to extend the designation to all private property as well. The Sierra Club earlier had filed suit to expand the mouse's habitat. In furtherance of its plan to extend the mouse's habitat to these private – now homeless – properties, FWS warned that it would take Escambia County to federal court if the county granted any building permits to owners seeking to rebuild on Perdido Key.

As it turned out, on September 15, 2004, the day before Hurricane Ivan hit Perdido Key, FWS employees had trapped a number of pairs of beach mice and taken them to a captive breeding facility in South Carolina to ensure that they would survive the storm. Yet, the Fishers and other former residents are unable to rebuild their homes because their government says that mice need their land.[2] At the same time, they still have to pay their mortgage and taxes on property the government has barred them from occupying. For the Fishers and other Perdido Key property owners, the government's cruel approach is proving more devastating than Hurricane Ivan. Yet, this was not the first time an agency of the government had punished human beings for the benefit of rodents.

Andy and Cindy Domenigoni owned a cattle ranch and grain farm outside the community of Winchester, in Riverside County, California. Their son was the fifth generation to work the land that Andy's ancestors settled 130 years earlier. In 1988, the family allowed an 800-acre section to lie fallow for two years in order to rest and rejuvenate the soil. One day in 1990, trespassing FWS biologists claimed that this land was home to the Stephens' kangaroo rat, also known as the k-rat, which FWS had declared an endangered species in 1988, three years after the Perdido Key beach mouse gained that status.

Without the Domenigonis' knowledge or consent, the FWS placed more than 1,600 acres of their ranch in an Endangered Species Act reserve study area as part of a Habitat Conservation Plan for the k-rat. The family found itself facing an FWS agent accompanied by an armed law enforcement officer. Their plans for grain planting on the 800-acre section, they were told, would constitute an illegal "take" of the k-rats biologists had found inhabiting that section. Under the Endangered Species Act, a "take" means not only to kill but to "harm" or "disturb" the species. These terms leave property owners vulnerable to the subjective interpretation of an FWS biologist, a reality the Domenigoni family quickly discovered. If they even disked the land, they could face a year in federal prison, a $50,000 fine for each and every "take" of a rat, substantial mitigation costs to restore the land, and impoundment of their farm equipment.

The Domenigoni family lost more than $75,000 in income for each of the three years they were unable to grow grain there and were forced to spend more than $175,000 on legal fees, biological surveys, and other related costs. Their total costs soared to more than $400,000, but this was not the worst of their woes. Because their farm lies in dangerous fire territory, for several years the local fire chief had notified farms in vulnerable areas to disk a firebreak around their homes for safety, a commonsense move that many had undertaken on their own. In 1993, however, the FWS forbade them from doing so because this would constitute a "take" of the k-rat. Because of the FWS' order, the Domenigoni family suffered further losses in the California Fire of October 1993, which also destroyed 29 homes and burned 25,100 acres in Riverside County.

One of the victims was Anna Klimko, who had obeyed the order of the FWS not to disk a firebreak around her home because of the k-rat. On November 19, 2003, John Stossel of ABC's *20/20* television news program reported on the California Fire and Anna's loss. As she kneeled in the ashes of her home, digging for whatever family keepsakes she could find, she posed this question: "For what? A rat." That is true, but it's actually a great deal more.

Wildfires, hurricanes, tornadoes, floods, and other disasters are common in America. The normal response of most human beings with any kind of compassion is to help the victims, as quickly as possible. That means helping people get a roof over their heads, and get their lives back to normal. Americans show a long record of providing such help, even though they are under no obligation to do so, and often at great sacrifice to themselves.

In the California case, an agency of the federal government *prohibited* people from taking measures that could easily have saved not only their property but their very lives. In the case of those kept homeless by federal mandate in Perdido Key, Florida, an agency of the federal government *prohibited* them from rebuilding homes destroyed by forces completely beyond their control, and through no fault of their own. This treatment was imposed by a government those citizens support with their hard-earned tax dollars and whose primary purpose is to protect their rights. Those citizens never considered that it was the purpose of the government to harass, criminalize, impoverish, and endanger them.

Such treatment is not only at odds with what Americans expect of government, but a long way removed from our country's philanthropic tradition and even normal human behavior. It is, in fact, the direct opposite, and for that to be the case, some other dynamic must be in place. This book will examine the forces in play, survey other cases – including some in which federal officials elevated the interests of flies above the needs of people – and tackle the hard questions that need to be faced.

What kind of ethos could motivate federal officials to elevate the concerns of mice and rats over those of human beings in their darkest hour of need? How did those beliefs affect efforts to combat deadly diseases such as malaria? How did they translate into laws such as the Endangered Species Act, along with policies and agencies empowered to enforce them at virtually any cost on human beings? What is the cost of such policies, not just to their victims like those described above, but to the broader taxpaying public?

How well do current polices designed to protect endangered animal and plant species actually perform their mission? How sound is the science involved? What is the record and practice when the science is shown to be wrong? What is the case for reform, and how has the government responded to reform efforts? Will the government continue to forbid families like the Fishers from rebuilding their houses after a natural disaster strikes, because of a beach mouse? What are the prospects that people like Anna Klimko will be able to protect themselves and their property against deadly wildfires, without taking a back seat to the interests of a rat?

In George Orwell's classic *Animal Farm*, the animals revolt and topple Jones, the disreputable farm owner. One of the first questions to emerge is the status of the wild, nondomestic creatures. Does the ideology of animalism include rats as well? The farm animals vote that, yes, rats are indeed comrades, and fully included in the ideology of animalism. As noted in this book, a related ideology that puts species above the needs of human beings fueled the crusade against DDT, ending its role as a lifesaver worldwide. The same beliefs fuel the Endangered Species Act and much current environmental policy.

Movements that wind up on the extreme side in practice are seldom seen that way in the beginning. They are not the calm, calculated "scientific" outlook of Bjorn Lomborg's *The Skeptical Environmentalist: Measuring the Real State of the World*.[3] Rather, they are the dogmatic certainty and rigid practices of the harsh, antipeople ideology played out in Florida, California, and across the nation; they are the enforcers who glibly dismiss as meaningless true stories of human misery, such as those described above and in the following chapters, while denying that they bear any responsibility for the human consequences, or that they themselves represent any kind of extremism in action.

In order to understand the Endangered Species Act of 1973, the statute which elevated a mouse in Florida and a rat in California to a higher status than people, one must understand the preservationist philosophical view from which it was developed.

Part I of this book tells that story, and how, birthed by Rachel Carson's *Silent Spring*, modern environmentalism became an extreme, highly politicized movement, based not on science, as it wants the world to believe, but on an outdated, counterproductive, and antipeople approach to the natural world.

The pesticide, DDT, which Rachel Carson demonized in *Silent Spring*, is used in Part I primarily as a vehicle to demonstrate that her book was largely the skilled advancement of politicized science. Although favoring restoration of the responsible use of DDT in those countries around the world where disease-carrying mosquitoes and other insects cause more than a million human deaths every year, this book does not suggest a return to the excessive and careless use of DDT that occurred in the United States during the 1950s and '60s.

Part II takes the Endangered Species Act of 1973 – the exclusionists' holy grail of environmental law – and describes how it came to be, how it is administered "whatever the cost," and how it is flawed and "broken." Part II also will show how the ESA has cost Americans billions of dollars in taxes and lost private land use, yet has accomplished very little biologically to aid the species or to justify the billions of dollars expended to implement and enforce it.

Part III tells the compelling, real-life stories of how the ESA, enforced by overreaching federal bureaucrats with a command-and-control approach, and promoted and advanced by exclusionist organizations, is responsible for loss of human lives, destruction of livelihoods and businesses, and the trampling of property owners' reasonable use of their land.

This book is ultimately a call for common sense and balance in crafting and enforcing the laws, policies, and practices that govern the relationship between the human species and the plant and wildlife species. We cannot escape the reality that sustainable civilization requires a constant balancing of our needs for a healthy environment, including clean water, clean air, and a full and diverse natural world, with our needs for jobs, places to live, transportation, food, schools, technological and medical advancement, and the like. That is not a simple or perhaps fully achievable objective. But it is a critical and necessary challenge if we are to remain a free, prosperous, and caring people.

NOTES

1. "Ivan blamed for 25 U.S. deaths," CNN, September 18, 2004, http://www.cnn.com/2004/WEATHER/09/

2. "Feds are warned: Retract 'mouse habitat' that bars hurricane victims from rebuilding – or face lawsuit," Pacific Legal Foundation Press Release of July 19, 2007, on the filing of its "60-day notice" informing the FWS of its intention to challenge the extended beach mouse critical habitat regulations in federal court.

3. Bjorn Lomborg, *The Skeptical Environmentalist – Measuring the Real State of the World*, Cambridge University Press, 2001.

PART ONE

FROM CONSERVATION TO EXCLUSION, FROM DDT TO ESA

CHAPTER 1

THE BIRTHING OF HUMAN EXCLUSIONISM

Conservation in America has been practiced for more than 300 years. The Massachusetts Bay Company restricted hunting of game species such as deer to avoid their depletion. Later, several New York counties limited the hunting of game birds such as grouse, quail, and turkey to certain months of the year to ensure their continued availability.[1] These efforts, some by private entities, aimed to protect the species in question and preserve them for human use. The evolution of conservation over the decades, and until the Endangered Species Act of 1973, proved meager, with few significant high points and several major low ones. When Congress did take steps to conserve wildlife, they were modest and erratically implemented.

One of the tragic low points was the decimation of the great herds of American Plains bison between 1830 and 1880. Yet, the federal government did nothing to preserve the nation's largest land animal until it stood on the brink of extinction.

According to estimates, between 25 million[2] and 60 million bison[3] roamed the Great Plains when the European migration to North America began in the early 17th century. But unlike the escalating bison decimation of the first two-thirds of the 19th century, the 1870s and '80s saw the wanton and reckless slaughter of bison by the millions. In his detailed history of the American Plains bison, Dr. William T. Hornaday,[4] wrote:

> *The ... causes of the extermination of the buffalo may be catalogued as follows: Man's reckless greed, his wanton destructiveness ... [and] [t]he total and utterly inexcusable absence of protective measures and agencies on the part of the National Government and of the Western States and Territories ... [and] [t]he perfection of modern breech-loading rifles .... Of all the deadly methods of buffalo slaughter, the still-hunt was the deadliest. Of all the methods that were unsportsmanlike, unfair, ignoble, and utterly reprehensible, this was in every respect the lowest and the worst. Destitute of nearly every element of the buoyant excitement and spice of danger that accompanied genuine buffalo hunting on horseback, the still-hunt was mere butchery of the tamest and yet most cruel kind.*[5]

In 1874, after much debate, both houses of Congress enacted a bison-protection law but President Grant killed the measure by holding it on his desk, without formal explanation. Two years later, with bison numbers declining into the mere "hundreds,"[6] a similar measure passed the House of Representatives, only to die in the Senate policy committee. This result, and the presumed reason for President Grant's earlier pocket veto – although he declined to say it publicly – was due to the popular belief that if bison were protected, the Indians, who relied on the bison for food and clothing, but who were increasingly and violently resisting westward migration, would have reason to remain in the Great Plains.

"Senate support for the bill probably died on June 25, 1876, along with General George Armstrong Custer and 264 soldiers from the 7th Cavalry," observes Shannon Peterson, author of *Acting for Endangered Species – The Statutory Ark*. "The Battle of Little Bighorn shocked the nation, reminding it that Indian resistance to westward expansion was not yet a thing of the past."[7]

> *In 1896, fearing the bison's approaching extinction, and having none of the animals to exhibit for posterity, the National Museum of*

*Natural History in Washington, D.C., commissioned Dr. Horna-
day to travel to the Great Plains to collect bison specimen for display
in the museum. When he returned with 25 buffalo specimen, Hornaday estimated from his observations that there were fewer than 100
Great Plains bison remaining in the United States.[8]*

Congress never did enact legislation prohibiting the killing of bison.
Federal protection came primarily through the creation of parks and preserves, the first of which, Yellowstone National Park, established in 1892,
provided invaluable habitat for the few remaining bison. It is worth noting
that during the 1870s, when the slaughter of bison on public lands was
rampant, six private individuals acquired and protected several bison on
their land. Nearly all bison in the country today are direct descendants of
these small stocks.[9] In 1905, during the presidency of Theodore Roosevelt,
the American Bison Society was founded with Dr. Hornaday as its first
president, and Roosevelt himself serving as honorary president. Roosevelt
was successful in persuading Congress to add several wildlife preserves,
and, with the help of a few private bison owners, the Society was able to
stock a number of preserves and parks. By 2007, the number of bison
on federal, Native American, and private land had increased to roughly
500,000.[10] Bison is the featured bill of fare at a restaurant chain, Ted's
Montana Grill, named after one of its founders, the environmentalist Ted
Turner.

Wildlife conservation came front and center in 1901 when Vice
President Theodore Roosevelt became president. Where the 19th century
pendulum began far toward indifference and wanton destruction of wildlife and forest resources, Roosevelt gave it a hefty push in the opposite
direction. Having initially gone west in 1883 to hunt big game, he had been
shocked to discover that the once abundant bison herds were depleted. On
later ventures to the west, he became increasingly alarmed to observe the
absence of other big-game species, as well as damaged grasslands and their
dependent species.

Roosevelt had always been a serious nature lover, with a deep venera-
tion for trees, particularly the conifers he encountered in the Rockies. As
his biographer Edmund Morris observed, "Walking on silent, moccasined
feet down a luminous nave of pines, listening to invisible choirs of birds,

he came close to religious rapture, as many passages in his books and letters attested.["11] As he entered the White House, wildlife conservation was at the top of his "to-do" list.

Also arriving on the scene at the end of the 19th century were Gifford Pinchot and John Muir, two other "talented, idiosyncratic, charismatic, and driven men," in the description of environmental historian Phillip Shabecoff. Together with Roosevelt, they "were to write the first pages of modern environmental history in the United States."[12]

As a young man with a keen interest in the out-of-doors, Pinchot pursued his father's suggestion of becoming a forester. The senior Pinchot had become wealthy as a lumberman, but regretted that his lumbering had done damage to the land. Forestry was a profession not yet recognized in the United States, so Pinchot studied scientific forestry in France. He returned with the European philosophy that the forests should be used to serve the needs of man, but must be protected from man's wanton misuse and overexploitation. He concluded that the "conservation" of the forests could be achieved only if the government controlled and managed the forests. In time he came to believe that all the nation's bounteous natural resources, including its land, water, minerals, and wildlife, should be available for people's consumption, use, and development, including for commercial purposes, so long as that usage was reasonable, efficient, and properly regulated by government.

"Conservation," Pinchot wrote, "is the most democratic movement this country has known for a generation. It holds that people have not only the right, but the duty to control the use of the natural resources, which are the great sources of prosperity." Pinchot viewed "the absorption of these resources by the special interests ... as a moral wrong ... unless their operations are under effective public control."[13]

Pinchot served as forestry advisor to Presidents Cleveland and McKinley, and to Roosevelt when he was governor of New York. When Roosevelt became president, Pinchot immediately became his chief advisor on all issues affecting the nation's forests and natural resources. For his part, Roosevelt wasted little time initiating Pinchot's conservation ideas of government control and management of the country's resources into his administration's policies and programs.

In his second year, he convinced Congress to enact the Reclamation Act of 1902, which delivered water and power to the west through the construction of a multitude of dams and irrigation canals, while at the same time restricting federal water for agriculture to farmers with 160 acres or less. In 1903, Roosevelt designated Little Pelican Island in Florida's Indian River as the first of several national wildlife refuges. In 1908, he held the first White House Conference on Conservation attended by all state governors. During his presidency, Roosevelt established "the first 51 Bird Reserves, four Game Preserves, and 150 National Forests. He also established the U.S. Forest Service, signed into law the creation of five National Parks, and signed the 1906 Antiquities Act under which he proclaimed a full 18 national monuments. The area of the United States placed under public protection by Theodore Roosevelt totals approximately 230,000,000 acres."[14]

Wildlife and natural resource conservation made great strides under the tutelage of the hard-charging Roosevelt and his advisor, Pinchot. Idealist John Muir, however, came to believe that their policies and programs did little more than disguise the continuing human assault on wild nature. Muir is known as a "preservationist" but his utopian view of the imminence of wild nature seeks to exclude human beings from it. That exclusionist view informed Rachel Carson's *Silent Spring*, the agenda of the modern environmentalist movement, and the enactment, implementation and enforcement of the Endangered Species Act of 1973.

Muir was born in Dunbar, Scotland, in 1838 and came to America with his family in 1849, a year after the Treaty of Guadalupe and 12 years before the Civil War, to work farms in Wisconsin. There John Muir studied natural sciences at the University of Wisconsin. Muir's father was "a religious zealot" of the fire-and-brimstone sort, though the son was tempered by a kind and loving mother.[15] In due time Muir himself would spawn zealotry based on a religious experience.

If Roosevelt experienced an almost religious rapture walking among the giant conifers, Muir's "transcendental rapture with nature"[16] occurred at age 26 while walking through Canadian swampland. There, he found the flower for which he had been searching, the Calypso borealis. One afternoon, two Calypso wild white orchids growing beside a yellow moss-covered embankment caught Muir's attention. "I never before saw a plant so full of life; so perfectly spiritual, it seemed pure enough for the throne of its Creator," he wrote. "I felt as if I were in the presence of superior beings who loved me and beckoned me to come. I sat down beside them and wept for joy."[17] This profound experience influenced the direction of his life. Muir's view that members of the natural world, like the two wild white orchids, were "superior beings" to man continued to evolve. From Canada he made his way – mostly on foot – to Florida, where he recorded these thoughts about the alligator:

> *Many good people believe that alligators were created by the Devil, thus accounting for their all-consuming appetite and ugliness. But doubtless these creatures are happy and fill the place assigned them by the great Creator of us all. Fierce and cruel they appear to us, but beautiful in the eyes of God. They, also, are his children, for He hears their cries, cares for them tenderly, and provides their daily bread .... With what dismal irreverence we speak of our fellow mortals! Though alligators, snakes, etc., naturally repel us, they are not mysterious evils. They dwell happily in these flowery wilds, are part of God's family, unfallen, undepraved, and cared for with the same species of tenderness and love as is be-stowed on angels in heaven or saints on earth .... Honorable representatives of the great saurians of an older creation, may you long enjoy your lilies and rushes, and be blessed now and then with a mouthful of terror-stricken man by way of dainty![18]*

Muir also recorded his reaction to a hunting adventure he was invited to join while in Florida:

> *Let a Christian hunter go to the Lord's woods and kill his well-kept beasts, or wild Indians, and it is well; but let an enterprising specimen of these proper, predestined victims go to houses and fields and kill the most worthless person of the vertical godlike killers,– oh! that is horribly unorthodox, and on the part of the Indians atrocious murder![19]*

Muir believed that nature's landscapes, species, and resources existed not to serve man, but separate and independent from their usefulness to man, and were fully deserving of – indeed demanded – recognition and preservation in their own right. Muir was outspokenly hostile toward man's perception that he rightfully dominated the earth:

> *How narrow we selfish, conceited creatures are in our sympathies! How blind to the rights of all the rest of creation! With what dismal irreverence we speak of our fellow mortals .... Well, I have precious little sympathy for the selfish propriety of civilized man, and if a war of races should occur between the wild beasts and Lord Man, I would be tempted to sympathize with the bears.*[20]

When Muir arrived in California's Sierra Nevada Mountains in May, 1868, and beheld the Yosemite Valley, he knew that this would be his home. Besides exploring the mountain passes and the valley meadows over several years, Muir's letters, articles, reported interviews, and conversations proclaimed the sanctity of the natural world to anyone who would listen. As he preached wild nature's authority to exist in its own right, independent of its value to man, Muir's reputation developed as the nation's leading voice for preserving all wildlife and natural resources.

Although Yosemite had become a national park in 1890, that status did not prevent timber companies, sheep herders, and other entrepreneurs from moving into the park to utilize its natural resources. This deeply troubled Muir and several academic followers of his teachings, who saw it as a direct affront to a philosophy that ranked animals and plants as superior beings.

The "balance-of-nature" school ushered in the transformation from the traditional anthropocentric view of human beings as earth's dominant species, to the biocentric view that elevated the natural world to a level equal with, and in time, above human beings. It viewed all life within the natural world – from the simplest plants in the forests and the unicellular organisms in the lagoons, to the thousands of diverse insect, bird, and other wildlife species, and man himself – as an interconnected part of a single system. If any element of that system is impaired or removed from performing its natural function, the web of life is reduced, all the interconnected elements are diminished, and the balance within the natural process is thrown out of kilter. Henry David Thoreau (1817-1862) was the intellectual philosopher of this school.

With his famous declarations that "in wildness is the preservation of the world" and "[t]he most alive is the wildest,"[21] Thoreau established the premise that nature without humans would naturally produce "the greatest regularity and harmony."[22] Thoreau was far from the only influence.

George Perkins Marsh (1801 - 1882), in his 1864 seminal book, *Man and Nature: Or, Physical Geography As Modified by Human Action*,[23] "was the first to raise concerns about the destructive impact of human activity on nature."[24] Marsh called man a "brute destroyer" and declared that man "is everywhere a disturbing agent. Wherever he plants his foot, the harmonies of nature are turned to discord." While Marsh accepted man's primary right to tame the wilderness, and to use the earth's natural resources for his benefit,[25] he condemned man's destruction of "the natural forces and processes that exist in a stable, harmonious balance."[26]

Aldo Leopold (1887 - 1948), the last of the major balance-of-nature intellectuals, introduced the "land ethic." According to Leopold, there was first an ethic guiding relations between individuals; later came an ethic informing the individual's relationship to the community; but, "[t]here is as yet no ethic dealing with man's relation to land and to the animals and plants which grow upon it." Leopold's land ethic "enlarge(d) the boundaries of the community to include soils, waters, plants, and animals, or collectively, the land. ... In short, a land ethic changes the role of Homo sapiens from conquerors of the land-community to plain member and citizen of it."[27]

In 1892, like-minded colleagues convinced Muir of the need to form an organization to advocate for the preservation of natural resources. This was the birth of the Sierra Club, and Muir was named as its first president and figurehead. Its primary mission was "to enlist the support and cooperation of the people and the government in preserving the forests and other natural features of the Sierra Nevada."[28] As the new organization and its charismatic leader's reputation and influence grew, the view that the natural world should be protected for its "wildness and beauty" – not for its usefulness to man – gained in acceptance and popularity.[29]

The key word in the Sierra Club's self-description is "preserving" (preservation), doubtless accurate at the time but even then distinct from "conservation," as it had been understood since colonial days. As historically practiced in America, conservation is inclusive and balanced, seeking prudent preservation of plants and animals both for their own sake, and for human use. The openly religious beliefs of Muir and his followers, by contrast, are really a theology of fundamentalist pantheism that displays a peculiar dialectic.

On the one hand, this belief is a kind of monism that proclaims to view human beings as just another animal species and not, as in the past, holding dominion over the earth and animals in any sense. The antithesis comes in its practice. In practice, fundamentalist pantheism seeks to *exclude* human beings from their own habitat, the property they rightfully own, as Paul and Gail Fisher and many others have discovered. The cause of accuracy compels the labeling of this kind of people-cleansing as *exclusionism*, with no other species does exclusionism so ruthlessly enforce its habitat cleansing. In a variation of *Animal Farm*, some species are less equal than others. The demonology of fundamentalist pantheism targets human beings alone. Consider the judgment of Greenpeace founder Patrick Moore.

He left an environmental movement that he believed fueled "ever-increasing extremism" because it was much more certain of what it was against than what it was for. Moore wrote that "environmental extremists are *anti-human*…. And they are just plain *anti-civilization*. In the final analysis, eco-extremists project a naive vision of returning to the supposedly utopian existence in the garden of Eden, conveniently forgetting that in the old days people lived to an average age of 35, and there were no dentists."[30] (Emphasis added.)

The result is human beings deprived of their most basic rights, the right to protect themselves from natural disasters such as wildfires, and their right to shelter. That is all part of their right to property, a basic *human* right. The attempt to distinguish property rights from human rights has no basis in law or reality. Property rights are about people, something Anna Klimko, among others, discovered the hard way. The extremist movement Patrick Moore describes is also at odds with traditional conservation of the type espoused by Pinchot. Consider, however, how from early times Muir's ethos fuels that opposition.

Two years into his presidency, President Roosevelt accepted Muir's invitation to spend a night camping in Yosemite's mountains. So euphoric was the president with the glorious surroundings, his late night conversation with Muir around a campfire, and the joy of waking to a lightly falling snow, that he proclaimed the experience "the grandest day of my life."[31] Yet, Roosevelt's fondness for Muir and his like devotion to pristine wilderness would soon be tested by one of the most contentious environmental contests in American history. Today few outside of the upper ranks of the exclusionist movement draw a distinction between "conservationism" and "preservationism," but this was not the case in 1906.

After suffering a devastating earthquake, the City of San Francisco proposed construction of a dam and reservoir in the Hetch Hetchy Valley as a source of water for its residents. Lying 15 miles north of the Yosemite Valley, and dubbed "Yosemite's twin" by Muir,[32] San Francisco's proposal for the damming of Hetch Hetchy required congressional approval. Gifford Pinchot, the president's close friend and natural resources advisor, who coined the term "conservation," strongly favored the dam.

Muir, on the other hand, attacked the proposal, as Phillip Shabecoff noted, "with the fervor of an Old Testament prophet."

> *These temple destroyers, devotees of ravaging commercialism, seem to have a perfect contempt for Nature, and instead of lifting their eyes to the God of the mountains, lift them to the Almighty Dollar. Dam Hetch Hetchy! As well dam for water tanks the people's cathedrals and churches, for no holier temple has ever been consecrated by the heart of man.*[33]

President Roosevelt was clearly torn between the two camps, both of which sought his support and waged vigorous campaigns to win a majority of votes in Congress. While in his heart he embraced Muir's vision of preserving pristine wilderness, with its natural resources, his practical side recognized that Pinchot's approach of allowing people to utilize natural resources under government management and supervision was a more realistic compromise position for the demands of the fast-growing west, which included San Francisco's need for water. Roosevelt eventually sided with Pinchot, favoring the dam.

It wasn't until 1913, a full four years after Roosevelt exited the White House, that Congress finally approved San Francisco's proposal for construction of the O'Shaughnessy Dam at Hetch Hetchy. Muir and the Sierra Club vigorously opposed the project right up to the congressional vote. The loss of the fight to preserve Hetch Hetchy deeply hurt Muir, and he died the following year.

Completion of the dam and flooding of the Hetch Hetchy valley occurred in 1923. Today, some 2.4 million residents of San Francisco, San Mateo, and Alameda counties, home to many affluent members of the Sierra Club, receive their water from the Hetch Hetchy reservoir as do communities in the San Joaquin Valley. The dam also generates electricity for the City of San Francisco, home to the national headquarters of the Sierra Club.[34] In this case, the exclusionist organization and its members show no philosophical objection to their own use of Hetch Hetchy water and electricity.

Although Muir and his Sierra Club lost the fight to save Hetch Hetchy, their pantheist-based exclusionist philosophy has continued its dominant influence on environmentalist thinking and action into the 21st century. Indeed, some followers continue the fight to remove the O'Shaughnessy Dam.[35] Philip Shabecoff, the first environmental reporter for the *New York Times*, writes:

> [T]*he modern environmental movement . . . has long since united behind the preservationist crusade conceived by Muir and others. While today's environmental organizations give lip service to* [Pinchot's approach of] *multiple use, they do so basically as a fall-back position. They know that the public, while increasingly sympathetic to protecting open space and wilderness, would not accept shutting out economic activity on all those parts of the federal domain that would otherwise be worthy of preserving in their pristine state. Today's environmentalists, or many of them, accept the exploitation of some public lands only to put themselves in a position to save others.*[36]

The progressive conservationism of the Roosevelt era also spawned a heightened recognition of the need to protect diminishing populations of migratory birds. Sports hunters, as well as market hunters of bird feathers for the decoration of fashionable women's hats, were blamed for the depletion of several species of migratory birds, including the snowy heron and the American egret in New York. Although the New York legislature enacted a law in 1906 to prohibit the possession for sale of the plumage of certain migratory birds, it soon became apparent that the wide range of these birds beyond state borders made such laws ineffective. Massachusetts came to the same recognition after trying to protect the heath hen. Dr. William Hornady pointed out in a 1911 *New York Times* commentary that unless a national law was enacted to protect the whooping crane, the trumpeter swan, and other migratory bird species, they would become as extinct as the Carolina parakeet.[37]

When the last of the once-estimated three billion passenger pigeons in the United States died in the Cincinnati zoo in 1914, the species' demise primarily due to hunting and habitat modification,[38] the federal government finally recognized that something had to be done on a national basis to protect migratory birds. In 1916, President Woodrow Wilson entered into a migratory bird protection treaty with Canada, and Congress ratified the treaty by enacting the Migratory Bird Treaty Act of 1918, making it a federal offense to capture, possess, sell, transport or kill any migratory bird protected by the treaty. Federal bird refuges on public lands were authorized in 1929. However, this enhanced statutory protection for migratory birds was effectively neutralized during the years of the Great Depression (roughly 1929 - 1933), when poaching of these birds for food increased dramatically, and the severe drought — causing dust-bowl conditions in much of the west — was damaging waterfowl habitat throughout the nation.

In January, 1930, the National Audubon Society testified at congressional hearings on protective legislation for the bald eagle that the symbol of America's national independence was on the verge of extinction.[39] Here is a description of the deadly treatment bald eagles and other birds of prey were subjected to in North America, as the Audubon Society must have informed Congress:

Birds of prey have been persecuted for hundreds of years in Europe and other parts of the world, usually as suspected predators of chickens or small livestock, such as goat kids or lambs .... Hawks, eagles, owls, falcons and other birds of prey that breed in North America were excluded from the 1918 Migratory Bird Treaty Act (MBTA), signed with Great Britain on behalf of Canada .... This exposed birds of prey to continued indiscriminate shooting for sport, hunting from aircraft, poisoning and even capture in pole traps, which catch birds by the feet and hang them upside down in nooses .... For generations in the 19th and 20th centuries, hunters gathered every fall on the rocky ridge to shoot these birds by the hundreds as they soared by. Dead hawks, falcons and eagles accumulated in huge piles, while wounded birds staggered around or lay helplessly immobile on the ground (Brett, 1973.) .... A bounty in Alaska resulted in the killing of some 150,000 .... [bald eagles] between 1917 and 1953 .... Bounty programs and random shooting of Bald Eagles from colonial times onward caused these birds to disappear from much of their original range, which encompassed the entire continent of North America, including arid regions in the Southwest.[40]

Despite the Audubon Society's testimony, Congress again failed to protect a clearly distressed species. It is worth noting that notwithstanding its own testimony in 1930 that the bald eagle was already in danger of extinction, the National Audubon Society not only failed to challenge, but actually promoted, Rachel Carson's 1962 claim in *Silent Spring* that DDT was primarily responsible for the near extinction of bald eagles and other birds of prey. DDT was not used in the United States until 1947.

At hearings of the newly constituted House Special Committee on Conservation of Wildlife Resources in 1934, the chief of the Bureau of Biological Survey testified that the numbers of migratory waterfowl in the United States had dropped by more than 75 percent since 1910.[41] Less than a month later, Congress enacted the Fish and Wildlife Coordination Act, which, in addition to providing some protection for migratory birds, directed the Department of Interior to assess the impact of residual sewage and commercial wastes on wildlife; it also directed dam-building agencies to assess the impact of dam construction on fish.

Later that year, Congress passed the Migratory Bird Hunt Stamp Act, which required hunters of ducks, geese, and other waterfowl to purchase from the federal government a license to hunt in the form of stamps. With the funds raised by the sale of these stamps, the federal government acquired waterfowl habitat, which over time substantially increased the national wildlife refuge system.

In 1936, President Franklin D. Roosevelt called the first of several annual North American Wildlife Conferences to highlight his administration's growing agenda to protect the nation's wildlife. Attended by representatives from federal and state agencies, Mexico and Canada, and a growing number of environmental organizations, these conferences advanced a more assertive role for the federal government in protecting species that were threatened with extinction. In 1938, the president of the General Wildlife Federation, who had been the head of the Bureau of Biological Survey, told Congress that it ought to expand the authority of the Bureau to allow it to prevent the extinction of all "valuable species."[42]

The year 1940 saw two isolated indications that Congress was beginning to recognize that wildlife species, especially charismatic species like the grizzly bear and the bald eagle, were diminishing in numbers, largely at the hand of man. In that year Congress moved the Bureau of Biological Survey from the Department of Agriculture to the Department of Interior, renamed it the U.S. Fish and Wildlife Service, and expanded its mission from a primarily scientific agency to a management agency for conserving fish and wildlife species.

Also, in 1940, coming a full decade after the first legislation to protect the nearly extinct bald eagle population was rejected, Congress finally enacted the Bald Eagle Protection Act, making it a federal crime to "take," meaning to kill, trap or otherwise harm, possess, sell, purchase, or trade in bald eagles or their parts.[43]

Beginning in 1941, Roosevelt's plans further to expand wildlife conservation measures succumbed to the urgency of World War II. And, except for an unsuccessful move in Congress in 1950 to enact special protection for bald eagles in the Alaska Territory, which had paid bounty on killed eagles since 1919 – and would until 1953 – little else occurred in the way of wildlife or natural resource protection during the 1940s and 1950s.

A major expansion occurred in the public's attitude toward wildlife and natural resource conservation during the 1960s. The "balance of nature" philosophy of the early naturalists, which, in reality, was not balanced, emerged as the science of ecology, which, in practice, was not very scientific. The conflicts would center on a book published in 1962.

NOTES:

1. Shannon Petersen, *Acting for Endangered Species - The Statutory Ark*, University Press of Kansas, 2002, p. 4.

2. Richard White, "Animals and Enterprise," in *The Oxford History of the American West*, ed. Clyde A Milner et al,. Oxford University Press, 1994, p. 249, as cited by Petersen, *op. cit.*, p. 6.

3. Several sources, including the naturalist, Ernest Thompson Seton, estimated their numbers at 60 million. Wind Cave National Park, http://www.nps.gov/wica/bison.htm; "History of the American Bison," http://www.buffaloexpress.com/buffexp/bison.cfm; "Bison bison," http://www.ultimateungulate.com/Artiodactyla/Bison_bison.html

4. For biographical information on Dr. William T. Hornaday; see http://usscouts.org/history/hornadaybiography.html

5. Hornaday, "Cause of the Extermination," *The Extermination of the American Bison*, 1886-87. http://www.nanations.com/buffalo/discovery_of_species.htm#Note Also, Project Gutenberg Ebook, http://www.gutenberg.org/files/17748/17748h/17748h.htm

6. Congressional Record, 44th Congress, 1st session, 23 Feb. 1876, p. H1238; as cited by Petersen, *op. cit.*, p. 7.

7. Petersen, *op. cit.*, p. 7-8.

8. "Killing of the Buffalo," *New York Times*, 26 July 1896, p. 20; as cited by Petersen, *op. cit.*, p. 8.

9. Valelrius Geist, *Buffalo Nation: History and Legend of the North American Bison*, Voyageur Press, 1996. Ike Sugg, "Where the Buffalo Roam, and Why," *Exotic Wildlife*, January/February, 1999; as referenced by Michael De Alessi, "Protecting Endangered Species," *Conservation Through Private Initiative: Harnessing American Ingenuity to Preserve Our Nation's Resources*, Reason Foundation, January 2005, p. 12.

10. "About North American Bison," http://www.notitia.com/bison/AboutBison.htm . Today, "bison is by far the fastest-growing sector of the meat business .... This year USDA-inspected slaughter houses will kill approximately 50,000 bison for human consumption." John Cloud, "Why the Buffalo Roam. Bison are flourishing again on the plains – because we like to eat them. Thoughts on a paradox," *Time*, March 26, 2007.

11. Edmund Morris, *The Rise of Theodore Roosevelt*, Coward, McCann & Geogheghan, 1979, p. 385; as cited in Shabecoff, *A Fierce Green Fire – the American Environmental Movement*, Hill and Wang:1993, p. 61.

12. Philip Shabecoff, *A Fierce Green Fire - the American Environmental Movement*, Hill and Wang: 1993, p.58.

13. Pinchot, *The Fight for Conservation*, 1910; as quoted in Robert McHenry and Charles Van Doren, eds., *A Documentary History of Conservation in America,* Praeger Publishers, 1972, p. 304; as cited by Shabecoff, *op. cit.*, p. 60.

14. "Theodore Roosevelt," U.S. Park Service, http://www.nps.gov/thro/tr_cons.htm

15. P.J. Ryan, "John Muir 1838-1914 National Park Service, The First 75 Years: Biographical Vignettes," undated. http://www.nps.gov/history/history/online_books/sontag/muir.htm

16. Shabecoff, *op. cit.*, p. 64.

17. Stephen Fox, *John Muir and His Legacy*, Little Brown and Company, 1981, p. 124; as cited by Shabecoff, *op. cit.*, pp. 63-64.

18. John Muir, Chapter 5, "Through Florida Swamps and Forests," *A Thousand-Mile Walk to the Gulf*, Edited by William Frederic Bade, Houghton Mifflin Company, 1916. http://www.yosemite.ca.us/john_muir_writings/a_thousand_mile_walk_to_the_gulf/

19. Muir, *op. cit.*, "October 22."

20. Muir, *op. cit.*, p. 148; Muir's classic statement of allegiance to the bears over civilized man is discussed by Fox, *op. cit.*, p. 52.

21. Henry David Thoreau, *The Writings of Henry David Thoreau*, Houghton Mifflin, 1906, p. 275. Shabecoff, *op. cit.*, pp.46-50; Robert Frazier Nash, *Wilderness in the American Mind*, 4th ed. 2001, p. 84.

22. Thoreau, *ibid*, p. 243.

23. Marsh, *Man and Nature: Or, Physical Geography as Modified by Human Action,* 1864; republished in 1874 as *The Earth as Modified by Human Action.*

24. David Lowenthal, "George Perkins Marsh: Renaissance Vermonter," 1958, as cited by The George Perkins Marsh Institute, http://www.clarku.edu/departments/marsh/georgemarsh.shtml

25. Lowenthal, *op. cit.*, p. 252.

26. Marsh, *op. cit.*

27. Aldo Leopold, "The Land Ethic," from *A Sand County Almanac*, 1948; as cited by Shabecoff, *op. cit.*, pp. 88-90.

28. Michael P. Cohen, *The History of the Sierra Club*, Sierra Club Books, 1988, p. 9.

29. Shabecoff, *op. cit.*, p. 66.

30. Patrick Moore, "Environmentalism for the 21st Century," *Greenspirit*, http://www.greenspirit.com/21st_century.cfm?msid=29&page=1

31. Roderick Nash, *Wilderness and the American Mind*, p. 138; as cited by Shabecoff, *op. cit.*, p. 65.

32. For a history of the Hetch Hetchy Valley, including a sketch of the original valley and a photo of the valley after the dam was built, see "Hetch Hetchy Valley," http://en.wikipedia.org/wiki/ Hetch_Hetchy_Valley, Hetch Hetchy

33. *Fox, John Muir and His Legacy, op. cit.*, p. 144.

34. "Hetch Hetchy Valley," http://en.wikipedia.org/wiki/Hetch_Hetchy

35. "Hetch Hetchy debate reborn," *Sacramento Bee*, Feb. 8, 2007, http://www.sacbee.com/341/ story/120442.html

36. Shabecoff, *op. cit*, p. 67.

37. Petersen, *op. cit.*, p. 10.

38. A.W. Schorger, *The Passenger Pigeon: Its Natural Hisotry and Extinction*, University of Oklahoma Press, 1955), pp. 199, 205, 214, 224-230; as cited by Petersen, *op. cit.*, p. 11.

39. U.S. House of Representatives, Committee on Agriculture, *American Eagle Protection*, hearing, 71st Congress, 2d session, January 31, 1930, Washington, D.C.; cited by Petersen, *op. cit.*, p. 15.

40. "Birds of Prey: Persecution and Hunting," *Endangered Species Handbook*, Animal Welfare Institute, 1983, http://www.endangeredspecieshandbook.org/persecution_birds.php

41. U.S. House of Representative, Special Committee on Conservation of Wildlife, *Conservation of Wildlife*, hearing, 73rd Cong., 2d session, 23 March 1934, p. 7; as cited by Petersen, *op. cit.*, p. 12.

42. Testimony of Jay Darling, U.S. Congress, House Select Committee on the Conservation of Wildlife Resources, *Conservation of Wildlife: Hearings on House Resolution*, 75th Congress, 3d session, May 5, 1938 (Washington, D.C.) p. 193; cited by Petersen, *op. cit.*, p. 14.

43. Yet, because of a lack of enforcement, the systematic killing of eagles went on for many years, with reports as late as 1970 telling of hunters in Wyoming stacking 770 eagle carcasses on the ground, while being paid $25 for every eagle shot. When the federal government finally began strictly enforcing the law, the decimation stopped. "Bald Eagle Bounces Back After Decades of Persecution," *National Geographic News*, June 20, 2002, http://www.news.nationalgeographic.com/ news/2002/06/0620_120620_baldeagle_2.html

CHAPTER 2

THE CARSON-OGENIC CRUSADE

ON A JUNE morning in 1963, Senator Abraham Ribicoff of Connecticut called his Senate special subcommittee on environmental hazards to order. Taking a line from President Lincoln's initial comment upon meeting the author of *Uncle Tom's Cabin*, Harriet Beecher Stowe, Ribicoff introduced the hearing's most celebrated witness: "Miss Carson ... we welcome you here. You are the lady who started all this. Will you please proceed."[1]

In 1963, neither Senator Ribicoff nor members of his committee could have known the full impact that Rachel Carson and her just-published book, *Silent Spring*,[2] would ultimately wield on all things environmental. As her biographer, Linda Lear, wrote 35 years later: "probably no one could have guessed that as she spoke, her vision was already shaping a powerful social movement that would alter the course of American history."[3]

As the 20th century came to a close, *Time* magazine named Rachel Carson as one of the "100 Most Important People of the Century."[4] *Time* headlined its commemorative article: "Before there was an environmental movement, there was one brave woman and her very brave book."

In 1994, the 25th anniversary edition of *Silent Spring* included an introduction by Vice President Al Gore: "Without this book, the environmental movement might have been long delayed or never developed at all. It led to environmental legislation at every level of government." Mr. Gore's film, *An Inconvenient Truth,* may have contained nine errors, as a British court recently ruled,[5] but the former vice president was certainly accurate here.

Like its author, *Silent Spring* ranks among the "most influential" books of the 20th century.[6] Philip Shabecoff, in his history of the American environmental movement, declared that *Silent Spring* "may be the basic book of America's environmental revolution."[7] While reporting on the environment for the *New York Times*, Shabecoff wrote: "I found myself bearing witness to the emergence of a major social movement, a movement that is becoming one of the most powerful political and cultural forces of our time."[8] Neither Shabecoff nor Carson biographer Lear characterize the movement that Carson birthed as "scientific." That is worth noting because, currently in its 40th anniversary edition, *Silent Spring* remains popular in bookstores and libraries.

High school and college students often find it on the reading list for science and environmental studies classes. The modern movement that Carson and her book spawned has profoundly influenced the environmental outlook of several generations of school students. Some text book publishers[9] and educators promote the one-sided view that producers – manufacturing companies, oil companies, the timber and forest products industries, the mining industry, pharmaceutical companies, builders, farmers and ranchers, and other interests – are responsible for destroying the environment. Even writers for kindergartners indoctrinate young children with the biased view that people who develop and produce are destroying the environment.

The illustrated children's book, *Rain Forest*, starts out in a beautiful forest and the animals are happy. But one day, men with bulldozers come and start cutting trees and clearing the land. The rains come and create a flood, which carries the men and their bulldozer to their deaths. The trees and animals remain safe.[10] Although the story is set in a South American rainforest, where, in real life, irresponsible and excessive tree-cutting has gone on for several decades, to impressionable young children *Rain Forest* inculcates the probable lifelong belief that any development and use of natural resources, anywhere, is ecologically harmful and morally wrong.

In the 2006 movie, *Hoot*, three junior high school students set out to stop the construction of a pancake restaurant in South Florida to save the habitat of the burrowing owl. Besides sabotaging the construction site, including stealing parts from and flattening the tires of the heavy equipment, these "environmentally conscious" kids kidnap and gag the "greedy land developer," spray paint a police car providing security, pull out the surveyors' stakes, release poisonous snakes on the project grounds, and put alligators in the portable toilets. Director and screenwriter Will Shriner, who also works as a comedian, explained *Hoot's* purpose: "If you don't send a positive message to young people to care about the environment, then there is really no chance .... The answers will come from the education and awareness of the generation that follows us."[11]

The message is actually negative and irresponsible, but increasingly common since *Silent Spring* first appeared in condensed version in three weekly issues of *The New Yorker* during June of 1962. Chapter I, "A Fable for Tomorrow," begins like this:

> *There was once a town in the heart of America where all life seemed to live in harmony with its surroundings ..... Then a strange blight crept over the area and everything began to change. Some evil spell had settled on the community: mysterious maladies swept the flocks of chickens, the cattle and sheep sickened and died. Everywhere was the shadow of death. The farmers spoke of much illness among their families. In the town the doctors had become more and more puzzled by new kinds of sickness appearing among their patients. There had been several sudden and unexplained deaths, not only among adults but even among children, who would be stricken suddenly while at play and die within a few hours.*

With these words, naturalist Rachel Carson launched an attack which, a decade later, would lead to the banning of DDT, a popular, effective and safe pesticide. To effectuate this mission, Carson demonized the established scientific and medical communities whose research and development of the chemical pesticide was single-handedly responsible for stopping typhus

– the second leading insect-borne killer disease in history. DDT also was saving millions of lives from malaria, the most prolific insect-borne killer disease of all time, and protecting public health around the world. On a larger and more lasting scale, Rachel Carson birthed the transformation of the balance of nature philosophy into the hardcore exclusionism we know today. A skilled writer, she was especially good at fear mongering.

"A Fable for Tomorrow" is a carefully contrived story that conjures up images of illness and death from the atomic fallout of two decades earlier. As biographer Linda Lear noted, Carson "cleverly [used] the public's knowledge [and fear] of atomic fallout as a reference point."[12]

Carson closed her opening chapter by acknowledging that she knew of no community that had experienced all the "mysterious maladies" she described. "Yet every one of these disasters has actually happened somewhere, and many real communities have already suffered a substantial number of them." She subtly suggested to her readers that recently deceased people in their communities who died of cancer were the victims of "the strange blight [that] crept over the area." She stirred fears that readers and their children would suffer a similar misfortune if DDT and other chemical pesticides continued to be used: "A grim specter has crept upon us almost unnoticed, and this imagined tragedy may easily become a stark reality we all shall know."

As we shall learn from scientists working in the field, Carson's theories about the effects of DDT on people bore only a tenuous connection to science. That crucial point failed to emerge at the time. The *New Yorker* and the Houghton Mifflin Company, Carson's publisher, recognized that *Silent Spring* contained the essential elements to create a media frenzy – the first step in the intended process to reverse the public's favorable view of DDT. Just two days after *The New Yorker's* third installment hit magazine stands, the *New York Times* editorialized in a piece titled "Rachel Carson's Warning," that if *Silent Spring* spurred the federal government to protect the public health instead of the chemical industry, Rachel Carson "would be as deserving of the Nobel Prize as was the inventor of DDT."[13]

Letters poured in to Carson from all over the country. So did requests for interviews from *Reader's Digest*, *Life* magazine, the *Washington Post*, the *London Sunday Times*, Eric Sevareid of *CBS Reports*, Hugh Downs of NBC's *Today Show*, National Educational Television, and countless others. In a special prepublication offering of *Silent Spring*, the president of the Board of the Book of the Month Club told club members that "[t]he portentous problem it presents – of worldwide indiscriminate poisoning of all forms of life, including human – is in the same dread category as worldwide nuclear warfare." Remarkably, the offering contained a review of *Silent Spring* by sitting Supreme Court Justice William O. Douglas, who called Carson's book "the most important chronicle of this century for the human race ... a call for immediate action and for effective control of all merchants of poison." The Club preordered 150,000 copies.[14]

Consumers' Union, the largest and most active consumer education organization in the country, preordered 40,000 copies of *Silent Spring* for its members.[15] And the Audubon Society, fearing Carson's prediction of future silent springs, took an active role in promoting the book with its thousands of members around the country.[16]

A reporter asked President Kennedy whether his administration was examining possible long-range dangerous side effects from widespread use of DDT. Kennedy responded that "since Miss Carson's book," his administration was indeed examining the matter.[17] Even the timing of unrelated events contributed to the escalating interest.

A year earlier reports had emerged from Europe and Canada that an increasing number of infants were being born with severely deformed limbs and organs. Within months, scientists discovered that a new drug, thalidomide, prescribed for, among other conditions, pregnant women suffering from morning sickness, was severely impairing early fetal development and causing the deformities. The tragic stories received extensive coverage in newspapers and television around the world. Although the U.S. Food and Drug Administration had rejected thalidomide two weeks before *Silent Spring's* release, a reporter asked Carson whether there was any relationship between the culprit drug and the chemical pesticides she condemned.

"It is all of a piece," Carson responded, "thalidomide and pesticides, they represent our willingness to rush ahead and use something new without knowing what the results are going to be."[18] That added to the growing fear of chemicals that the serialized version of *Silent Spring* had initiated.[19] While the media, the publisher, and activist organizations aligned with Carson's thesis generated eager anticipation of *Silent Spring's* arrival at the bookstores, *The New Yorker's* serialized version was continuing to create a firestorm of controversy.

The U.S. Department of Agriculture, at the time responsible for approving use of DDT and the other chemical pesticides, and the companies that produced them, recognized that it had to respond to the increasingly heavy criticism Carson's charges were generating. Representative was the response of a spokesman for the Department's Agricultural Research Service, who accused Carson of "putting down everything that favors her case and ignoring all else. The balance of nature," he pointed out, "is a wonderful thing for people who sit back and write books or want to go out to Walden Pond and live as Thoreau did. But I don't know of a housewife today who will buy the type of wormy apples we had before pesticides."[20]

The response had merit, in that Carson had all but stated that DDT was causing people to become sick and die. However, the exchange recalls that it was not science that destined Rachel Carson to become the mother of modern environmentalism. Rather, it was her natural gift for writing, and her intense love of nature, both evident from childhood. At 10 years of age she wrote a moving story about a young pilot killed in World War I that was published in *St. Nicholas Magazine for Children*, the same respected children's literary magazine that had introduced the stories of young William Faulkner, F. Scott Fitzgerald, and E. E. Cummings. Several other published stories followed.

Her early love of "the out-of-doors and the whole world of nature" Carson attributed to her mother.[21] An amateur naturalist of the conservation school known as "nature study," Mrs. Carson spent many hours with her young daughter, exploring the woods and fields, and talking about the birds, insects, and other wildlife that lived along the Allegheny River near their home.[22] Deriving its authority from natural theology, nature study was premised on the notion that preserving nature was a holy mission or "divine obligation."[23] Young Carson's early reading of nature-study authors depicting the wonders of unspoiled nature, together with her mother's frequent admonitions that natural creatures and objects should be observed, but never disturbed, created in her a lifelong obligation to preserve the balance of nature.[24]

Carson chose English as her college major, primarily to enhance her already formidable composition skills, but during her third year a charismatic biology professor reignited her childhood passion for nature and wildlife. Carson duly changed her major to zoology and set out to combine her two interests by writing about living science.

Like many young people returning to small hometowns following college graduation, Carson's brief return to her hometown prompted her to roam some of the same routes that she and her mother had walked when she was younger. In a few weeks she would be leaving for graduate school at Johns Hopkins University, and her walks were "a farewell gesture to her childhood and to the natural surroundings that nurtured her."[25] But to Carson's dismay, the town's two coal-driven power plants – one of which employed her father, her sister and her brother – emitted a foul-smelling sulphur odor, and dispensed waste into the Allegheny River. As Carson biographer Linda Lear described the scene:

> [B]etween the two power stations, new businesses and industries sprang up ... each seemingly more environmentally damaging than the last. In the three decades since the Carsons had settled into the once wildly beautiful valley of the lower Allegheny, there was no doubt that industry had brought technological progress, higher income, and regular work, but it had also produced environmental blight.... When Rachel stood on the long front porch of the farmhouse that June, the horizon she looked out on was dominated not by the farms and field of her childhood but by smokestacks of the power generators. She felt little sadness about leaving Springdale. The memory of the defilement industrial pollution brought would remain.[26]

After earning her master's degree in zoology, Carson wrote and taught for three years. In 1936 she joined the United States Bureau of Fisheries, where she was soon writing articles on marine zoology. The publication of her article, "Undersea," by the *Atlantic Monthly* in September, 1937, launched her career as a natural-science writer. Her first book, *Under the Sea-Wind*, published in 1941, received little attention, but in 1951, two years after becoming the chief publications editor of the Fisheries Bureau, her second book, *The Sea Around Us*, brought her national acclaim and the financial independence to retire from Fisheries. Her last book of the trilogy, *The Edge of the Sea,* was published in 1955.

By the time Carson's professional writing career began, she had fully embraced the "balance of nature" philosophy of the naturalist intellectuals – Thoreau, Marsh, Muir, and Leopold. When *The Sea Around Us* earned her the 1952 John Burroughs Medal for excellence in nature writing, Carson issued this warning:

> *Mankind has gone very far into an artificial world of his own creation. He has sought to insulate himself, in his cities of steel and concrete, from the realities of earth and water and the growing seed. Intoxicated with a sense of his own power, he seems to be going farther and farther into more experiments for the destruction of himself and his world.*[27]

As Robert James Bidinotto observed, "All these ideas [of the balance of nature naturalists] lay like dry, rotting timber on a forest floor, waiting for a spark. And the spark that ignited the organized environmentalist movement was Rachel Carson's 1962 book, *Silent Spring*."[28] True to form, Carson concluded *Silent Spring* with this statement:

> *The "control of nature" is a phrase conceived in arrogance, born of the Neanderthal age of biology and philosophy, when it was supposed that nature exists for the convenience of man. The concepts and practices of applied entomology for the most part date from that Stone Age of science. It is our alarming misfortune that so primitive a science has armed itself with the most modern and terrible weapons* [referring to chemical pesticides like DDT], *and that in turning them against the insects it has also turned them against the earth.*[29]

Such was the influence of *Silent Spring* on that June morning in 1963, that Senator Ribicoff was likely unaware of anyone less than worshipful of Rachel Carson's work and the suspect science behind it.

NOTES:

1. Linda Lear, *Rachel Carson: Witness for Nature*, Henry Holt and Company, New York, 1997, p. 3.

2. Rachel Carson, *Silent Spring*, Houghton Mifflin Company, New York, 1962.

3. *Ibid,* p. 4.

4. Peter Matthiessen , *Time,* March 29, 1999. See also: Kevin Markey, 100 Most Important Women of the 20th Century, *Ladies Home Journal Books,* p. 60; Gail Meyer Rolka, *100 Women Who Shaped World History,* 100 Series, Bluewood Books, p. 94; Deborah Felder, *The 100 Most Influential Women of All Time: A Ranking Past and Present,* Citadel Press, 2001.

5. "Gore climate film's nine 'errors': A High Court judge who ruled on whether climate change film, An Inconvenient Truth, could be shown in schools said it contains nine scientific errors," *BBC News,* October 11, 2007, http://news.bbc.co.uk/2/hi/uk_news/education/7037671.stm

6. The Boston Public Library, http://www.bpl.org/research/AdultBooklists/influential.htm and *National Review,* http://www.nationalreview.com/100best/100_books.html, and others.

7. Philip Shabecoff, *A Fierce Green Fire - The American Enviornmental Movement,* Hill and Wang, 1983, p. 99.

8. Shabecoff, *op. cit.,* p. xiv.

9. For example, a science textbook used in Texas for the past 20 years, Environmental Science: Creating a Sustainable Future by Dr. Daniel D. Chiras, Ph. D., was rejected by the Texas State Board of Education in 2003 for further use in Texas schools because of its blatant environmentalist agenda. Dr. Chiras has charged censorship on the part of the Board and has sued its members, claiming that his constitutional right of free speech has been violated. http://dir.salon.com/story/news/feature/2003/11/05/textbooks/index.html

10. Helen Cowcher, *Rain Forest,* 1988.

11. CNSNews.com, Cybercast News Service, May 1, 2006, http://www.cnsnews.com/ViewPrint.asp?page=/SpecialReport/archive/200605/SPE20060501a.html

12. Linda Lear, Introduction to the 40th anniversary edition of *Silent Spring,* p. xv.

13. *New York Times* editorial, July 2, 1962, *op. cit.,* p. 411.

14. Book-of-the-Month Club News, September, 1962, as cited by Lear, *op. cit.,* p. p. 419.

15. Lear, *op. cit.,* p. 411.

16. *Ibid,* p. 408.

17. Presidential News Conference, August 29, 1962; cited at Lear, *op. cit.,* p.419; President Kennedy was apparently referring to the *New Yorker* serialized version, as Silent Spring, the book, was not published until September, 1962.

18. *New York Post,* September 14, 1962, as cited by Lear, *op. cit.,* p. 412.

19. Carson was referring to what later became known as the "precautionary principle," discussed by J. Gordon Edwards in "DDT: A Case Study in Scientific Fraud," *Journal of American Physicians and Surgeons,* Vol. 9, No. 3, Fall, 2004, p. 86.

20. Lear, *op. cit.,* p. 413.

21. *Ibid*, p. 7.

22. *Ibid*, p. 16.

23. Renowned nature-study botanist, Liberty Hyde Bailey, as related by his associate, Cornell professor Anna B. Comstock in her *Handbook of Nature Study*, p. xi-xv, 1-24; cited by Lear, *op. cit.*, p. 14.

24. Lear, *op. cit.*, p. 15.

25. *Ibid*, p. 54.

26. *Ibid*, p. 55.

27. "Design for Nature Writing," remarks at the presentation ceremony of the Burroughs Medal, April 7, 1952, and published in *Atlantic Naturalist* 7, 5 May/August, 1952, pp. 232-234; as cited by Lear, *op. cit.*, p. 221.

28. Robert James Bidinotto, "Environmentalism or Individualism?" 2003, p. 7, www.econot.com/page4.html . This article is a concise treatment of the origins and history of modern environmentalism, and its incompatibility with the founding principles and values of America.

29. *Silent Spring, op. cit.*, p. 297.

CHAPTER 3

![gray bar]

POLITICIZED SCIENCE

IN LATE JANUARY, 1944, a young college biology graduate named Gordon Edwards entered Italy as a combat medic with the U.S. Army following the invasion at Anzio. At the time, typhus was taking a toll in and around Naples.

"[We] went to sleep every night while being fed upon by bedbugs and fleas, and there was no way to escape them," Edwards wrote. "We had heard about 'cooties' (body lice) causing typhus, which killed more than three million people in Europe and vicinity during and after World War I."[1]

The great fear was that lice-borne typhus would infect U.S. soldiers and the civilian population, and become an epidemic that would quickly spread across the continent. "Blitz Plague," a *Saturday Evening Post* article of August, 1942, described typhus-carrying lice as "the mass killer which has slaughtered 200 million people in Europe and Asia alone, diverted the stream of history, and done more than any other single factor to determine the outcome of wars."[2] When Napoleon's Grand Army invaded Russia in 1812 with half a million men, the epidemic of the lice-borne diseases typhus and trench fever killed more than 150,000 of them, and was the chief cause of Napoleon's retreat.[3] In Italy during the winter of 1944, the military liberation of Europe from Nazi occupation had just begun.

The incipiency of typhus had to be stopped before the disease became widespread.

In 1939, while searching for an insecticide to prevent moths from damaging wool fabrics, Swiss scientist, Dr. Paul Muller, picked up on a chemical formula that had been developed, but never tested, by an Austrian chemistry graduate student in 1874.[4] Muller discovered that the chemical was "effective in controlling mankind's worst insect pests, including lice, fleas, and mosquitoes."[5] Dr. Muller called the chemical DDT, and in 1948 he received the Nobel Prize in Medicine and Physiology.

When typhus reappeared in and around the Naples area in 1944, Dr. Joseph Jacobs at the pharmaceutical firm of Merck & Co. in New Jersey was assigned the task of replicating Muller's formula. On an emergency basis, Jacobs produced a batch of 500 pounds of DDT powder that was immediately flown to Italy.

"One day," Gordon Edwards wrote, "I was ordered to dust every soldier in our company with an insecticidal powder that had just been received. For two weeks I dusted the insecticide on soldiers and civilians, breathing the fog of white dust for several hours each day."[6]

The emergency effort worked. DDT stamped out the blood-sucking lice and stopped the century-old killer disease typhus in its tracks.[7] President Franklin D. Roosevelt expressed his thanks for the emergency effort through a telegram of the Surgeon General, which read: "It is estimated that 5,000 lives were probably saved by destroying the typhus-carrying body lice infesting our soldiers."[8] DDT dusting also was directly responsible for saving from certain death large numbers of Europeans. As the Allies liberated Nazi concentration/death camps, they dusted DDT on the prisoners who had managed to survive the Nazis and the typhus-carrying lice.

When the war in Europe ended, Edwards, the Army medic, came home to earn a doctorate in entomology from Ohio State University. After a brief stint as a seasonal ranger at Glacier National Park in Montana, he went to California where Dr. J. Gordon Edwards, Ph.D., taught biological science, including medical entomology, at San Jose State University for the next 44 years. Following his retirement in 1990, Emeritus Professor Edwards continued to lecture and write, and maintained a full-time presence as the

Senior Curator of the University's entomology museum that bears his name.[9] His teaching, research, writings, and lectures span 50 years. Dr. Edwards is one of the world's leading authorities on DDT and its effects on wildlife and humans.

"At least 80 percent of the world's human infectious diseases are transmitted by insects, mites, or ticks (*Science* magazine, June 9, 1972). They have caused the death of hundreds of millions of people by infecting them with the pathogens that cause typhus, bubonic plague, yellow fever, malaria, dengue fever,[10] sleeping sickness, encephalitis, elephantiasis, leishmaniasis, and yaws."[11] "Many medical historians believe malaria has killed more people than any other disease in history, including the Black Plague, and may have contributed to the collapse of the Roman Empire."[12]

The millions of malaria-caused deaths, and billions of body- and brain-damaging illnesses, continued worldwide until shortly after World War II, when the use of DDT largely eliminated the disease-carrying mosquito in country after country. One of the leading malaria-fighting organizations in the world in recent years is Africa Fighting Malaria.[13] On September, 2005, Africa Fighting Malaria's Drs. Roger Bate and Richard Tren presented written testimony to the U.S. Senate Environment and Public Works Committee on malaria-related issues, including DDT's post-World War II malaria eradication success. Their testimony began with this statement:

> *This committee seeks to understand the influence of science in public policy and consequences of the misuse of that science in such policy. There can be few more compelling and tragic examples of the abuse of science and misuse in ongoing public policy than that of DDT and public health ....*

> *DDT is safe for human use and there has never been a peer-reviewed replicated study showing any harm from the chemical, even though billions have been exposed to it (hundreds of millions in moderate to high doses).*

Their testimony included this historical sampling of DDT's malaria-fighting impact:

• Southern European countries, which began to utilize spraying of DDT only months following V-E Day, fully eradicated malaria within a few years.

• The U.S. government began DDT spraying shortly after the war ended, and completely eliminated malaria by 1952.

• In South America, Bolivia's DDT spraying eradicated malaria and other mosquito-borne diseases by 1947, leading the Pan American Health Organization to undertake a similar program on a hemispherewide basis. By 1950, many Central and South American countries had fully eradicated malaria, as well as dengue and yellow fever.

• On the African continent, South Africa's use of DDT spraying began in 1946 and by 1948 had eliminated the disease in 80 percent of the country (except in the low lying areas adjoining Mozambique, then Portuguese East Africa, and Zimbabwe, then Southern Rhodesia). Malaria cases in Transvaal Province dropped to about one-tenth of the number of cases reported in 1942/43.

• On the Indian subcontinent, where malaria cases far exceeded the numbers in South Africa, India began spraying DDT in 1951, and by 1957, reduced deaths from malaria almost 100 percent. In Sri Lanka (formerly Ceylon), 2.8 million malaria cases in 1946 dropped to 110 by 1961, and to 17 cases by 1965.

• The Republic of China (Taiwan) had more than one million malaria cases in 1945, but DDT spraying reduced the number to only nine cases in 1969, and to zero not long thereafter.[14]

In writing *Silent Spring*, Carson recognized that with DDT successfully eradicating malaria-carrying mosquitoes around the world, making vegetables and fruits more healthy and attractive, and being a handy and reliable means of ridding one's house and yard of pesky insects, the popular pesticide would not likely be discredited by claims of its still speculative effects on birds alone. To cause consumers to turn against DDT, she would have to shock and scare them by characterizing the pesticide as a silent killer of people. Thus, *Silent Spring* cleverly mixes tenuous accounts and references regarding DDT's unproven effects on birds with carefully worded intimations of its dire effects on people, thus conveying the impression that DDT was a killer of all life.

"Everywhere was the shadow of death," Carson declared in her first chapter. But in her stretch to declare DDT as a killer of people, she was unable to credit the pesticide with saving lives. This is why *Silent Spring* makes no mention of the millions of lives saved, or the illnesses DDT single-handedly prevented between 1945 and its publication in 1962.

"Carson vividly describes the death of a bird that she thought may have been poisoned by a pesticide," Dr. Edwards wrote, "but nowhere … does she describe the death of any of the people who were dying of malaria … and other diseases that are transmitted by insects."[15]

Silent Spring's utter silence on DDT's unprecedented lifesaving credentials raises doubts about Carson's professed admiration for Dr. Albert Schweitzer, to whom she dedicated the book. In a letter lamenting the death of her mother, Carson wrote: "Her love of life and all living things was her outstanding quality …. More than anyone else I know, she embodied Albert Schweitzer's 'reverence for life.'"[16] Surely Carson knew that Dr. Schweitzer's "reverence for life" was so profound that he had permanently moved his family to Africa half a century earlier so he could medically minister to the wretched victims of insect-borne diseases, among other illnesses – the very victims the DDT she condemned was saving by the millions.

When *Silent Spring* hit bookstore shelves in September, 1962, Dr. Gordon Edwards was a young, dedicated environmentalist. He belonged to several environmental organizations, and his nature articles had appeared in *The Indiana Waltonian, Audubon Magazine,* and other environmental periodicals. From the advance publicity, Edwards had high hopes for a book written by a fellow biologist. "I eagerly read the condensed version of *Silent Spring* in *The New Yorker* magazine and bought a copy of the book as soon as I could find it in the stores. As I read the first several chapters of the book, I noticed many statements that I realized were false."[17]

Because Carson came from the biology community, Edwards at first was inclined to overlook her broad use of literary license. But as he read further, it became clear that she "was really playing loose with the facts and was also deliberately wording many sentences in such a way as to make them imply certain things without actually saying them. She was carefully omitting everything that failed to support her thesis that pesticides were bad, that industry was bad, and that any scientists who did not support her views were bad. . . it slowly dawned on me that Rachel Carson was not interested in the truth about those topics, and that I was being duped, along with millions of other Americans."[18]

Edwards then went back and read *Silent Spring* again, "but this time my eyes were open and I was not lulled into believing that her motives were noble and that her statements could be supported by logic and by scientific fact." He recorded his findings about Carson's significant errors, misinterpretations, mischaracterizations, and omissions, and read the scientific articles and reports she cited in the book. He was disturbed to discover that many of them not only failed to support the contention for which she had cited them, but actually contradicted the point she was attempting to make.[19]

Of the numerous factual and scientific disappointments Edwards found in Carson's book, the one surrounding her dedication of *Silent Spring* to Dr. Albert Schweitzer ranked at the top because he knew she had deliberately misled her readers in an attempt to add credibility to her attack on DDT. Edwards wrote:

> *On the first page of the book . . . Rachel Carson wrote: 'Dedicated to Dr. Albert Schweitzer, who said "Man has lost the capacity to foresee and to forestall. He will end by destroying the earth."' Surely she knew he was referring to atomic warfare,[20] but she implied that he meant there were deadly hazards from chemicals such as DDT. Because I had already found a great many untruths in her book, I got a copy of Dr. Schweitzer's autobiography, to see whether he even mentioned DDT. He wrote [p.262]: "How much labor and waste of time these wicked insects do cause us, but a ray of hope, in the use of DDT, is now held out to us."* [21]

On page 16 of *Silent Spring*, Carson claimed: "This industry [referring to the makers of DDT and other chemical pesticides] is a child of the Second World War. In the course of developing agents of chemical warfare, some of the chemicals created in the laboratory were found to be lethal to insects. The discovery did not come by chance; insects were widely used to test chemicals as agents of death for man." Dr. Edwards writes: "Carson thus seeks to tie insecticides to chemical warfare. However, DDT was never tested as an 'agent of death for man.' It was always known to be nonhazardous to humans! Her implication is despicable."[22]

On pages 17 and 18, after stating in great detail how violently poisonous arsenic is to humans and vertebrate wildlife, Carson writes: "Modern insecticides are still more poisonous," making special mention of DDT as an example. "This implication that DDT is horribly deadly," Edwards writes, "is completely false."[23] "Human volunteers in Georgia ingested up to 35 milligrams daily, for nearly two years, and did not experience any difficulties then or later" (citing research by W. J. Hayes, "The effect of repeated oral doses of DDT in man," *Journal of the American Medical Association*, 1956; 162: 890-897). "Workers in the Montrose Chemical Company had 1,300 man-years of exposure, and there was never any case of cancer during 19 years of continuous exposure to about 17 mg/man/day" (*citing* Laws, Curley, and Biros, "Men with intensive occupational exposure to DDT," *Archives of Environmental Health*, 1967; 15: 766-775).[24]

While DDT was *Silent Spring*'s most prominent target, Carson's clever association of it with truly toxic chemicals caused readers to view DDT as similarly dangerous. For example, on page 24, after quoting "so experienced a pharmacologist as Dr. Lehman" that chlordane is "one of the most toxic of insecticides – anyone handling it could be poisoned," she tells this story: "One victim who accidentally spilled a 25 percent industrial solution on the skin developed symptoms of poisoning within 40 minutes and died before medical help could be obtained."

As Dr. Edwards explained: "The actual details regarding this accident were readily available at the time, but Carson evidently chose to distort them. The accident occurred in 1949 in the chemical formulation plant, when a worker spilled a large quantity down the front of her body. The liquid contained 25 pounds of Chlordane, 39 pounds of solvent, and 10 pounds of emulsifier (*Journal of the American Medical Association*, August 13, 1955.) Carson's reference to this as a '25 percent solution' spilled on the skin certainly underplays the severity of that drenching, which was the only account known of such a deadly contamination during the history of chlordane formulation."[25]

On page 187, Carson again reveals her lack of concern for human lives threatened by diseases transmitted by insects:

Only yesterday mankind lived in fear of the scourges of smallpox, cholera, and plague that once swept nations before them. Now our major concern is no longer the disease organisms that once were omnipresent; sanitation, better living conditions, and new drugs have given us a high degree of control over infectious disease. Today we are concerned with a different kind of hazard that lurks in our environment – a hazard we ourselves have introduced into our world as our modern way of life has evolved.

"Surely Carson was aware," Edwards writes, "that the greatest threats to humans are diseases such as malaria, typhus, yellow fever, Chagas's disease, African sleeping sickness, and a number of types of ... tick-borne bacterial and rickettsial diseases. She deliberately avoids mentioning any of these, because they could be controlled only by the appropriate use of insecticides, especially DDT. Carson evidently preferred to sacrifice those millions of lives rather than advocate any usage of such chemicals."[26]

These examples only scratch the surface of significant errors, misrepresentations, and omissions that Dr. Edwards found in *Silent Spring*. He described numerous others in various articles.[27] They are classic examples of politicized science, personal opinion, and even outright misrepresentation, camouflaged by the white coat of the laboratory.

In the arena of the environment, self-anointed experts – usually environmental activists – advance a dubious scientific theory as fact, primarily to promote a politico-environmental agenda. In contrast to legitimate science, the politicized version tends to be speculative, anecdotal, unauthoritative, lacking in empirical data, and offered without peer review within the scientific community. The most telling characteristic of politicized science, however, is its convenient confirmation of the predetermined result desired by its proponents.

"They are anti-science and technology," Patrick Moore says of his former eco-extremist colleagues. "Science is invoked to justify positions that have nothing to do with science. Unfounded opinion is accepted over demonstrated fact."[28] In short, politicized science is a matter of environmental extremists first determining the policy they want – often with like-minded government bureaucrats joining in – and then finding "experts" to support it. Under the discipline of legitimate science, policy would be established based upon demonstrated scientific data.[29]

Gordon Edwards credits Carson's use of politicized science with changing him "from an 'environmentalist' to a scientist with a desire to keep truth in science and environmentalism." After *Silent Spring's* publication, he began to feel uncomfortable with fellow environmentalists, lamenting their transformation from "dedicated nature enthusiasts" to "environmental extremists at work." The meetings of the Audubon Society and the Sierra Club that he attended as an academic ecologist "became frustrating, because everyone else praised Rachel Carson, while I knew that she had exaggerated, fabricated, and prevaricated throughout the book."[30] Yet, despite Dr. Edwards' desire "to keep truth in science and environmentalism," Carson's doomsday message was gathering steam.

On the *New York Times* best-seller list for most of the fall, publisher Houghton Mifflin reported *Silent Spring* flying out of bookstores at the rate of 106,000 copies a week.[31] Adding to the fear factor that the book was generating, on October 22 – one month after *Silent Spring* hit the bookstores – President Kennedy went on television to inform the American people of the recently discovered Soviet military buildup in Cuba, including the ongoing installation of offensive nuclear missiles. As Carson biographer Linda Lear noted, "In *Silent Spring* Carson deliberately employed the rhetoric of the Cold War"[32] and the crisis over pesticides "was for her perfectly analogous to the threat of radioactive fallout."[33] Yet, despite strong criticism of *Silent Spring* from the established science community, major newspapers, news magazines, and television networks embraced Carson and her thesis.

She was challenging the establishment, condemning industry, and embracing a populist cause, and her role as a woman in the men's world of science made her an attractive underdog in the fight. Alone or alongside her opponents, she regularly was portrayed in the more sympathetic and appealing light. One prominent commentator for the *New York Times* exemplified the type of warm embrace Carson received from the media, writing: "Evidence continues to accumulate that she is right and that *Silent Spring* is the 'rights of man' of this generation."[34]

One of those influenced was the mother of future Vice President Al Gore. "I particularly remember my mother's troubled response to Rachel

Carson's classic book about DDT," Gore wrote. "My mother was one of many who read Carson's warnings and shared them with others."[35] Many others also got the word through television.

On April 3, 1963, CBS aired "The Silent Spring of Rachel Carson," a highly promoted and long-awaited program with respected television journalist Eric Sevareid. The demure author, sitting calmly in her wood-paneled study, stated her concerns about chemical pesticides to a television audience estimated at between 10 and 15 million people. The program only enhanced Carson's credibility and for many who would never read the book, this CBS special would be their only exposure to *Silent Spring* and its unsettling message of impending disease and death from DDT.

While showing Carson reading passages from her book, the camera cut away, leaving only her voice, as viewers watched selected dramatic scenes of DDT being excessively and carelessly applied. The chemical industry's representative on the program, a Ph.D. with outstanding credentials, made a valid and prophetic point when he said, "If man were to faithfully follow the teachings of Miss Carson, we would return to the Dark Ages, and insects and disease and vermin would once again inherit the earth." But CBS crowned Carson with the white hat of environmental virtue.[36] By the end of the program, she had been catapulted into near-celebrity status, wielding enormous influence.

The day following the airing of the CBS program, Senate Majority Leader Hubert Humphrey announced that he was forming a special subcommittee on environmental hazards, to be chaired by Senator Abraham Ribicoff, that would hold public hearings to review the use and application of DDT and the other chemical pesticides targeted by Carson's book.[37]

In the Senate hearing room, jammed with friends and foes, and the media hanging on her every word, Rachel Carson testified: "We still talk in terms of conquest. We still haven't become mature enough to think of ourselves as only a tiny part of a vast and incredible universe. Man's attitude towards nature is today critically important simply because we have now acquired a fateful power to destroy nature. But man is part of nature and his war against nature is inevitably a war against himself."[38]

The military analogy is of great interest. This "war" that Carson saw as inevitable would empower government employees – all of whom live in modern dwellings, drive automobiles, work in government buildings on land where species formerly lived, and make ample use of modern technology – to exclude their fellow human beings from their own property, and forbid them to take measures against deadly natural disasters. Carson, meanwhile, was fighting a battle of her own.

Less than a year following her Senate testimony, Rachel Carson, then only 57, succumbed to the cancer that had been advancing during the years she was writing *Silent Spring*. Her legacy of politicized science would yield deadly consequences around the world.

NOTES

1. J. Gordon Edwards, "Mosquitoes, DDT, and Human Health," *21ˢᵗ Century Science & Technology Magazine*, Fall 2002, p. 16. www.21stcenturysciencetech.com/articles/Fall02/Mosquitoes.html

2. Edwards, "Mosquitoes, DDT, and Human Health," *op. cit.*, p. 17.

3. Dr. Didier Raoult and 10 other French researchers, *The Journal of Infectious Diseases*, 2006: 193: pp. 112-120, http://www.journals.uchicago.edu/JID/journal/issues/v193n1/34959/brief/34959.abstract.html

4. "Paul Muller - Biography," www.Nobelprize.org/medicine/laureates/1948/mullerbio.html

5. J. Gordon Edwards, "DDT: A Case Study in Scientific Fraud," *Journal of American Physicians and Surgeons*, Volume 9, Number 3, Fall 2004, p. 83; citing EJL Soulsby and WR Harvey, "Disease transmission by arthropods," *Science* 1972; 178: 1153-1155.

6. Edwards, "Mosquitoes, DDT, and Human Health, *op. cit.*, p. 16.

7. *Ibid.*

8. Joseph J. Jacobs, *The Anatomy of an Entrepreneur*, ICS Press, 1991, pp. 84-87.

9. The J. Gordon Edwards Museum of Entomology, Department of Biological Sciences, San Jose State University, One Washington Square, San Jose, CA 95192-0100.

10. The World Health Organization reported in July, 2007, that dengue fever is raging across Asia, but also has reached epidemic levels in Latin America. Carried and spread by the infected mosquitoes in much the same way as malaria, dengue fever is a noncontagious virus for which there is no cure or vaccine. In addition to excruciating muscle and joint pain, high fever, and nausea, the most serious form of dengue fever can cause internal bleeding, liver enlargement, circulatory shutdown, and death – especially in children. According to the WHO, the average annual number of cases reported globally has increased from 15,497 in the 1960s, to 884,462 in the first five years of the current century. "Dengue fever hitting Asia may be worst in years," *MSNBC*, July 30, 2007, reporting on *Associated Press* story, http://www.msnbc.man.com/id/20040971/wid/11915773?GT1=10212.

According to *Directors of Health Promotion and Education*, http://www.dhpe.org/infect/dengue.html, "no effective mosquito control efforts are underway in most countries with dengue."

11. Edwards, "Mosquitoes, DDT, and Human Health," *op. cit.*, p. 16.

12. Todd Seavey, "The DDT Ban Turns 30 – Millions Dead of Malaria Because of Ban, More Deaths Likely," *Special Reports*, American Council on Science and Health, June, 2002, http://www.acsh.org/publications/reports/ddt2002.html

13. Africa Fighting Malaria is a health advocacy organization based in Johannesburg, South Africa, and Washington, D.C. It monitors the activities of aid agencies and health groups in Africa and other parts of the world, and advises on policies to combat malaria and other diseases. No organization has been more persistent or effective in fighting the preservationist-influenced ban on DDT than Africa Fighting Malaria. Dr. Roger Bate, Ph.D., is the U.S. Director of Africa Fighting Malaria, and a Resident Fellow at the American Enterprise Institute for Public Policy Research, in Washington, D.C. Dr. Richard Tren, Ph.D., is South African Director of the organization.

14. Drs. Bate and Tren's full written testimony to the Senate Committee, "Science in Environmental Science Making," September 28, 2005, can be viewed at www.aei.org/publications/pubID.23259,filter.all/pub_detail.asp

15. J. Gordon Edwards, "The Lies of Rachel Carson," *op. cit.,* p. 46. www.21stcenturysciencetech.com/articles/summit02/Carson.html

16. Lear, *op. cit.*, p. 338.

17. Edwards, "The Lies of Rachel Carson," *op. cit.,* p. 41.

18. *Ibid.*

19. *Ibid.*

20. Dr. Schweitzer had made two highly publicized condemnations of atomic weapons: an article, "A Dedication of Conscience," also broadcast on radio from Oslo, Norway, by the Nobel Peace Prize Committee on April 24, 1957; and a book, *Peace or Atomic War?*, Henry Holt & Co, 1958.

21. Edwards, "DDT: A Case Study in Scientific Fraud," *op. cit.*, p. 83, citing Schweitzer A., *Out of My Life and Thought: an Autobiography*. New York, NY.: Henry Holt; 1949. Because this example of Carson's duplicity disturbed him so, Dr. Edwards made reference to it in several of his articles.

22. Edwards, "The Lies of Rachel Carson," *op. cit.*, p. 42.

23. *Ibid*, p. 41.

24. Edwards, "DDT: A Case Study in Scientific Fraud," *op. cit.,* p. 84.

25. Edwards, "The Lies of Rachel Carson," *op. cit.,* p. 44.

26. *Ibid*, p. 46.

27. Edwards, "Mosquitoes, DDT, and Human Health"; "DDT: A Case Study in Scientific Fraud"; "The Lies of Rachel Carson," *op. cit.*; "100 things you should know about DDT," *JunkScience.com: All the Junk That's Fit to Debunk,* www.junkscience.com/ddtfaq.htm; *op. cit.*

28. Moore, "Environmentalism for the 21st Century," *Greenspirit*, http://www.greenspirit.com/21st_century.cfm?msid=29&page=1

29. David Stirling, "Politicized Science Equals Bad Science," *Los Angeles Times*, August 4, 2000.

30. Edwards, "Remembering Silent Spring and Its Consequences," Prepared for address to Doctors for Disaster Preparedness, Oregon Institute of Science and Medicine, August 3, 1996, p. 1, http://www.oism.org/ddp/epa.doc

31. Lear, *op. cit.*, p. 426.

32. For example, on p.3 (40th Edition): "In the gutters under the eaves and between the shingles of the roofs, a white granular powder still showed a few patches; some weeks before it had fallen like snow upon the roofs and the lawns, the fields and streams."

33. Lear, *op. cit.*, p. 428.

34. Brooks Atkinson, "Critic at Large," *New York Times*, April 2, 1963, cited by Lear, p. 447.

35. Al Gore, *Earth in the Balance*, Houghton Mifflin Company, 1992, p. 3.

36. Lear, *op. cit.*, pp. 448 - 450.

37. Lear, *op. cit.,* pp, 450, 451.

38. John Burnside, "The Legacy of Silent Spring," *AlterNet: EnviroHealth*, p. 3, http://www.alternet.org/envirohealth/27336/

CHAPTER 4

"GOING WILD AGAINST DDT"

WHILE DR. EDWARDS' status as a biologist and self-avowed environmentalist made him somewhat unique among scientists offended by Carson's *Silent Spring*, the established scientific community resented her attacks. "Whose voice do we hear, that of science or of the sustaining industry?"[1] became Carson's standard line in speeches. It did not seem to concern her that royalties from her best-selling book made her vulnerable to the same question.

To these scientists, Carson had done more than challenge the use of an effective pesticide that had saved millions of lives around the world. She was assaulting their integrity and professionalism, the body of research to which some had devoted their careers. Numerous scientists of impeccable credentials publicly challenged Carson's condemnation of DDT and other chemical pesticides. Occasionally, one of their "guest commentaries" would appear in a mainstream newspaper, as when a Fellow of the American Association for the Advancement of Science and a member of the National Association of Science Writers, wrote that *"Silent Spring* is NOT a scientific work. It is full of error, perhaps not evident to the lay reader, but clear indices of a writer who has ventured into an unknown field and has absorbed all sorts of evidence, some of it sound, some of it worthless, and given everything equal billing."[2]

But for the most part, the embrace of Carson's crusade by the mainstream media largely relegated her disbelievers to industry-sponsored trade publications and events. For example, the principal scientist and head of economic entomology at the Illinois Natural History Survey and Illinois Agricultural Experiment Station, wrote: "In her reckless misinterpretation of scientific facts, Miss Carson has done irreparable harm to the orderly process of protecting human life from hazards far worse than the ogres she conjures up."[3]

Two highly respected biochemists affiliated with the American Cyanimid Corporation, who had spent years in chemical research and promoting the public use and value of DDT, feared that Carson's attack could lead to legislation banning use of the effective pesticide. One gave numerous speeches in which he characterized Carson as "a fanatic defender of the cult of the balance of nature."[4] The other biochemist wrote that while Carson may not advocate the total ban of chemical pesticides, "[s]he merely states that they produce cancer and deformed babies. In light of such statements it is not necessary to advocate halting their use."[5]

Dr. Frederick J. Stare, Ph.D., M.D., of the Harvard Medical School recognized Carson as a "literary luminary," but criticized her scientific conclusions as "baloney."[6]

Dr. Cynthia Westcott, a respected entomologist with a Ph.D. in plant pathology, known around the country as "The Plant Doctor," wrote in an early review of *Silent Spring* for the *National Gardener*, that Carson's thesis that DDT and other pesticides were a threat to human health "can only be conjecture; no proof has yet been offered of any link with human cancer or other ailments.... Throughout *Silent Spring*, we are given pills of half truth, definitely not tranquilizing, and the facts are carefully selected to tell only one side of the story."[7] Unlike Carson's public attacks on the scientific community, however, Dr. Westcott used a personal letter to tell her that she "deplored" her suggestion that entomologists and other scientists were out for private gain.[8]

Just as the demonizing of DDT was Carson's vehicle for taking the balance-of-nature philosophy to a new level, in the post-*Silent Spring* decade, the increasingly aggressive exclusionist organizations adopted Carson's politicization of science to advance their agenda to an even more intense level. As Edwards noted, "The pseudo-environmentalists were going wild against DDT. Clifton Curtis of World Wildlife Fund, for example, wrote that 'DDT is so potent that as long as it is used anywhere in the world, nobody is safe' – and provided no data to back up his assertion."[9] Many organizations, including Greenpeace, the Sierra Club, the Environmental Defense Fund, the Natural Resources Defense Council, and the curiously named Physicians for Social Responsibility, were vehemently condemning DDT, which became a tipping-point issue.

"If the environmentalists can win on DDT," Dr. Charles Wurster, chief scientist for the Environmental Defense Fund, declared in 1969, "they will achieve, and quite probably retain in other environmental issues, a level of authority they have never had before ... much more is at stake than DDT."[10]

Wurster thus confirmed that political power was one of the movement's main objectives, and that Carson's demonizing of DDT had shown them the way to achieve that power. In 1967, the Audubon Society, one of Carson's early and most active supporters, created a political arm called the Environmental Defense Fund (EDF). Its primary purpose was to lobby the government, file lawsuits, influence the media, and motivate public opinion to achieve a ban of DDT.[11] One of the founders of EDF, civil rights attorney Victor Yannacone, urged Dr. Wurster, as the organization's chief scientist, to conduct a scientific experiment that would demonstrate DDT's harmful effect on the environment. Wurster complied by placing marine algae in tanks filled with sea water and then adding sufficient DDT to get concentrations of 500 parts per billion (ppb). Wurster reported that the DDT killed the algae.[12]

Wurster's experiment came to the attention Dr. Paul Ehrlich,[13] Stanford University biologist, founder of the organization Zero Population Growth, and author of the 1968 best-seller *The Population Explosion*, whose predictions turned out spectacularly wrong. Ehrlich wrote a story in *Ramparts* magazine called "Ecocatastrophe" which recalled the genre of *Silent Spring*:

The end of the ocean came late in the summer of 1979, and it came even more rapidly than the biologists had expected. There had been signs for more than a decade, commencing with the discovery in 1968 that DDT slows down photosynthesis in marine plant life. It was announced in a short paper in Science, but to ecologists it smacked of doomsday. They knew that DDT and similar chlorinated hydrocarbons had polluted the entire surface of the earth, including the sea.[14]

Two years later, other scientists performing the same experiment that Wurster conducted found that 600 ppb of DDT did not kill the algae, and that 700 ppb of DDT actually benefited the algae.[15] Dr. Edwards characterized Wurster's contrived experiment as a hoax, and Ehrlich's scenario based upon it as demonstrating the great damage that politicized science does to legitimate science. Yet, "thousands of school children were required to read Ehrlich's article, and teachers warned that 'it shows how humans are endangering the earth with pesticides.'"[16]

In "Ecocatastrophe" Ehrlich also wrote that the U.S. Department of Health, Education and Welfare had shown "unequivocally" the increasing death rate from the excessive use of chemicals such as DDT. "They [HEW] estimated that Americans born since 1946 (when DDT usage began) now [in 1968] had a life expectancy of only 49 years, and predicted that if current patterns continued, this expectancy would reach 42 years by 1980, when it might level out." In his attempt to scare people about DDT, Ehrlich allowed his zeal to obscure his scientific judgment, because "[i]n 1980, life expectancy at birth for both males and females in the United States was 73.7 years," according to Drs. Bate and Tren, "31.7 years longer than Ehrlich predicted in his alarmist and misleading publication."[17]

In 1969, with the frontal attack on DDT at full throttle, the Director General of the World Health Organization (WHO) issued a remarkable public statement on DDT that is worthy of note, especially in light of later events:

DDT is so safe that no symptoms have been observed among the 130,000 spraymen or the 535 million inhabitants of sprayed houses (over the past 29 years of its existence.) No toxicity was observed in the wildlife of the countries participating in the malaria campaign.

Therefore, WHO has no grounds to abandon this chemical which has saved millions of lives, the discontinuation of which would result in thousands of human deaths and millions of illnesses. It has served at least two billion people in the world without costing a single human life by poisoning from DDT. The discontinuation of the use of DDT would be a disaster to world health.[18]

At the same time, the U. S. Center for Disease Control in Atlanta, concerned that the assault on DDT might be making political headway, issued this warning:

A decision to ban the production of DDT in the U.S. would result in a denial of the use of DDT to most of the malarious areas of the world. The available evidence on the very slight risks, if any, does not justify the U.S. making a unilateral decision that would so adversely affect the future economic and social well-being of so many other nations of the world. The mere banning of the use of DDT within the U.S. may raise unwarranted fears in the minds of those responsible for decision making in other governments who will not be fully informed of the known facts about the benefits and risks involved in the continued use of DDT in malaria eradication.[19]

The spring of 1970 witnessed the largest political protests in American history. Months of demonstrations and rallies against the Vietnam War dissuaded President Lyndon Johnson from seeking a second term, but the most vociferous protests followed President Richard Nixon's April 30 announcement that he was ordering an attack against Communist sanctuaries on the Cambodian-Vietnam border to protect American troop withdrawals. "For hundreds of thousands, even millions, of students, faculty, and staff at more than half of the nation's colleges, 'business-as-usual became unthinkable .... Expressions of protest across the country took every conceivable form and were carried out under every conceivable banner, slogan and cry."[20]

On May 4, four students were killed by National Guard troops at an antiwar rally at Kent State University in Ohio. The rest is history. But while the Vietnam War was the primary object of this spring of protests, there were others. As Phillip Shabecoff noted, one week prior to Nixon's televised address,

> [o]n April 22, 1970 ... some 20 million Americans, many of them young, massed in the streets, on campuses, on riverbanks, in parks, and in front of government and corporate buildings to demonstrate their distress and anxiety over the state of the environment. It was called Earth Day. A revolution, of sorts, had begun .... A series of well-publicized ecological insults in the years following the publication of Silent Spring, including: a huge spill from an oil rig off the coast of Santa Barbara, California; the Cuyahoga River in Cleveland bursting into flames because of the heavy concentration of inflammable industrial chemicals in its waters ... the dense smog blanketing many of our major cities ... and dozens of other notorious episodes directed the country's attention to the worsening condition of the natural landscape .... April 22, 1970 is as good a date as any to point to as the day environmentalism in the United States began to emerge as a mass social and cultural movement.[21]

This highly charged atmosphere proved ideal for the Environmental Defense Fund to challenge the safety of DDT. With the goal of obtaining a ruling banning its nationwide production and use, the EDF filed a complaint with the Environmental Protection Agency (EPA), the new federal agency created through executive order by President Nixon with jurisdiction over chemical pesticide. As the EPA's first Administrator, Nixon appointed William Ruckelshaus. The EDF challenge to the safety of DDT was the first major issue to come before the agency. Administrator Ruckelshaus named the respected hearing examiner, Edmund Sweeney, to preside at the high-profile hearing, and to rule for or against DDT based on the scientific evidence presented.

One of the primary witnesses called by the Environmental Defense Fund to support its anti-DDT position, and representative of its witnesses as a class, was Dr. Samuel S. Epstein, M.D. Author of numerous books and articles on cancer prevention, chair of several professional committees and associations, including, for nearly two decades, the Rachel Carson Council,[22] Dr. Epstein was the 1998 recipient of an award regarded as the "Alternative Nobel Prize." His views are widely considered "alternative" because during his career he has vehemently championed the cause of preventing cancer, while condemning in harsh terms those government bodies and nonprofit organizations that work to advance the diagnosis, treatment, and cure of cancer. He has referred to the National Cancer Institute and the American Cancer Society as "the Cancer Establishment." At the heart of Dr. Epstein's professional career has been the "precautionary principle."

> *Precautionary doctrine holds that, if anyone raises doubts about the safety of a technology, the technology should be severely restricted, if not banned outright, until it is proven to be absolutely safe .... The net result is that the precautionary principle repeatedly stifles risk-taking, innovation, economic growth, scientific and technological progress, freedom of choice, and human betterment. Had* [the precautionary principle] *governed scientific and technological progress in past centuries, numerous historic achievements would have been ... stopped dead in their tracks: airplanes, antibiotics, aspirin and automobiles; biotechnology, blood transfusions, CAT scans and the contraceptive pill; electricity, hybrid crops ... microwaves, open heart surgery, and organ transplants; pesticides, radar and refrigeration; telephones, televisions, water purification and x-ray – to name a few .... Had today's technophobic zealots been in charge in previous centuries, we would have to roll human progress back to the Middle Ages – and beyond, since even fire, the wheel and organic farming pose risks, and none would have passed the "absolute safety" tests the zealots now demand.*[23]

Accordingly, in Dr. Epstein's view, only the total removal of all carcinogenic substances from human use or contact will insure the prevention of cancer. In this vein, preventing cancer in humans requires banning the use or consumption of *any substance* that, when pumped through a tube (called gavage) into the stomach of a laboratory mouse or rat in massive doses – hundreds or even thousands of times greater than the amount any human might ingest over many years, or even a lifetime – cause the development of tumors in the small rodents' stomachs.

Epstein predictably testified that because DDT had been shown to be carcinogenic, and that, in his opinion, even the presence of one molecule of a carcinogen was unsafe for humans, DDT ought to be banned. That was the natural extension of Rachel Carson's thesis in *Silent Spring*, which, after a decade of popularization by the media, had succeeded in leading much of the public also to believe that contact with any amount of DDT could cause cancer.

In language reminiscent of Carson's effort to marginalize scientists working in industry, Dr. Epstein declared as recently as 2000: "Time and again, we see that government and industry are both willing to sacrifice human lives on the altar of profits.... [I]f for economic gain [a] CEO puts in place practices that damage public health – in other words, kills or injures innocent people – I think we should lock him up and throw away the key."[24] That is indeed a curious statement coming from one whose testimony a quarter century earlier contributed significantly to the total banning of the one effective chemical insecticide responsible for saving the lives of millions of innocent people from malaria and other insect-borne diseases.

Still riding Rachel Carson's *Silent Spring* bandwagon, the media picked up on Dr. Epstein's testimony and reported it widely. The periodical *Science* highlighted his testimony in its "Point of View" column.[25] But the balance-of-nature philosophy did not translate to balance in the media, which failed to give similar coverage to the testimony of scientific experts such as U.S. Surgeon General Jesse Steinfield, M.D., and John Higginson, Director of the International Agency for Research on Cancer. They, and many others, testified that DDT did not cause cancer in humans. And *Science* magazine refused to publish the point of view of Dr. W. H. Butler of the British Medical Research Council, whose testimony fully contradicted Epstein's position.[26]

Judge Sweeney heard scientific testimony from 125 witnesses over the course of nearly eight months, creating a transcript of more than 9,300 pages. His professionalism and objectivity stand out in the introduction of his Examiner's Report. Judge Sweeney ruled that DDT should not be banned. In his findings, he wrote:

> *No Hearing Examiner will ever enjoy the privilege that I had in listening to so many leaders in the field of scientific and medical achievement .... No restrictions were placed on the number of*

witnesses they could present, other than the necessary exhortations concerning relevance and materiality. The pros and cons of DDT have been well aired. I think the right of cross-examination spurred a genuinely sober assessment of the facts available on the question of the benefits and risks of DDT. DDT is not a carcinogenic [cancer risk], *mutagenic* [mutations], *or teratogenic* [threat to developing fetuses] *hazard to man. The uses of DDT under the registration involved here do not have a deleterious effect on freshwater fish, esturarine organisms, wild birds or other wildlife .... The evidence in this proceeding supports the conclusion that there is a present need for the essential uses of DDT.*

Judge Sweeney rejected the proposition that DDT was unsafe to humans and wildlife as advanced by the Environmental Defense Fund and the scientists who supported it. Instead, his findings and conclusions were consistent with the position of reputable scientific organizations such as the National Academy of Sciences, which had written: "To only a few chemicals does man owe as great a debt as to DDT. In little more than two decades DDT has prevented 500 million human deaths due to malaria that otherwise would have been inevitable."[27] And the World Health Organization had stated: "The discontinuation of the use of DDT would be a disaster to world health."[28]

Judge Sweeny's ruling should have ended the DDT debate on scientific grounds, but that was not the case. Defeated on the front of scientific testimony, the Carson-ogenic forces shifted the battle to another, as Gordon Edwards observed.

"It was highly unusual, but even before the EPA publicly released Judge Sweeney's Report, the Environmental Defense Fund had obtained all of the details, and had already moved to file an Appeal."[29] Although the normal process would have had a judicial officer hear the appeal, "because of the importance of the question, rather than refer it to the judicial officer, Mr. Ruckelshaus decided to rule on the appeal himself."[30]

The decision of the EPA boss to short-circuit the process and handle the appeal himself made a mockery of what had been a careful and serious scientific inquiry. It ranks as a classic example of how politicized science trumps legitimate science to reach the preordained goal. Not only was he an attorney with no significant scientific background, but:

> *Ruckelshaus never attended a single day of the seven months of EPA Hearings on DDT, and his Special Assistant, (Marshall Miller), told reporters that Ruckelshaus had not even read the transcripts (Santa Ana Register, 23 July 1972.) He turned the transcript of the Hearings over to a 29-year old judicial officer, Charles Fabrikant, who also 'had no special background in science.' Two non-scientists in Fabrikant's office prepared anti-DDT tracts based upon Environmental Defense Fund propaganda, rather than on the hearings transcript and the data of the experts. (They included claims from EDF literature that appeared nowhere in the entire 9,300 pages of the Hearing transcript.) Fabricant synthesized a report based upon those tracts, and prepared the document that became the infamous 'Ruckelshaus Opinion and Order on DDT.'* [31]

The order issued on June 2, 1972, and banned DDT's production and use in the United States retroactive to January 1, 1972.

Although at the time Ruckelshaus denied that his unilateral and arbitrary reversal of the science-based findings was political, he later acknowledged that in such decisions "the ultimate judgment remains political."[32] This proved a watershed moment.

The total ban of DDT for purely political reasons marked the beginning of a pattern of environmental decision making by government agencies in response to pressure and influence from exclusionists – many inside the agencies – on the basis of political expediency and public perception, not scientific evidence.[33] Another key reality escaped notice, but Gordon Edwards was paying attention.

At the time he officially banned DDT based on Environmental Defense Fund propaganda, "Ruckelshaus was himself a member of the Environmental Defense Fund and ... [later] solicited donations for the group on his personal stationery. On that stationery, he said 'I hope you will read this brochure explaining some of the critical problems EDF has fought to solve, and I hope you will join.' The brochure claimed that 'EDF scientists blew the whistle on DDT by showing it to be a cancer hazard,' and 'three years later, when the dust had cleared, EDF had won.'"[34]

Long before the ban, Dr. Edwards had searched for a personal way to demonstrate that DDT was not harmful to humans – even if consumed in amounts far in excess of what any people would normally ingest in their entire lifetimes. "After hearing DDT accused of being extremely toxic to humans, and after studying the U.S. Public Heath Service's report of tests in which human volunteers ingested up to 35 mgs of it per day for nearly two years, with no adverse effects,[35] and after reviewing Dr. Edward Laws' report on the workers who absorbed 400 times as much DDT as normal Americans, daily, at the Montrose Chemical Company,[36] and remembering my own days ... during the war in Europe ... I thought I should try to convince people that the environmental extremists were wrong. Thereafter, at the beginning of each DDT speech I made,[37] I would publicly eat a tablespoon of DDT powder." *Esquire* magazine published a full-page photograph of Dr. Edwards eating a tablespoon – about 12 mgs – of DDT powder in its September, 1971, issue. The caption stated that he was eating 200 times the normal intake.[38]

If the anti-DDT propaganda of Rachel Carson and her extremist followers had been true, Gordon Edwards should have perished from DDT contact as early as 1944, when he dusted the troops and civilians in Italy. And by the standards of anti-DDT hysteria of the early 1970s, he should have dropped dead soon after ingesting 200 times the normal amount, following the first of his numerous speeches on DDT's effects on humans. Instead Gordon Edwards, conservationist, environmentalist, and outdoorsman, proved them wrong again.

He lived on, healthy and active, until July, 2004, when he suffered a fatal heart attack climbing one of Glacier National Parks more than 200 mountains over routes he helped pioneer since he first began climbing there in 1947. He was 84 years old. That was more than long enough for Dr. Edwards and other men of science to see the deadly consequences of the ban on DDT.

NOTES

1. Women's National Press Club, Dec. 5, 1962, where she "charged that basic scientific truths were being compromised 'to serve the gods of profit and production.'" Lear, *Rachel Carson: Witness for Nature, op. cit.*, p. 426.

2. Dr. R. Milton Carleton, Ph.D, *"Silent Spring:* Merely Science Fiction Instead of Fact," *Chicago Sunday Sun-Times*, September 23, 1963; cited by Lear, *op. cit.*, p. 431.

3. George C. Decker, Ph.D., "Pros and Cons of Pests, Pest Control and Pesticides," *World Review of Pest Control*, Spring, 1962, pg. 6-18; cited by Lear, *op. cit.*, pp. 431, 432.

4. Reference to Robert White-Stevens, Ph.D; Lear, *op. cit.*, p. 434.

5. Thomas H. Jukes Letter of May 12, 1963; cited in Lear, *op. cit.,* p. 434.

6. Frederick J. Stare, "Some comments on Silent Spring," *Nutrition Reviews*, January, 1963; cited by Lear, *op. cit.*, p. 433, and footnote 13, p. 574.

7. Cynthia Westcott, Ph.D., "Half Truths or Whole Story? A Review of Silent Spring," *National Gardener*, 1962; cited by Lear, *op. cit.*, pp. 435-36.

8. Lear, *op. cit.*, p. 437.

9. Curtis' allegations are refuted, among other places, by Claus and Bolander in *Ecological Sanity*, David McKay Company, 1977, pp. 288-550; as cited by Edwards, "Mosquitoes, DDT, and Human Health," op. cit., p.25.

10. *New York Times* and *San Francisco Chronicle*, November 30, 1969, as cited by Edwards in "Remembering Silent Spring and Its Consequences," p. 4; *Seattle Times*, October, 1969, as cited by Patrick Poole, "The Green-Big Tobacco Death Alliance," *FrontPageMagazine.com*, October 18, 2006; also Drs. Tren and Bate, "Malaria and the DDT Story," IEA Research Paper No. OP 117, http://ssrn.com/abstract=677448

11. For more information on EDF, later shortened to "Environmental Defense," see www.environmentaldefense.org reprint of "The Birth of Environmentalism," from the 1990 book, *Ahead of the Curve,* by Robert E. Taylor.

12. Wurster, "DDT reduces photosynthesis by marine phytoplankton," *Science* 1968; 159: 1474-1475; as cited by Edwards, "Remembering Silent Spring and its Consequences," *op. cit.*, p. 4.

13. The biographical sketch of Dr. Ehrlich provided by The National Center for Public Policy Research states: "Since the release of (*The Population Explosion*) in 1968, Ehrlich has been one of the most frequently cited 'experts' on environmental issues by the media, despite the fact that his predictions on the fate of the planet, more often than not, have been wrong." http://www.nationalcenter.org/dos7111.htm

14. Paul Ehrlich, "Ecocatastrophe," *Ramparts*, September 3, 1969, pp. 24-28.

15. *Science*, Issue 167: 1970.

16. Edwards, "Remembering Silent Spring," *op. cit.*, p. 5.

17. Bate and Tren, "Science in Environmental Policy Making," September 28, 2005, p. 6, http://*www.aci.org*

18. Lisa Makson, "Rachel Carson's Ecological Genocide," *FrontPageMagazine.com*, July 31, 003, p. 3, www.frontpagemag.com/Articles/ReadArticle.asp?ID=9169

19. Edwards, "Mosquitoes, DDT, and Human Health," *op. cit.*, p. 26.

20. "The Vietnam War," http://www.vietnamwar.com/PoliticalProtests.htm

21. Shabecoff, *op. cit.*, pp. 103-104.

22. "An Interview With Samuel Epstein, An Epidemic Of Cancer Deception: The Establishment, Why We Can't Trust Them," *The Sun*, March, 2000, http://www.healthy-communications.com/prepedemic3-02-02.html

23. Paul Driessen, "Roots of Eco-Imperialism," *Eco-Imperialism*, Free Enterprise Press, Bellevue, WA, 2003-2004, pp. 27-28; for more explanation of the precautionary principle, see Michael Fumento, *Science Under Siege: Balancing Technology and the Environment,* Wm. Morrow Company, New York, 1993, pp. 45-77; Patrick Moore's speech: "Environmentalism in the 21st Century, *Greenspirit, op. cit.*

24. "An Interview with Samuel Epstein," An Epidemic Of Cancer Deception: The Establishment, Why We Can't Trust Them," *op. cit.,* p. 8.

25. *Science*, Issue 175, 1972, p. 610.

26. James P. Hogan, "Kicking the Sacred Cow: Saving the Mosquitoes – The War on DDT," www.jamesphogan.com/books/kicking_the_sacred_cow.php?section=5

27. *The Life Sciences*, Washington, D.C., 1970, p. 432.

28. Edwards, "Mosquitoes, DDT, and Human Health," *op. cit.,* p. 24.

29. Edwards, "Remembering Silent Spring," p. 34, http://*www.oism.org/ddp/ddt.htm.*

30. June 3, 1982 affidavit testimony of John Quarles, General Counsel for EPA, U.S. District Court for the Northern District of Alabama; as cited by Edwards, "EPA and the Reasonable Certainty of No Harm," (Prepared for address to Doctors for Disaster Preparedness, Seattle, Washington, 6 June 1999), p. 6.

31. Edwards, "Remembering Silent Spring," *op. cit.*, p. 33.

32. Ruckelshaus' letter to Allan Grant, President of the American Farm Bureau Federation, April 26, 1979; as cited by J. Gordon Edwards, "DDT: A Case Study in Scientific Fraud," *Journal of American Physicians and Surgeons*, Vol. 9, No. 3, Fall, 2004.

33. Marjorie Mazel Hecht, "Scientist Score DDT Ban," *21st Century Science & Technology Maazine*, Summer, 1992, p. 48.

34. Edwards, "Remembering Silent Spring," *op. cit.*, p. 34.

35. W. J. Hayes, "The effect of known repeated oral doses of DDT in man," *Journal of the American Medical Association*, 162: 890-897, 1956.

36. Edward Laws, *et al.*, "Men with intensive occupational exposure to DDT," *Archives of Environmental Health* 15: 766-775, 1967.

37. According to Dr. Edwards, his DDT speeches averaged about one per week. See "Mosquitoes, DDT, and Human Health," *op. cit.*, p. 5.

38. Edwards, "Remembering Silent Spring," *op. cit.*, p. 37.

CHAPTER 5

THE TRAGIC LEGACY: ECOLOGICAL GENOCIDE

The world environmental movement, while trying to be a friend to nature, has unfortunately often been an enemy of man.

— Dr. Roger Bate, Director, Africa Fighting Malaria[1]

THE WORLD HEALTH Organization's earlier prediction of the worldwide consequence of a United States ban of DDT could not have been more accurate. After boldly declaring in 1969 that "the discontinuation of the use of DDT would be a disaster to world health," beginning in 1975 – just three years after Ruckelshaus banned DDT's manufacture and use in the United States – the WHO began yielding to pressure from North America and Europe, both influenced by "Carson-ogenic" ideology, to replace the aggressive and enormously successful 30-year malaria-control approach of total mosquito vector eradication, with one of passive response.

Under direction of the WHO, together with its partner, the United Nations Environment Program, the highly effective and popular use of indoor residential spraying,[2] gave way to programs promoting insecticide-treated bed nets and drug treatment therapies – programs that do not have as their primary objective the full eradication of the mosquito-carriers of malaria. According to Dr. Donald Roberts of the Uniformed Services University of the Health Sciences in Bethesda, Maryland, "Neither ... [drug] treatment nor use of insecticide-treated nets will result in dramatic reductions of malaria."[3] Dr. Roberts is emphatic: "DDT is the best insecticide we have today for controlling malaria. DDT is long-lasting, the alternatives are not. DDT is cheap, the alternatives are not. End of story."[4]

Dr. Roberts also points out the enormous economic boost malarial countries receive when hundreds of thousands of their people are *not* victims of malaria or other infectious diseases. India provides a vivid example. In the pre-DDT year, 1940, the country had 100 million cases of malaria with 2.5 million deaths annually. Its people produced less than 25 million tons of wheat and experienced massive starvation, while trying to cope with and control malaria took 60 percent of India's Gross Domestic Product. By the 1960s, as Drs. Bate and Tren testified, when, due to DDT, malaria cases had been reduced to less than 100,000, with fewer than 1,000 deaths, India's economic stability enabled its people to produce in excess of 100 million tons of wheat.[5]

In 1977, exclusionist organizations sued to prohibit the U.S. Agency for International Development (USAID) from exporting DDT to other countries. After the USAID issued Regulation 16 Guidelines in 1986, Secretary of State George Schultz telegraphed orders to all U.S. embassies that "[t]he U.S. cannot, repeat cannot, participate in programs using . . . DDT."[6]

After three decades of unrelenting pressure by the powerful exclusionist cabal to influence donor countries, including the United States, to cut off funding for DDT spraying in the poor malarial nations of the world, the number of deaths and sicknesses from the disease is currently greater than at any point in history. As of 2003, "there are some 300 to 500 million reported cases of malaria each year, 90 percent of them occurring in Africa. According to the World Health Organization, about two and a half million people die of the disease each year, again, mostly in Africa, the majority of them poor children ... about one child being lost to malaria every 30 seconds."[7] "It's worse than it was 50 years ago," says Dr. Robert Desowitz, malaria expert at the University of North Carolina, Chapel Hill.[8]

"The resurgence of a disease that was almost eradicated 30 years ago is a case study in the danger of putting concern for nature above concern for people," decries Nizam Ahmad, a Bangladesh analyst of health conditions affecting developing countries.[9]

Over the last three decades, "[t]he case study of DDT and its place in malaria control," Drs. Bate and Tren told senators, "is a perfect example of how bad science and scaremongering allow government officials, UN agencies and private companies to put their own interests, commercial or otherwise, ahead of those that they are assisting."[10] Uganda serves as a prime example of how these forces come together to prevent African nations from protecting their people from malaria.

According to the WHO, Uganda had more than 12 million cases of malaria in 2003, with 93 percent of its 27 million people constantly living in fear of the disease. Remembering its past eradication of the disease through the use of DDT, Uganda, a few years ago, renewed its effort to again acquire and use DDT to control the active mosquito vector. But, "on February 2, 2005, the UN news agency IRIN reported that the European Union had cautioned Uganda against using DDT." On April 26, 2005, the EU tightened the screw "when the chief of the EU mission in Uganda said there could be dire consequences for [Uganda's] exports to Europe – which account for more than 30 percent of Uganda's total exports – if DDT was detected" on its horticultural exports.[11]

A month later, on September 23, 2005, Dr. Gerhard Hesse of the German corporation, Bayer Crop Sciences, a major manufacturer of a less effective and more expensive alternative to DDT, sent an email to malaria scientists acknowledging that "DDT use is for us a commercial threat," following which he restated his company's support for the European Union's threat to impose trade sanctions against those countries that seek to use DDT for malaria control.[12]

The WHO's current malaria response program is called Roll Back Malaria, which, as the name suggests, simply responds to the continuous onslaught of malaria, rather than aggressively eradicating the mosquito vector with DDT before it can infect. Suggesting the presence of corruption surrounding this program, Bate and Tren write that "Bayer Crop Sciences reported sales of more than $7 billion in 2004, and Bayer's Dr. Hesse is a board member of the World Health Organization's Roll Back

Malaria coalition."[13] "The outrageous tragedy is that children in Uganda and elsewhere are paying with their lives and facing a blighted future so that a coalition of industrial concerns and public agencies can maintain their power base and profits."[14]

While politicized science and scaremongering are certainly seminal factors in the continuing embargo on DDT, as is the multibillion dollar incentive to companies manufacturing DDT alternatives, there is an even more sinister reason that the people of African and other developing countries are dying by the millions from malaria.

Columnist John D'Aloia, Jr., poses these poignant questions:

> *What would you call an action, knowingly taken, that resulted in the deaths of tens of millions of people, people who lived in a certain part of the world? Does the word "genocide" come to mind? Consider these grim statistics – 50 million killed since 1972; almost 90 percent of the victims are in sub-Saharan Africa.*[15]

When the Environmental Defense Fund began its efforts in the late 1960s to have DDT banned, Dr. Edwards reported that Dr. Charles Wurster, its chief scientist, was asked whether many people would die if EDF achieved its objective. Edwards writes that he responded: "Probably ... so what? People are the cause of all the problems; we have too many of them. We need to get rid of some of them, and this [referring to malaria] is as good a way as any."[16]

Some may find this comment shocking, but it serves as an example of the extremism that flows from fundamentalist pantheism and its agenda of politicized science. In this view people are the problem; there are "too many" of them. Therefore, to complete the syllogism, we need to "get rid" of some of them, with the moral detachment of General Buck Turgidson in *Dr. Strangelove*. The agent of choice for this deadly exclusion is malaria, thriving again because of the ban on DDT.

When the campaign to ban DDT in the early 1970s was gathering steam, "the Audubon Society distributed hundreds of thousands of yellow propaganda leaflets stating: 'DDT should be banned throughout the land, and banned from export.' And on February 25, 1971, the Sierra Club's president stated: 'The Sierra Club wants a ban, not just a curb, on persistent pesticides, even in the tropical countries where DDT has kept malaria under control."'[17] As Dr. Edwards noted: "These actions were taken despite the full knowledge that a ban on DDT would result in the death of ... million[s] [of] Third World inhabitants."[18]

"Millions" gives some definition to what Dr. Wurster meant by "some." By any account many will simply have to die. Advocates of this view are quite up-front about it.

In his 1990 book, *The Discipline of Curiosity*, Alexander King, founder of the depopulationist organization known as the Malthusian Club of Rome,[19] which has been active in more than 40 countries, wrote: "My own doubts came when DDT was introduced. In Guyana, within two years it had almost eliminated malaria. So my chief quarrel with DDT in hindsight is that it has greatly added to the population problem."[20]

In a 1991 interview with the United Nations' *UNESCO Courier*, famed oceanographer and environmental icon, Jacques Cousteau, revealed the overriding concern of many eco-activists when he asked: "Should we eliminate suffering diseases? The idea is beautiful, but perhaps not a benefit in the long run. We should not allow our dread of diseases to endanger the future of our species. This is a terrible thing to say. In order to stabilize world population, we must eliminate 350,000 people per day. It is a horrible thing to say, but it's just as bad not to say it."[21]

Edwin J. Cohn of the USAID's Office of Policy Development was less gentlemanly than Cousteau when he said about the fecundity of women in malarial countries: "Rather dead than alive and riotously reproducing."[22] Consider also National Park Service biologist, David Graber, whose commentary in the *Los Angeles Times* stated:

> I know scientists who remind me that people are part of nature, but it isn't true. Somewhere along the line ... we quit the contract and became a cancer. We have become a plague upon ourselves and upon the Earth .... Until such time as Homo sapiens should decide to rejoin nature, some of us can only hope for the right virus to come along.[23]

It was a classic statement of what Greenpeace founder Patrick Moore said about his former extremist colleagues. "Humans are characterized as a cancer on the Earth .... They are anti-science and technology."[24]

For senior University of Texas ecology professor, Eric Pianka, the right virus has already come along. Pianka was the recipient of the Distinguished Scientist Award for 2006 from the Texas Academy of Science. In March, 2006, at the 109th meeting of that Academy, Dr. Pianka openly advocated the extermination of 90 percent of the earth's population – more than five billion human beings – by way of airborne Ebola. He decried that "the Earth as we know it will not survive without drastic measures. Then, and without presenting any data to justify this number, he asserted that the only feasible solution to saving the Earth is to reduce the population to 10 percent of the present number." When the question and answer session concluded, "immediately almost every scientist, professor and college student present stood to their feet and vigorously applauded the man who had enthusiastically endorsed the elimination of 90 percent of the human population. Some even cheered." [25]

Today, the large and influential exclusionist organizations avoid expressing publicly the elitist and antipeople philosophy reflected in the sampling of comments above. Nor do media advisors for the World Health Organization, the United Nations agencies, or the donor community of wealthy nations of North America or Europe, allow their clients to be so candid. Yet, the dogged withholding of the safest, cheapest, and most effective malaria-eradicating insecticide in history to the poor countries whose people are dying by the millions and sustaining brain-damaging illnesses by the billions, leads to no other logical conclusion. The exclusionists are getting what they want, a kind of people cleansing.

"Stunning Photographs Show the Horror of Genocide in Darfur," reads the headline in the *San Francisco Chronicle*.[26] In the article, the photographer, former Marine Captain Brian Steidle, the U.S. representative to the Africa Union peacekeeping mission, tells how Arab-dominated Sudanese government forces, side-by-side with Arab militias, are systematically killing thousands of non-Arab Darfurians. "Darfur is a region in Sudan, the largest country in Africa ... [Darfurians] are being killed because they're black," explained Steidle. He told of seeing Sudanese planes and helicopters bomb, strafe, and burn villages, "shooting indiscriminately with their antipersonnel rockets into [one] village of 20,000 . . . I saw 37 villages burned in one day," Steidle recalled. Nearly 200,000 Darfurians have been killed and two million more have been displaced. That this is a "genocide" is undeniable, as the universal use of the word in media accounts of the five year carnage makes clear.

Also in Africa, continuing for more than three decades, over 50 million black people have died, while billions more have suffered permanent brain damage and other lifelong debilitations. Yet, even now one rarely reads of this systematic extermination in the general print media, hardly ever is DDT mentioned as a certain antidote, and virtually never is the word "genocide" applied to it.

Michael Critchton, M.D.,[27] declared in a 2003 speech:

> *So I can tell you some facts. I know you haven't read any of what I am about to tell you in newspapers, because newspapers literally don't report them. I can tell you that DDT is not a carcinogen and did not cause birds to die and should never have been banned. I can tell you that the people who banned it knew it wasn't carcinogenic and banned it anyway. I can tell you that the DDT ban caused the deaths of tens of millions of poor people, mostly children, whose deaths are directly attributable to a callous, technologically advanced western society that promoted the new cause of environmentalism by pushing a fantasy about a pesticide, and thus irrevocably harmed the third world. Banning DDT is one of the most disgraceful episodes in the twentieth century of America. We knew better, and we did it anyway, and we let people around the world die and didn't give a damn.[28]*

The forced submission of a specific population to death from an avoidable disease for the purpose of holding down the population to protect wildlife species can only be considered ecological genocide. That has become possible because the politicized science and exclusionism from Rachel Carson's book, have affected popular thinking. Consider *Time* magazine's interview with Bill and Melinda Gates about their commitment of $258 million to fight malaria in Africa. Melinda Gates said:

> *"When we were in Mozambique, seeing the mothers with babies dying of malaria, I think for both of us it really gave us a face to what we're trying to do in the whole area of malaria," said Melinda Gates. Bill Gates described their approach to a solution: "Malaria deaths have doubled over the past 20 years because of drug resistance,*

population increase, and it's a great example of the whole global vacuum. Inventions that exist [were] *not being put to use, the creation of new approaches and new drugs was not being funded very well, and the ultimate solution, which is a vaccine, people had largely given up on.'*[29]

These generous and well-intentioned philanthropists appear unaware of some realities. The mosquito vector and its larvae must be eradicated as a first step in reducing malaria-caused death and suffering in Africa – a feat only DDT has proven capable of achieving. Bill and Melinda Gates also appear unaware that hundreds of millions of dollars in vaccine research has proven a dismal failure. As Dr. Edwards wrote in 2004:

After 25 years, [US] *AID's malaria vaccine research project is still proving to be a disaster. In a 6-year effort, during which perhaps 18 million human beings died of malaria, U.S. Navy researchers sequenced the genome of the parasite causing falciparum malaria, which has about 6,000 genes, compared to fewer than 30 in a typical virus. Th[is so-called] 'breakthrough' was announced at a* [2002] *joint press conference in Washington, D.C., called by Science and Nature. The genome of the Anopheles gambiae vector, which contains nearly 300-million DNA base pairs, has also been sequenced. To date, there is no evidence that knowing the sequences will lead to any methods of controlling malaria transmission.*[30]

The Gates' enormous financial contribution to fight malaria in Africa would fund interior residential spraying of DDT throughout the malarial countries of Africa and perhaps the world. Yet not one penny will be dedicated to the use of DDT. Sadly, millions of poor Africans will die, and others will sustain permanent brain damage, while the Gates-funded vaccine research is under way.

The cause of this disaster is clear to all but the willfully blind. "Carson and those who joined her in the crusade against DDT have contributed to millions of preventable deaths," said former U.S. Surgeon General and retired U.S. Navy Vice Admiral Dr. Harold M. Koenig. Debunking the vast increase in human cancer that Carson implicitly predicted from DDT's continued use, Dr. Koenig added:

Sure more people are dying now of cancer than they did in the past, because they are no longer dying of other causes at earlier ages, especially infectious diseases. The longer people live, the greater chances they have of dying of cancers. We know of some things that have greater association with cancers. These include the use of tobacco in any form, excessive sun exposure, obesity, stress and lack of exercise.[31]

According to a 2001 study reported in the *Journal of Clinical Oncology*, utilizing data from the National Centers for Health Statistics on cancer mortality between 1950 and 1990,[32] Carson's implicit predictions of cancer-increase from DDT use have proven utterly wrong. While the mortality rates for "all cancers" during those four decades increased 8 percent, mortality from lung cancer alone increased 223 percent, while mortality from cancers other than lung cancer fell 17 percent. The study concluded:

It is widely recognized that the increase in lung cancer [during this 40 year period] *resulted almost solely from increases in cigarette smoking .... The focus on all-cancer mortality also led to the widespread perception of a cancer epidemic caused by environmental pollution. A typical commentary blamed 'increasing cancer rates' on 'exposure to industrial chemicals and run-away modern technologies whose explosive growth has clearly outpaced the ability of society to control them.'* [33] *There is no denying the existence of environmental problems, but the present data show that they produced no striking increases in cancer mortality. In reality, the cancer 'epidemic' consisted of one disease, cancer of the lung, and was due to one lifestyle factor, cigarette smoking.*[34]

Dr. Koenig concluded: "As far as I know, there is no association between DDT or any other insecticides and cancer. To categorize Carson's work as research is a big stretch. It was really just hysterical speculation."[35]

The exclusionists were wrong on DDT, with deadly consequences. But as Charles Wurster observed, that campaign armed them with new authority on other environmental issues. In fact, they would soon have a federal statute of their very own.

NOTES

1. Bate, "Malaria Rates Underscore Need to Set Aside Costly Taboos," *Journal of the South African Institute of International Affairs*, Dec. 1, 2004, http://www.aei.org/publications/pubID.21641,filter.all/pub_detail.asp

2. As Drs. Bate and Tren described, interior residential spraying, "IRS" (as it is called) is a process whereby "sprayers apply a small amount of DDT, usually 2g of active ingredient per square meter, on the inside walls of houses and under the eaves outside where most mosquitoes rest between blood meals . . . Because of its long lasting action – up to one year – DDT vastly improved malaria control compared with alternative insecticides that had to be applied every one to two weeks." Senate Committee testimony, "Science in Environmental Policy Making," *op. cit*, p. 3.

3. Donald Roberts, "To Control Malaria, We Need DDT," *21 Century Science & Technology* magazine, Fall 2002, p. 34.

4. Lisa Makson, "Rachel Carson's Ecological Genocide," *FrontPageMagazine.com*, July 31, 2003, p. 2, http://www.frontpagemag.com/Articles/ReadArticle.asp?ID=9169

5. *Ibid*, p. 3

6. Edwards, "DDT: A Study in Scientific Fraud," *op. cit.*, p. 87.

7. Todd Seavey, "The DDT Ban Turns 30 – Millions Dead of Malaria Because of Ban, More Deaths Likely," American Council of Science and Health, June 2002, http://www.acsh.org/publications/reports/ddt2002.html.

8. Makson, *op. cit.*, p. 3.

9. *Ibid*, p. 2.

10. Bates and Tren, "Science in Environmental Policy Making," *op. cit.*, p. 2,

11. *Ibid*, p. 12.

12. Bate and Tren, "Science in Environmental Policy Making," *op. cit.*, p. 12; "Deadly Mosquito Standoff," *Washington Times,* October 21, 2005.

13. Bate and Tren, "Deadly Mosquito Standoff," *op. cit.*

14. Bate and Tren, "Science in Environmental Policy Making," *op. cit.*, p. 13.

15. John D'Aloia, "Return DDT," *eco-logic Powerhouse*, Oct. 13, 2004, www.eco.freedom.org/el/20041001/trackside.shtml .

16. According to Dr.Edwards in "Remembering Silent Spring" (p.7), Victor Yannacone, a founder of EDF, was told of Wurster's comment, and related it in a speech at the Union League Club in New York on May 20, 1970. Dr. Edwards wrote: "Yannacone told me that such comments were leading him to consider withdrawing from the Environmental Defense Fund, because he was formerly a civil rights attorney and was beginning to feel that he was working with the wrong people." Yannacone later resigned from EDF. Wurster's comment also was reported by Congressman John

Rarick, who chaired the House Hearings on the Federal Pesticide Control Act of 1971, pp. 266-267, in Serial No. 92-A. Although neither Yannacone nor Wurster testified at the hearing, Wurster later sent a letter to the committee (made part of the record) reading as follows: "I wish to deny all of the statements of Mr. Yannacone. His remarks about me, attributed to me, and about other trustees of EDF are purely fantasy and bear no resemblance to the truth. It was in part because Mr. Yannacone lost touch with reality that he was dismissed by EDF, and his remarks of May 1970 [in the Union League Club speech] indicate that his inability to separate fact from fiction has accelerated." It is not unfair to characterize Dr. Wurster's denial as vague and general in that it did not indicate which of Yannacone's remarks attributed to him were inaccurate, or in what manner they were inaccurate. Considering the nature of the specific comment attributed to him, one can think of more specific and emphatic forms of denial than Wurster chose to use.

17. Both organizations' comments cited by Edwards in "Remembering Silent Spring," *op. cit.*, p. 7,

18. *Ibid*, p. 7.

19. The Malthusian Club of Rome is named after Thomas Robert Malthus (1766 – 1834), the British political economist best known for his gloom and doom predictions on population. In his "Essay on the Principle of Population," he postulated on the factors that would depopulate the earth, such as diseases and epidemics, famine, pestilence, plague, and war. Although few of his predictions came to pass in industrialized countries, a few of them, such as malaria, are still harshly evident in developing countries.

20. Edwards, "Remembering Silent Spring," *op. cit.*, p. 7.

21. UNESCO Courier (French language edition), November 1991; also referenced by G. Edward Griffin, *The Creature from Jekyll Island: A Second Look at the Federal Reserve,* American Media: 1994.

22. R.S. Deowitz, *Malaria Capers*, W. W. Norton Co, New York, N.Y., 1991; as cited by Edwards, "DDT: A Case Study in Scientific Fraud," *op. cit.*, p. 85.

23. D.M. Graber, "Mother Nature as a hothouse flower," *Los Angeles Times Book Review*, October 22, 1989, p. 10.

24. Moore, "Environmentalism for the 21st Century, *Greenspirit,* http://www.greenspirit.com/21st_century.cfm?msid=29&page=1

25. Forrest M. Mims, III, chairman of the Environmental Science Section, Texas Academy of Science, and author of 60 books. See his account of Professor Pianka's troubling remarks, "Meeting Doctor Doom," in the Web magazine, *The Citizen Scientist,* http://www.sas.org/tcs/weeklyIssues_2006/20060407/feature1p/index.html

26. *San Francisco Chronicle*, March 9, 2006, p. B1.

27. Michael Critchton: A.B. degree, *summa cum laude,* from Harvard University; M.D. degree from Harvard Medical School; post-doctoral fellowship at the Salk Institute for Biological Studies. His novels include *The First Great Train Robbery, The Andromeda Strain, Jurrassic Park*, and *State of Fear.* Critchton is a frequent lecturer, essayist and a courageous, outspoken opponent of "consensus science."

28. Commonwealth Club, San Francisco, September 15, 2003.

29. "Riches to the Poor," *Time*, November 7, 2005, p. 103.

30. Edwards, "DDT: A Case Study in Scientific Fraud," *op. cit.*, p. 87.

31. Makson, "Rachel Carson's Ecological Genocide," *op. cit.*, p. 2-3.

32. DDT and related insecticides were in use in the U.S. between 1945 and 1972.

33. "A typical commentary" is a reference to Dr. Samuel S. Epstein's 1990 article, "Losing the war against cancer: Who's to blame and what to do about it," *International Journal of Health Service* 20: 53-71.

34. Brad Rodu and Philip Cole, "The Fifty-Year Decline of Cancer in America," *Journal of Clinical Oncology*, Vol. 19, Issue 1 (January), 2001, pp. 239 - 241, http://www.jco.org/cgi/content/full/19/1/239

35. Makson, "Rachel Carson's Ecological Genocide," *op. cit.*, pp. 2 and 3.

PART TWO

THE ENDANGERED SPECIES ACT OF 1973

CHAPTER 6

"WHATEVER THE COST"

BETWEEN 1962 AND 1972, a period that witnessed the first Earth Day (1970), the creation of the Environmental Protection Agency (1970), the banning of DDT (1972), and much of the Vietnam War, Congress enacted an array of species protection bills and other environmental laws that responded to public concerns. These included the Wilderness Act in 1964, the first Clean Water Act in 1965, the Endangered Species Preservation Act of 1966, the Clean Air Act (1967), the Wild and Scenic Rivers Act (1968), the Endangered Species Conservation Act of 1969, the National Environmental Policy Act of 1969, the Wild Free-Roaming Horses and Burros Act (1971), and the Marine Mammal Protection Act (1972).

During these years, major newspapers continued to report ongoing concerns expressed by biologists, government officials, and preservationist groups that species familiar to the public were still declining, and editorialized for stronger laws. Very active in this regard, for example, was the *New York Times*. In several issues during 1967 and 1968, it reported and editorialized that the FWS considered 78 species of birds, fish, mammals, reptiles, and amphibians to be endangered, and that 250 other species were facing extinction, including the "blue whale, the polar bear and the leopard, the fearsome tiger and the humble alligator."[1] These efforts led to Congress' enactment of the Endangered Species Conservation Act of 1969.

Yet, while these laws, including those protecting endangered species, contributed substantially to their purpose, the preservationist community clamored for more. The organizations and thousands of their mobilized supporters lobbied Congress and the White House to enact greater protections for endangered species.

In late 1972, President Nixon called on Congress to enact a stronger species protection law. He stated that "even the most recent act to protect endangered species, which dates only from 1969, simply does not provide the kind of management tools needed to act early enough to save a vanishing species."[2] Shortly following the President's comments, identical endangered species bills were introduced in the House and Senate. However, with the war in Vietnam quickly becoming Nixon's war, 1972 was an especially contentious election year and neither measure moved out of its first committee.

When a reelected Nixon and the heavily Democratic Congress returned to work in early 1973, four similar endangered species bills were introduced early in the session – a Democrat-sponsored bill in the House and the Senate, and Nixon administration bills in both houses. These measures contained several significant changes from then-existing law. One provision – later, "Section 4" of the ESA – required the Secretary of Interior to determine whether "any species" should be listed as endangered or threatened. A species was defined as "fish or wildlife or plants," and the measures further defined "fish or wildlife" as "any mammal, fish, bird ... amphibian, reptile, mollusk, crustacean, arthropod or other invertebrate."[3]

News coverage and editorial support in the months leading up to introduction of legislation, as well as the year-long congressional deliberations on the measures themselves, focused almost entirely on larger, charismatic species such as wolves, eagles, grizzly bears, whales, and other species popular with and familiar to the public. As House members and Senators discussed the bills during committee hearings and in public comments, little, if any, reference was made to the less familiar "fish or wildlife or plant species" that also were protected by the measures. From these discussions and comments, one could easily be lulled into the misunderstanding – as apparently were several members of Congress, as well as associations and organizations representing industry and land users – that the thousands of little known, obscure species were not the bills' primary beneficiaries, or that their inclusion need not be taken seriously.

Another major provision, which became the ESA's "Section 7," that elicited no significant interest on the part of Congress prohibited the "take" of any listed species. A "take" means to "harass, harm, pursue, hunt, shoot, wound, kill, trap, capture or collect" a listed species.[4] And even though in committee testimony the wildlife director of Friends of the Earth stated that the degradation of a listed species' habitat would fit the definition of a "take" under the bills, "no member of Congress questioned the organization's representative on this point or raised the issue elsewhere."[5]

What is curious and indeed remarkable in light of the acrimony that has accompanied the ESA over the past 35 years is the absence of any serious debate on any of the bills' provisions during congressional deliberations. What little exchange there was concerned whether the new federal endangered species law would preempt the states' historical authority to manage wildlife. Once proponents responded that the states would continue to be free to enact more restrictive species protection laws if they so chose, that issue also went away.

Before the July vote in the Senate, even a member not regarded as friendly to further species protection, Senator Ted Stevens (R-Alaska), stood to offer his support, declaring that although "the bill is not perfect, I believe it takes a major step in the protection of American endangered and threatened species."[6] The Senate vote was 92-0; eight Senators did not vote. The members of the House were no less enthusiastic.

The primary author of House Resolution 37, Congressman John Dingell (D-Michigan), commented before the vote that he had not heard "a whisper of opposition to its passage at the earliest opportunity."[7] Dingell's comment was quite accurate; when HR 37 came before the House in September, it passed 390-12, with 32 members not voting. Even the 12 members who voted "no" chose not to speak against the bill in prevote deliberations. Nor did opposition materialize when the minor differences between the Senate version and the House version were resolved in the conference committee. On December 19, the Senate unanimously approved the conference committee report, and on December 20 it was approved in the House, 390-4; 73 House members did not vote. No members voiced opposition to the conference committee report in either house.

On December 28, 1973, President Nixon issued this statement from the White House:

> *I have today signed ... the Endangered Species Act of 1973. At a time when Americans are more concerned than ever with conserving our natural resources, this legislation provides the Federal Government with the needed authority to protect an irreplaceable part of our national heritage – threatened wildlife.*
>
> *This important measure grants the Government both the authority to make early identification of endangered species and the means to act quickly and thoroughly to save them from extinction .....*
>
> *Nothing is more priceless and more worthy of preservation than the rich array of animal life with which our country has been blessed. It is a many-faceted treasure, of value to scholars, scientists, and nature lovers alike, and it forms a vital part of the heritage we all share as Americans.*
>
> *I congratulate the 93rd Congress for taking this important step toward protecting a heritage which we hold in trust to countless future generations of our fellow citizens. Their lives will be richer, and America will be more beautiful in the years ahead, thanks to the measure that I have the pleasure of signing into law today.*

How is it that a measure later characterized as the most important environmental law in history could pass through both houses of the United States Congress, and be signed by the President, with virtually no debate or opposition? Indeed, as Congressman Dingell remarked before the House voted on the conference committee report, "[i]t would be no exaggeration to say that scarcely a voice has been heard in dissent."[8] Nor was Dingell referring only to his colleagues in the Congress. With two minor exceptions,[9] no special interests voiced opposition to the bill. Even the conservative National Rifle Association supported the bill.[10]

Shannon Peterson, Ph.D., attorney, ESA researcher and author, offers the most likely explanation:

> *Few at the time opposed the ESA because no one anticipated how it might interfere significantly with economic development or personal property interests .... The timber industry, other natural resource industries, and private property groups declined to fight the law in 1973 because they failed to see how it might affect them.*[11]

Those who declined to oppose the ESA because they didn't recognize how it would affect them got a rude awakening in June, 1978, in the first legal challenge to the Act to reach the Supreme Court. The Supreme Court declared: "The plain intent of Congress in enacting the statute was to halt and reverse the trend toward species extinction, *whatever the cost.*" (Author's emphasis.)[12]

The use of the broad, absolute language, "whatever the cost," is rare in Supreme Court parlance. To understand the "species-first – people-last" attitude that came into full dominance following the Supreme Court's use of those imperious words, the circumstances surrounding the case warrant consideration.

In 1967, the Tennessee Valley Authority (TVA), a public corporation owned by the federal government, proposed to Congress the construction of the Tellico Dam and Reservoir Project on the Little Tennessee River. That river begins in the mountains of northern Georgia, runs through national forestland in North Carolina, and into Tennessee where it converges with the Big Tennessee River near Knoxville. As proposed, the shallow, fast-moving waters of the Little Tennessee River would flow into – and the river itself would be inundated by – a deep reservoir more than 30 miles in length. Conceived as a multipurpose project to benefit the people of the region, the Tellico Dam was designed to stimulate shoreline development, generate hydroelectric power to heat 20,000 additional homes, provide flood control and recreation, and enhance employment opportunities in "an area characterized by underutilization of human resources and out-migration of young people."[13] Congress approved and appropriated start-up funding for construction of the dam and reservoir, and the project got under way later in 1967.

In 1973, with construction at the halfway point, a University of Tennessee ichthyology professor discovered just upriver from the construction site an estimated 10,000 to 15,000 members of a previously unknown species of perch, which became known as "the snail darter," after its primary food source. Also during 1973, while continuing its annual practice of appropriating funds for the dam's construction, Congress was holding hearings on, and at year's end enacted, the Endangered Species Act.

Two years later, as the dam was approaching completion, a University of Tennessee law student named Hiram Hill, who had become familiar with the snail darter's discovery through some ichthyology graduate students, persuaded his environmental law professor, Zygmunt Plater, to utilize the new ESA to list the snail darter as an endangered species. Hill, together with local environmental activists, farmers trying to save their farmland, members of the Cherokee Nation who before Andrew Jackson's March of Tears had lived in the area, and other locals looking for a way to stop the dam's completion, petitioned Secretary of Interior, Cecil D. Andrus, to list the snail darter as endangered. After considering comments from interested parties, including the TVA on behalf of the federal government, Andrus complied:

> *The snail darter occurs only in the swifter portions of shoals over clean gravel substrate in cool, low-turbidity water. Food of the snail darter is almost exclusively snails which require a clean gravel substrate for their survival. The proposed impoundment of water behind the proposed Tellico Dam would result in total destruction of the snail darter's habitat.*[14]

Nonetheless, in December, 1975, Congress and the President again approved funds for the completion of the Tellico project. Early in 1976, with construction nearing completion, Secretary Andrus designated the area of the Little Tennessee River occupied by the snail darter as its "critical habitat."[15] Under Section 7 of the ESA, "all Federal agencies must take such action as is necessary to insure that actions authorized, funded, or carried out by them do not result in the destruction or modification of this critical habitat area."

The Secretary's designation was tantamount to halting construction of the dam. To the people in charge at the TVA, however, the image of a dry, nonoperating, and isolated Tellico Dam inspired fear. The TVA proposed to Secretary Andrus a relocation of the snail darter population to the nearby Hiwassee River. Over several months TVA experimented with transplanting the fish. Although that yielded some promising results, Andrus summarily concluded that transplantation was not feasible.

Late in 1976, after Secretary Andrus declined to take the step of suing TVA to stop the project, Hill and his copetitioners filed suit in federal District Court to enjoin the completion of the dam and filling of the reservoir. In deciding whether to grant the injunction stopping the project, the judge utilized a commonsense balancing approach: while an operating Tellico Dam would likely terminate the snail darter's continued existence on the one hand, granting the injunction would amount to scrapping the entire Tellico Dam project, including millions of dollars of already expended public funds, as well as the dam's anticipated benefits to the people of the region, on the other.

Weighing both sides, the judge decided that granting the injunction under these circumstances would lead to the absurd result of requiring "a court to halt impoundment of water behind a fully completed dam if an endangered species were discovered in the river on the day before such impoundment was scheduled to take place. [I] cannot conceive that Congress intended such a result," the judge's ruling stated.

Such a balancing test, Hill and the other preservationists feared, could establish a dangerous precedent that might thwart future implementation of a law purposely crafted – as they viewed it – to favor species over people. So he and his copetitioners appealed the District Court's ruling to the Sixth Circuit Court of Appeals. While the appeal was under consideration, Congress and the President again approved funding for completion of the Tellico Dam. Early in 1977, however, the Sixth Circuit Court of Appeals found that the District Court had abused its discretion in utilizing a balancing approach, stating: "Courts are ill-equipped to calculate how many dollars must be invested before the value of a dam exceeds that of the endangered species."[16] The Court of Appeals reversed on the grounds that the likely destruction of the snail darter's critical habitat constituted a "blatant statutory violation" of the ESA.[17] The appellate court's decision surprised many in Congress and other potentially affected parties by declaring: "Conscientious enforcement of the Act requires that it be taken to its logical extremes."

The appellate court ordered the District Court to halt all Tellico Dam construction activity. TVA immediately petitioned the U.S. Supreme Court to review the Sixth Circuit's decision, which it agreed to do.[18] In the meantime, a now-awakened Congress began a series of oversight hearings to vent shock and anger over the appellate court's opinion.

Several members introduced bills to limit the scope and reach of the ESA. What in 1973 had been a cordial deliberative process with virtually no disagreement now became a lively and heated debate on a most contentious subject. Both the House and Senate Appropriations Committees issued strongly worded reports urging completion and operation of the dam. The House Report called on TVA to work with the Department of Interior "to relocate the endangered species to another suitable habitat so as to permit the project to proceed as rapidly as possible." It further recommended a special appropriation of $2 million to facilitate the relocation of the snail darter.[19] The report of the Senate Appropriation Committee proved even stronger:

> *This committee has not viewed the Endangered Species Act as preventing the completion and use of these projects that were well under way at the time the affected species were listed as endangered. If the* [ESA] *has* [the effect of preventing completion and use of the dam], *which is contrary to the Committee's understanding of the intent of Congress in enacting the Endangered Species Act, funds should be appropriated to allow these projects to be completed and their benefits realized in the public interest, the Endangered Species Act notwithstanding.*[20]

The Senate Report concurred in the House Committee's recommended appropriation to relocate the snail darter.

The Supreme Court's much-awaited decision in *TVA v. Hill* issued in June, 1978. To the cheers of environmentalists and the dismay of private landowners, agricultural and timber interests, and other commercial users of the land, it was a landmark decision announcing that "[t]he plain intent of Congress in enacting [the ESA] was to halt and reverse the trend toward species extinction, *whatever the cost.*" (Emphasis added.) In rejecting the District Court's balancing of the interests of wildlife with humans, Chief Justice Warren Burger, writing for a six-member majority, stated:

> *It may seem curious to some that the survival of a relatively small number of three-inch fish among all the countless millions of species extant would require the permanent halting of a virtually completed dam for which Congress has expended more than $100 million. The paradox is not minimized by the fact that Congress continued to appropriate large sums of public money for the project, even after congressional Appropriations Committees were apprised of its apparent impact upon the survival of the snail darter. We conclude, however, that the explicit provisions of the Endangered Species Act require precisely that result .... Concededly, this view of the Act will produce results requiring the sacrifice of the anticipated benefits of the project and of many millions of dollars in public funds. But examination of the language, history, and structure of the legislation under review here indicates beyond doubt that Congress intended endangered species to be afforded the highest of priorities[21] ... the plain language of the Act, buttressed by its legislative history, show clearly that Congress viewed the value of endangered species as "incalculable."[22]*

Not seeing it that way at all, Justices Powell, Blackmun, and Rehnquist dissented. Justice Powell, joined by Justice Blackman, and relied upon in Justice Rehnquist's separate dissent, wrote:

> *Nor can I believe that Congress could have intended this Act to produce the "absurd result" – in the words of the District Court – of this case. If it were clear from the language of the Act and its legislative history that Congress intended to authorize this result, this Court would be compelled to enforce it. It is not our province to rectify policy or political judgments by the Legislative Branch, however egregiously they may disserve the public interest. But where the statutory language and legislative history, as in this case, need not be construed to reach such a result, I view it as the duty of this Court to adopt a permissible construction that accords with some modicum of common sense and the public weal.[23]*

Justice Powell pointed up the value of a commonsense balancing approach when considering the merit of wildlife species. "Although the snail darter is a distinct species," he observed, "it is hardly an extraordinary one. Even ichthyologists familiar with the snail darter have difficulty distinguishing it from several related species …. Moreover, new species of darter are discovered in Tennessee at the rate of about 1 a year; 8 to 10 have been discovered in the last five years …. All told, there are some 130 species of darters, 85 to 90 of which are found in Tennessee, 40 to 45 in the Tennessee River system, and 11 in the Little Tennessee itself."[24]

Justice Powell further recognized the ESA's potential economic and social impact in the years to come by noting that "[t]he act covers every animal and plant species, subspecies, and population in the world needing protection. There are approximately 1.4 million full species of animals and 600,000 full species of plants in the world. Various authorities calculate as many as 10 percent of them – some 200,000 – may need to be listed as endangered or threatened. When one counts in subspecies, not to mention individual populations, the total could increase to three to five times that number."[25]

Whether the Court majority's harsh interpretation of the ESA reflected Congress' actual intent and purpose, or was an excessively strict reading of the Act, as the dissenting opinions suggest, the *TVA v. Hill* decision would enjoy a long afterlife – though not for the Tellico Dam or the snail darter. Within the year, a still-angry Congress amended an energy bill which President Jimmy Carter grudgingly signed into law, exempting Tellico Dam from the provisions of the ESA. Two months later the reservoir was filled and the dam went into full operation. Even the dam's predicted extinction of the snail darter came to naught. In August, 1984, the FWS reduced the snail darter's status from endangered to threatened because a thriving population of snail darters was found in the Hiwassee River where TVA biologists had transplanted them during their experiment in 1976. Other natural populations of snail darter as well were found in Tennessee, Alabama, and Georgia.[26] Yet, the primacy given the ESA by the Supreme Court's *Hill* decision had several significant and lasting effects.

Gone was the practical and commonsense approach utilized by the federal District Court – a balancing of the costs and benefits of preserving a species against its economic and social impacts on people. For example, a case very similar to the Tellico Dam construction project occurred in July, 2006. A federal District Court stopped construction on the $320 million Grand Prairie Irrigation Project in Arkansas solely on the unconfirmed report of a single kayaker who claimed to have spotted the ivory-billed woodpecker in a swamp some 14 miles from the project. The last confirmed sighting of this species, presumed extinct in North America, occurred in 1944. But based on this kayaker's report, two exclusionist organizations sued the U.S. Army Corps of Engineers, contending that the project would kill trees in which the woodpecker lived and that the noise from its pumping stations would cause the bird stress.

According to the Justice Department lawyer representing the Army Corps, a one-month delay in construction would cost the Corps $264,000 and a six-month delay would cost $3 million. Following the instruction of *Hill*, however, the judge stopped construction on the irrigation project, stating: "When an endangered species is allegedly jeopardized, the balance of hardships and public interest tip in favor of the protected species." Although the Corps had conducted a study showing that the woodpecker – if one had in fact been spotted – would not be harmed by the project, the judge halted the project until much more extensive studies were conducted.[27] If Justice Powell's dissenting position had carried the day in *Hill*, federal District Courts would have retained the discretion and flexibility to customize their rulings on the ESA to comport with common sense and balance.

The *Hill* decision also emboldened the federal environmental bureaucracy in implementing and enforcing the ESA. Most people who work in regulatory capacities for NOAA Fisheries (which, under the ESA, is lead agency for anadromous fish), and the FWS (as to all other species) choose those positions because they personally embrace a heightened enforcement role for the federal government. Because habitat for most plant and wildlife species is situated on or adjacent to land owned by farmers, ranchers, timber companies, and other private parties, ESA enforcers view the owners of private property as the Act's primary violators. With the natural propensity of regulatory bureaucrats to find ways to expand their authority over time, the Supreme Court's declaration that species extinction was to be halted and reversed "whatever the cost" virtually assured that they would increasingly adopt a "command-and-control" mind-set in performing their mission. Numerous examples are described in this book.

Yet, *Hill* had its most profound effect on exclusionist organizations by affirming their hard-line attitude toward species preservation. To them, the Court's words: "whatever the cost," was an echo of John Muir's call for the preeminence of wild nature, the fulfillment of Rachel Carson's politicized attack on science and technology, and the culmination of what the Environmental Defense Fund's Dr. Charles Wurster had in mind in 1969 when he said that if the environmentalists can win on DDT, they would gain a level of authority they have never had before.

Politically they had won on DDT. By their victory in *Hill*, they were now legally empowered not only to advance, but to enforce, wildlife preservation without restraint. As a practical matter, the "whatever the cost" mandate gave impetus to the antihuman, anticivilization ideology that Greenpeace founder Patrick Moore abandoned. Eco-extremists, Moore explains, "reject consensus politics and sustainable development in favor of continued confrontation and ever-increasing extremism. They ushered in an era of zero tolerance and left-wing politics.... They are anti-business."[28]

As much as the *Hill* decision could have been helpful in insuring that the ESA would be implemented and enforced so as to achieve balance between plant and wildlife species and human interests, it was the ESA itself, not the Supreme Court, that created the imbalance. Although the Court could have adopted a construction of the ESA that better accorded with common sense and the prudent expenditure of public funds, it was indeed the political branches that created the ESA. The negative effects would soon be evident.

NOTES

1. Shannon Peterson, *Acting for Endangered Species – The Statutory Ark*, University of Kansas Press, 2002, p. 25, citing "78 Species Listed Near Extinction," *New York Times*, March 12, 1967; "Civilization's Prey," *New York Times* editorial, September 9, 1967; "Traffic in Savagery," *New York Times* editorial, September 19, 1968.

2. Nixon, *Public Papers of the Presidents of the United States*, 1972, p. 183; as cited by Petersen, *op. cit.*, p. 27.

3. ESA, 16 *U.S. Code* 1532, "Definitions," Section 3 (16) and (8).

4. *Ibid*, Section 3 (19).

5. Petersen*, op. cit.,* pp. 33-34.

6. Statement of Senator Stevens, reprinted in Committee on Environment and Public Works, *Legislative History*, p. 361, as cited by Petersen, *op. cit.,* p. 29.

7. Statement of Representative Dingell, reprinted in Committee on Environment and Public Works, *Legislative History*, p. 196, as cited by Petersen, *op. cit.,* p. 29.

8. *Ibid*, pp, 479-480, as cited by Petersen, *op. cit.*, p.29.

9. The fur industry was concerned that the law would affect its activities, and state fish and game agencies expressed concern about the federal preemption issue. Petersen, *op. cit.*, p. 30.

10. Statement of the executive vice president of the NRA, Subcommittee on the Environment, *Endangered Species Act of 1973*, p. 123, as cited by Petersen, *op. cit.,* p. 30.

11. Petersen, *op. cit.,* p. 30-31.

12. *Tennessee Valley Authority v. Hill*, 437 U.S. 153, 184 (1978).

13. TVA testimony at Hearing on Public Works for Power and Energy Research Appropriation Bill 1977, before a Subcommittee of the House Committee on Appropriations, 94th Congress, 2nd Session, pt. 5, p. 261 (1976.)

14. 40 *Federal Register* 25597, June 17, 1975.

15. 41 *Federal Register* 13926, October 9, 1976.

16. *Hill v. T.V.A.*, 549 F. 2d 1064, 1072 (1977).

17. *Ibid, pp.* 1069, 1075.

18. Recognizing the drastic impact the ruling would have on all who owned or might seek to use or develop private property in the future, Pacific Legal Foundation was the only public interest legal organization to file a brief urging the Supreme Court to adopt the District Court's commonsense balancing approach.

19. H.R. Report No. 95-379, p. 104 (1977).

20. Senate Report No. 95-301, (1977).

21. U.S. Supreme Court Opinion, *T.V.A. v. Hill*, 437 U.S. at 172-173.

22. *Ibid,* p.188.

23. *Ibid,* p.196.

24. *Ibid,* Justice Powell's dissenting opinion, p. 197, footnote 3.

25. *Ibid,* Justice Powell's dissenting opinion, p. 204, footnote 13.

26. "U.S. To Downgrade Status of Snail Darter," *New York Times*, July 8, 1984.

27. *National Wildlife Federation et al v. Army Corps of Engineers* (Eastern District of Arkansas); "Woodpecker Halts Arkansas Irrigation Project," *Associated Press*, July 20, 2006, as reported in http://www.forbes.com/technology/ebusiness/feeds/ap/2006/07/20/ap2893076.html

28. Moore, "Environmentalism in the 21st Century," *Greenspirit, op.cit.*

CHAPTER 7

ANTIPEOPLE BIAS, OTHER PERVERSE FEATURES

In 2003, 30 years after President Nixon signed the Endangered Species Act into law, Craig Manson, Assistant Secretary of Interior for Fish, Wildlife and Parks (Director of the FWS), issued an official statement declaring:

> *The Endangered Species Act is broken. The flood of litigation over critical habitat designation is preventing the Fish and Wildlife Service from protecting new species and reducing its ability to recover plants and animals already listed as threatened or endangered. Imagine an emergency room where lawsuits force doctors to treat sprained ankles while patients with heart attacks expire in the waiting room .... This is a classic example of good intentions failing the test of reality.[1]*

Secretary Manson's diagnosis of the ESA was actually generous to the Act. The "Citizen Suits" provision that allows and encourages "the flood of litigation" he bemoaned is only one of the Act's serious flaws. The ESA is broken – conceptually, morally, and practically – and it has been from the day it became law.

THE ESA PERPETUATES A PRESCIENTIFIC MYTH ABOUT NATURE

The ESA is broken conceptually because the goal it was enacted to achieve, the restoration and preservation of all native species, is based on a myth. That myth is the "balance of nature," the idea that nature, undisturbed by man, is perfectly balanced, and operates in universal harmony, constancy, and stability. It is a common, but erroneous belief that the North American continent perfectly accommodated the balance of nature, and that all wildlife and plant species naturally thrived until the arrival of the Europeans, who disturbed that balance.[2]

The exclusionist community has been highly successful in injecting into popular culture the belief that every species of flora and fauna, from the most simple to the more complex, not only is essential to earth's balance, but interdependent on one another. Each species in nature would continue to live and perform its given role if only man's destructive ways were constrained. "For example," explains Michael Barbour, "the preservation of endangered species and ecosystems is currently argued on the basis of a nature described as tightly organized, interdependent, and highly co-evolved. 'Everything is connected to everything else,' was the way Barry Commoner expressed it in his first law of ecology in his 1975 book *Making Peace with the Planet*. The loss of an endangered species to extinction, according to this view of nature, will have repercussions that ripple out through the surrounding ecosystem of which it was once a part."[3]

When the naturalist-philosophers of the late 19th and first half of the 20th centuries – Henry David Thoreau, George Perkins Marsh, John Muir, Aldo Leopold, and later Rachel Carson – popularized the romantic notion of nature consistently in balance, except for human intrusion, they were largely restating philosophical beliefs that originated as far back as Cicero's *The Nature of the Gods*, in 44 B.C. George Perkins Marsh expressed much the same view 18 centuries later in *Man and Nature*. Marsh's view of the unchanging permanence and balance of the natural world was accepted without question for another 100 years. As biology and environmental sciences professor Daniel Botkin observed: "The perception of nature as highly ordered has been common among scientists, naturalists, and conservationists in the twentieth century. Not only was the environment thought to be highly ordered, but species were perceived to interact in a highly ordered way."[4]

But "[s]omething profoundly important happened among American ecologists during the decade of the 1950s." With improved biological observations, more extensive experimentation, and more thorough datakeeping and analyzes suggesting that nature was not so harmonious, constant, or stable, but rather dynamic, erratic, and volatile, ecologists started to challenge the popular, age-old belief in the balance-of-nature.[5]

By the early 1970s, with advanced scientific methods such as digital-recording systems that could be read directly by computers,[6] biologists began to create computer models of forests and other ecosystems that allowed them "to mimic nature realistically." Through this process, these scientists discovered that in ways large and small, the natural world is constantly undergoing change, increasing or reducing the members of every plant and wildlife species, as well as their habitat. By the late 1970s, with accumulated and persuasive evidence that little, if anything, about nature is balanced, most ecologists understood that the balance of nature was an unrealistic perception of the natural world – indeed, a myth. The reality is, as Dr. Botkin explained, "a nature of chance," "a nature with inherent randomness," "a nature with 'risk.'"[7]

In *The Beak of the Finch*, science writer Jonathan Weiner beautifully depicts a vivid example of the real natural world. A historical affirmation of the inherent randomness of nature is evident in this passage:

> *All told there are somewhere between two million and thirty million species of animals and plants alive on the planet today* [1994]. *Something like a thousand times that many species – about two billion, by the most conservative guess – have evolved, struggled, flourished, and gone extinct since the first shelly fossils were laid down in the Cambrian explosion, about 540 million years ago.*[8]

With that backdrop, *The Beak of the Finch* is the story of the enduring finches of Daphne Major, the small, volcanic island in the Galapagos archipelago, just south of the equator some 600 miles off the west coast of

South America. There, in 1835, Charles Darwin took specimen of 13 finch species back to England for study. His stay on the island, although short, was an experience he later described as "the origin of all my ideas – the origin of *The Origin of the Species*."[9]

Daphne Major is an unforgiving landscape, "like the frame of a work of tragic art in which someone has tried to put everything of life and death in a single place .... It is an island's island, with just one half-safe place to land, one dented place to camp .... If Alcatraz [describes] the impossibility of escape, then Daphne Major suggests the near impossibility of life .... The bizarre flora and fauna hang on here drought after drought, deluge after deluge."[10] Because the finches have no predators and few competitors on the island, Daphne Major exemplifies nature undisturbed by man; it provides an ideal research site for studying the effects of nature's continuously changing conditions on the birds.

But where Darwin's observations on Daphne Major lasted only nine days, Peter and Rosemary Grant, the biologist stars of *The Beak of the Finch*, have spent several months of every year for nearly three decades on the island observing "Darwin's finches." The finches were given this moniker because Darwin theorized that Daphne Major's then-13 distinct species had evolved from a common ancestor over centuries of time in order to adapt and survive in their environment. Although he was unable to actually see it occurring, Darwin also – correctly, it turns out – theorized that the finches would continue evolving to survive in their constantly and naturally changing environment.

Early on in their long run of annual visits, the Grants learned that Daphne Major was usually, and some years excessively, wet in the first half of the year, but exceedingly dry in the second half. In a wet season, grasses and small plants sprout between the lava-rocks, the insects multiply and grow plump, flowers bloom and produce seeds, the trees small nuts, the cacti become succulent, and the finches thrive, mate, and produce young in large numbers. But during the dry seasons, which often extend into multi-year droughts, life can squeeze the finches ruthlessly. Weiner writes:

> *It is the twenty-fifth of January, 1991. There are four hundred finches on the island at this moment, and the Grants know every one of the birds on sight .... In other years there have been more than a*

thousand finches on Daphne Major .... The flock was down to three hundred once. The number is falling toward that now. The birds have gotten less than a fifth of an inch of rain in the last forty-four months: in 1,320 days, 5 millimeters of rain.[11]

The Grants have discovered that in the harshest of times the different finch populations struggle mightily to find withered seeds and nuts for sustenance, and their beaks' shapes and strengths are tested to find, break, and consume them. The finches whose beaks cannot reach or crack the hardened seeds die of starvation, sometimes in vast numbers. Those whose beaks have adapted sufficiently to allow their survival until the rains return are rewarded and replenished quickly. In the mating process, and over several generations, a female and male – each with minutely improved beak characteristics – will produce offspring with the best of both parents' beak qualities. In this brutal process, and over many years, a degree of evolution, or even a new species of finch, emerges into the world. The Grants' work has demonstrated that in the raw and ever-changing natural environment, even without the disturbing hand of man, species extinction and new species evolution is reality.

Yet, notwithstanding science's discrediting of the balance of nature view during the last half-century, exclusionist environmentalists have refused to let go of it. As Professor Botkin observed:

> *In the social and political movement known as environmentalism, ideas of stability may have been less formal, but the ... underlying beliefs of a balance of nature dominated. Although environmentalism seemed to be a radical movement, the ideas on which it was based represented a resurgence of prescientific myths about nature blended with early-twentieth-century studies that provided short-term and static images of nature undisturbed.[12]*

It is important to recognize, as Dr. Botkin stated, that environmentalism is a "social and political movement," not a scientific one. While often dressed in the white coat of the laboratory to garner credibility, a closer look reveals little more than conviction based on emotion. Because so much of the large exclusionist organizations' programs depend on fund raising appeals, the movement could not afford to accept the new scientific reality of nature as it has emerged since the 1950s. The hard truth is that emotion-based appeals bring in the dollars, whereas the disciplined regime of science does not.

The lobby that crafted and influenced the passage of the ESA in 1973 firmly believed in and sought to restore the continent's balance of nature by first protecting, and then preserving, the species from the normal and necessary endeavors of man. "Biologists today understand," says Randy Simmons, "that there is no balance of nature, there is no ecological stasis, there is only change. Therefore, the Endangered Species Act cannot restore a balance of nature by restoring species."[13]

It can, however, inflict major suffering on people, and does.

THE ESA'S DISREGARD FOR PEOPLE

As earlier noted, when Hurricane Ivan struck the Florida Keys in September, 2004, many homes and businesses on Perdido Key were destroyed by the Category-3 storm. But instead of the federal government assisting the residential and business property owners, including Paul and Gail Fisher, to get their lives back to normal, the government is using the destruction of Ivan to expand the critical habitat of the listed Perdido Key beach mouse to the vacant lots that prior to Ivan accommodated the homes and businesses of the now displaced owners. As countless cases demonstrate, the ESA is broken morally because it disregards and disrespects people.

From Congress' enactment, President Nixon's execution, and the Supreme Court's lofty interpretation that nothing shall interfere with preserving even the most obscure species, *i.e.*, "whatever the cost," the ESA has been interpreted by the courts, implemented and enforced by the federal government, and championed by the exclusionist community as indifferent and even hostile to human needs, human rights, and human dignity. In weighing the value, practicality, and cost of preserving hundreds of plant and wildlife species and their habitat against the value of people-needs such as jobs, homes, transportation – even the national defense[14] – the ESA's bias automatically tilts against the interests of people. The use of land lies at the heart of the conflict.

A full 75 to 80 percent of all listed species have habitat on private propery.[15] Prior to the ESA, what people could do with their property was primarily a matter for local governments. Since 1973 the designations of critical habitat put local property owners at the sole mercy of the federal government. The ESA authorizes the Services to take regulatory control of all or a portion of the owner's property with no obligation on the part of the government to compensate him for the economic or social impact its action imposes.

When private land is designated as critical habitat for a listed species, the property owner can make little use of it – even the construction of a fence – without first obtaining the permission of the FWS. Receipt of such approval rests on whether the proposed land use will "harm" a listed species or its habitat in the opinion of FWS biologists. Even when granted, approval is frequently accompanied by onerous and excessively expensive conditions which make the proposed land use impractical. At this juncture, the conflict between the ESA's critical habitat restrictions and the property owner's constitutional right to the reasonable use of his property becomes palpable. Yet, few property owners faced with critical habitat land use restrictions are in a financial position to challenge or resist the federal government.

Most owners simply capitulate to the government's demand and accept the lost use of their land rather than engage in a protracted legal fight that will cost them hundreds of thousands of dollars in attorney fees and court costs, frequently more money than their proposed land use is worth. Besides the heavy economic burdens, the government's arbitrary and drawn-out process for reviewing land use proposals, even where ultimately approved, can be exceedingly frustrating to property owners.

During the 35 years the ESA has been on the books, numerous property owners denied use of their land by ESA regulations have filed lawsuits charging the federal government with taking private property for the "public use" of species protection and preservation, and seeking "just compensation" under the Fifth Amendment. In as clear a statement of a public use as there can be, Congress' "findings" to the ESA declare that endangered or threatened "species of fish, wildlife, and plants are of aesthetic, ecological, educational, historical, recreational, and scientific value to the Nation and its people."[16]

Curiously, with one recent exception mentioned below, neither a federal agency nor a federal court has yet recognized or declared the ESA as serving a "public use," or that the imposition of severe land use regulations under the ESA constitutes a "taking" of private property requiring "just compensation" under the Fifth Amendment. The referenced exception occurred in 2001, in a ruling that many hope will someday become accepted legal precedent.

In *Tulare Lake Basin Water Storage District v. United States*, a federal trial court found that the government's diversion of contract irrigation water from agricultural water users for the benefit of threatened chinook salmon and delta smelt violated the property rights of the water users. In a judgment requiring the government to pay the water users several million dollars for their losses due to the government's cut-off of the water, the judge stated:

> *The Fifth Amendment to the United States Constitution concludes with the phrase: "nor shall private property be taken for public use, without just compensation." The purpose of that clause is ... "to bar Government from forcing some people alone to bear public burdens which, in all fairness and justice, should be borne by the public as a whole...." The federal government is certainly free to preserve the fish; it must simply pay for the water it takes to do so.*[17]

Because the government's posttrial settlement of the judgment with the water users eliminated an appeal – and only appellate court opinions create precedent, this case established no judicial precedent. But exclusionists shudder at the prospect that an appellate court could find ESA land use restrictions as a Fifth Amendment "taking," requiring just compensation. Recognizing that compensating property owners impacted by critical habitat regulations is not an obligation the federal government – and especially its taxpayers – would be inclined to assume, exclusionists fear that the government would instead choose to moderate – that is, to balance – its imposition of ESA land use restrictions, thus giving people's lives, livelihoods, and property rights as much consideration as the species.

That this fear is real was apparent in 2003, when natural resources and land use lawyer, and former Department of Interior Solicitor, William G.

Myers III, was nominated by President George W. Bush to the U.S. Ninth Circuit Court of Appeals. Myers has long believed, as the "Takings" clause of the Fifth Amendment clearly provides, that when a property owner is prohibited by government from using his land because it is – fortuitously – habitat for a plant or wildlife species, the government effectively has taken his land for a "public use," in which case he is entitled to "just compensation." In vigorously opposing Myers' nomination and stymieing it in the Senate Judiciary Committee for three years, the Sierra Club stated in a fund raising letter: "[Myers] argues . . . that property rights are . . . 'fundamental' . . . in which case the government may not intrude upon them, except in very narrow circumstances. *This view . . . would doom environmental protection.*" (Emphasis added.)

This statement makes clear the exclusionists' view that the ESA as a statute takes precedence over the Fifth Amendment to the United States Constitution. It is no wonder they tremble at the prospect that judges like Myers and others who respect the Constitution could be setting judicial precedent as members of the federal appellate courts.[18] Yet, as much as preservationists fear judges in high places who respect property rights, they loathe the rare member of Congress with courage to challenge their ongoing assault on private property.

As Chair of the House Resources Committee, California Congressman Richard Pombo pushed several bills that threatened the exclusionists' agenda for the country. One of those required the federal government to compensate property owners when ESA regulations destroyed or significantly diminished the value of their land. On a 229-193 vote, Pombo's bill gained passage in the House of Representatives, the only modification of the ESA in 35 years that would have helped balance the species-people relationship. For that, and similar people-oriented efforts in other legislative areas, the large exclusionist organizations made him their top congressional target in the November, 2006, elections.

Although the seven-term congressman was highly respected for his support of private property rights and his work on several natural resource issues critical to the country, the Defenders of Wildlife, together with the Center for Biological Diversity, the Sierra Club, the League of Conservation Voters, and several wealthy individuals,[19] devised a plan to "revise" Pombo's image in the minds of his constituents. Through the use of mass mailings, and campaign speeches by celebrities, including former president Bill Clinton and television's *Alias* star, Jennifer Garner, Pombo was painted as an "extremist," a "radical," a "villain" to the environment. Through innuendo, it was suggested that Pombo was involved in the Washington, D.C., scandal involving convicted lobbyist, Jack Abramoff (although there was no evidence before or since the election to substantiate such smears). And, according to *Wall Street Journal* editorial writer, Kimberley A. Strassel, because Pombo had declined to hold a hearing on supposed human rights abuses in the Marianas Islands (a U.S. territory), mailings accused him of supporting "forced abortion," "child prostitution," and "sweatshop labor."

It was vicious, but it worked. Pombo was defeated. As Strassel noted, "The broader Democratic victory slipped the Resources chairmanship [that Pombo had occupied to Representative Nick] Rahall, who may hail from rural West Virginia, but votes like a resurrected Rachel Carson."[20] And with the House Resources Committee in the hands of ultra-greens, Pombo's bill reforming the ESA died a sudden death.

Meanwhile, the ESA is broken practically in numerous ways. One bears resemblance to Newton's Law that every action generates an opposite reaction.

THE ESA'S PERVERSE INCENTIVE

The ESA's disregard for people, demonstrated through the government's and exclusionist organizations' command-and-control approach toward property owners, has generated ill-will and sometimes outright hostility by landowners toward the ESA's goal of preserving species. Addressing the harsh effects of the ESA, one researcher voiced the findings of many:

> *In nearly every corner of the nation, landowners who happen to have threatened or endangered species on their lands, or who simply have habitat that might be used by endangered species, are routinely prevented from using their lands or property, including such activities as harvesting trees, planting crops, grazing cattle, irrigating fields,*

clearing brush along fence-lines, discing firebreaks around homes and barns, or building a home.[21]

Whether real property is owned as a future homesite, an investment for retirement, as a place to conduct business, or for later development, it is often the owner's primary financial asset. A sudden and drastic diminution in value is the last thing property owners want. Yet, for most property owners, there is little economic value in land that is occupied by or situated near the habitat of a listed plant or wildlife species. As Sam D. Hamilton, Southeast Regional Director of the FWS, acknowledged regarding the ESA's effect: "The incentives are wrong here. If I have a rare metal on my property, its value goes up. But if a rare bird occupies the land, its value disappears."[22]

Three decades of onerous, value-reducing restrictions on farmers, ranchers, timber companies, home builders, and other property owners have fostered an adversarial relationship. Property owners stand on one side, outnumbered by government regulators and exclusionists on the other, with endangered species often caught in the cross fire. To avoid this situation, some landowners take early steps to remove existing or potential species habitat, in order to rid their property of the burden that results from hosting an endangered species. A prominent example of a species caught in this ESA-induced cross fire is the endangered red-cockaded woodpecker, a small black and white bird, with the male bearing a patch of red feathers on its cheek.

Spending its life within a few miles of its hatch-nest, the woodpecker's habitat requirements are unusually specific: it will only nest in mature pine forests, in the cavities of trees between 60 and 70 years of age, and where the forest floor is open and free of hardwood trees or brush. In recent decades the red-cockaded woodpecker has resided primarily in the Carolinas and Florida.

The family of Ben Cone, Jr., owned several thousand acres of land containing pine forests in Pender County, North Carolina. In 1982, Mr. Cone inherited this forestland, and for nearly a decade after, maintained it primarily for the benefit of native wildlife, planting special grasses for wild turkey, selectively logging 30-50 acres of timber on a five-year basis to create open areas, and conducting controlled burns to enhance foraging for quail and deer. Although he had observed a few red-cockaded woodpeckers on the land in the 1970s, they posed no particular concern, as he was not commercially logging at the time. In fact, given its habitat requirements, the latent effect of Cone's various efforts on behalf of other wildlife species made his pine forest even more attractive habitat for the woodpecker.

When Cone decided in 1991 to begin commercial logging operations on his property, FWS informed him that 29 red-cockaded woodpeckers in 12 colonies were calling it home. Under the FWS guidelines, a circle with a half-mile radius was drawn around each colony, and in that circle no trees could be harvested, lest it be deemed a violation of the ESA, subjecting the violator to civil damages, and potentially to criminal prosecution, with substantial fines and even jail time.

This removed some 1,560 acres of Mr. Cone's property from his use and placed it under the control of FWS. And although the imposition of this critical habitat for the preservation of the red-cockaded woodpecker on Cone's land was for the benefit of all members of the public, that is a "public use" in the words of the Fifth Amendment, the federal government paid Cone nothing for virtually confiscating his land. At the same time, he remained bound to continue maintaining it and paying the property taxes at its assessed value before the government's intervention.

Instead of the ESA helping protect the woodpecker by preserving its habitat, the government's command-and-control approach had the opposite effect. It turned what had been – and from all indications would have remained – a friendly and accommodating relationship between an endangered species and a landowner into an unnecessarily adversarial one. Not long after the FWS had taken control of this sizeable piece of Mr. Cone's property, he commented: "I cannot afford to let those woodpeckers take over the rest of the property. I'm going to start massive clear-cutting. I'm going to a 40-year rotation, instead of a 75- to 80-year rotation."[23] And so he began annually to clear-cut 300-500 acres, being certain never to allow any tree (of those he still controlled) to reach the old age that made it attractive for nesting by the red-cockaded woodpecker.[24]

By the time Cone had clear-cut 700 acres, the government recognized the long-term counter-productiveness of its approach. It decided to return the use of his property to him if he would delay any further logging for four years and pay $45,000 to create woodpecker habitat on government land. Cone accepted the government's offer because it would allow him to regain control of his property, but it rankled him that "I bought my own timber back for $45,000 and four years."[25] Most ordinary landowners, not having the financial resources or chutzpah of Ben Cone, are not offered such opportunities by the government. Nor was Cone's experience with the red-cockaded woodpecker an isolated or aberrational one.

In a study examining the extent to which North Carolina forest land-owners engage in the practice of preemptively destroying the endangered woodpecker's habitat to avoid losing the use of their property, researchers found a consistent pattern. Reviewing data on more than 1,000 forest properties over the period 1982-90, they discovered that the closer the property was to known locations of the woodpecker, the greater the probability that the forests would be harvested – the FWS' term for it is "panic cutting" – before the trees reached woodpecker-nesting age.[26] This practice has occurred with other species as well.

In 1989, landowners in and around Tri County, Texas, "began destroying ash juniper forests [habitat for the golden-cheeked warbler] in order to thwart ESA regulations."[27] It is difficult to know the extent to which preemptive habitat destruction actually occurs. Certainly, as *Science Under Siege* author Michael Fumento points out: "many people don't destroy the habitats on their land and don't destroy the endangered species." However, "for these decent folk, the reward is to have their private property infringed for the good of all of the rest of us."[28]

The counterproductive effect of the ESA's command-and-control approach is evident, but exclusionists refuse to accept it. One who does – at least in principle – is Michael Bean, longtime wildlife program director for Environmental Defense, often referenced in the literature as the original behind-the-scenes crafter of the ESA. In a 1994 Fish and Wildlife Service training seminar on the red-cockaded woodpecker, Bean opined that preserving endangered species depends on preserving people's rights, including their private property rights. He stated:

> *Because... red-cockaded woodpeckers tend to prefer ... long-leaf pine over other species, landowners thinking about what species to plant after harvest or on former forest land ... regard the choice of*

planting long-leaf as a foolish choice because of the greater potential for having woodpecker problems in the future ....

Now it's important to recognize that all of these actions that land-owners are either taking or threatening to take are not the result of malice toward the red-cockaded woodpecker, not the result of malice toward the environment. Rather, they're fairly rational decisions moti-vated by a desire to avoid potentially significant economic constraints. In short, they're really nothing more than a predictable response to the familiar perverse incentives that sometimes accompany regulatory programs, not just the endangered species program but others. What is clear to me after close to 20 years of trying to make the ESA work, is that – from the outside, in deference to you trying to do it from the inside [referring to the FWS employees he was addressing] *– is that on private lands at least, we don't have very much to show for our efforts other than a lot of political headaches.*[29]

The ESA remains good at creating headaches, and a lot more, for many people across the nation. The "flood of litigation" Assistant Secretary Manson mentioned when he described the ESA as "broken" presents a particularly serious problem.

CITIZEN SUITS – THE TRUE "GREEN REVOLUTION"

Under a provision called "Citizen Suits,"[30] ordinary citizens can bring legal action in federal court to compel the government to enforce the ESA, or to stop a person, corporation, or even a government agency from vio-lating the ESA. Citizen suits came about during the Act's drafting in 1973, when the exclusionist lobby persuaded Congress to include a private party right-to-sue provision out of purported concern that political pressure might otherwise dissuade federal agencies from enforcing the ESA. Quite obviously, this rationale raises the question whether the regulatory agen-cies of government at any level possess the independence and dedication to duty to perform their responsibilities in the face of political pressures.

However, as Bruce Benson notes, "[a]lthough these actions are called citizen suits, most of them are not brought by individuals alarmed about the failure to protect the environment. A large majority are brought by environmental organizations."[31] While the ESA gives implementation and enforcement responsibilities primarily to the FWS and NOAA Fisheries, Dana Joel Gattuso observes that litigation under the "citizen suits" provision has become

> *an epidemic that not only compromises human needs but, ironically, compromises the protection of endangered species. ESA lawsuits are so routine that [FWS] staff spends more time and dollars handling litigation than saving species. The FWS reports that as much as two-thirds of its budget for placing endangered species on the protection list is consumed fulfilling court orders and settlement agreements.[32]*

According to Kay Goode, then assistant field supervisor for ESA enforcement at FWS' Sacramento office, the Service has been sued so often by organizations claiming her failure to enforce the ESA that her staff members jokingly refer to their office as "litigation central." *Sacramento Bee* reporter Tom Knudson's article "Litigation Central" is one in a five-part series on environmentalist organizations published by the *Bee* in April, 2001. As Knudson stated, suits by such groups to compel the designation of critical habitat have "so swamped the Fish and Wildlife Service that it has halted the biological evaluations necessary to add new species to the federal endangered species list."[33]

ESA citizen suits offer the challenging litigants a unique "win-win-win" situation. Their first "win" comes with the opportunity such suits provide to directly develop ESA law in the courts. As with their initial success in *TVA v. Hill*, "[t]hese suits allow environmental groups to influence the interpretation and enforcement of environmental statutes."[34] Such litigants are "the engine that propels the field of environmental law."[35]

As Knudson wrote: "Since 1995, most cases brought have not been about dams, nuclear power or pesticides, but about rare and endangered species. The flood of suits has turned judges into modern day Noahs who decide which species are saved – and which aren't. But the judges – guided by law, not science – aren't always the best-equipped to make biologically correct decisions."[36]

In 2003 the organization American Rivers, and nine other similar groups, sued the Army Corps of Engineers for failing to reduce water levels on the Missouri River to benefit three wildlife species.[37] They alleged that higher water levels were jeopardizing the habitat of piping plover, least terns, and pallid sturgeons by denying these species shallow-water sandbars upon which to breed. In ruling for the species, and with full recognition of the harm her ruling would inflict on people, federal District Judge Gladys Kessler wrote:

> *Navigation will be interrupted for the remainder of the summer and barge companies will lose revenues. Water quality may be affected and there may be higher water purification costs. Hydroelectric resources will be affected* [referring to the numerous electricity-generating dams on the river], *and consumers may suffer higher costs.* [Nevertheless] *there is no dollar value that can be placed on the extinction of an animal species – the loss is to our planet, our children and future generations.*[38]

Where the Army Corps in this case had chosen – for scientific, economic, and practical reasons – not to lower the Missouri's normal seasonal water levels, the citizen suit empowered the preservationist petitioners not only to challenge that determination, but ultimately to control the interpretation and enforcement of the ESA. Says Dana Joel Gattuso, "Environmental groups fuel the judicial absurdity and artfully use the courts to drive their political agenda."[39]

The exclusionist organizations' second win is their likelihood of success in court. The congressional scheme in creating and empowering the government regulatory agencies was that, by reason of their expertise in their respective statutory fields, such agencies were to be given substantial deference – absent an "abuse of discretion" – whenever their determinations were challenged in court. Numerous federal appellate court cases have recognized and upheld this principle in most statutory contexts. Yet, when the FWS, NOAA Fisheries, and even the Army Corps of Engineers make a determination under the ESA, the courts regularly find an abuse of discretion, and rule in favor of the challengers. Recognizing the leverage the likelihood of success offers these litigators, the Services and Corps are inclined to settle many of their suits out of court, rather than spend the time and resources litigating cases the courts are likely to overturn anyway.

These organizations' third win involves the principle of "follow the money." Citizen suits provide successful litigants the award of attorney fees. Where a suit is litigated and the court issues a final ruling that favors the challenging party, the court also will order that the government pay the organization's attorney fees. Where the suit is resolved by the government agreeing to settle the issue, the settlement agreement will include attorney fees as agreed upon by the government and the organization. Whether by court order or settlement agreement, attorney fees paid to exclusionist plaintiffs are funded by the taxpayers. As Knudson noted:

> *On April 15, 1998, when millions of Americans were filing their taxes, the Southwest Center for Biological Diversity* [now the Center for Biological Diversity] *was filing a lawsuit to protect Alaska's Queen Charlotte goshawk. Six weeks later, the center's legal team was in California to sue over the Sacramento splittail. Then came another California case concerning 39 species, from the Pacific pocket mouse to the California gnatcatcher. No environmental group in America files more endangered species cases at a more frenetic pace than the Southwest Center.... Public records show that from 1994 to 1999 alone, the Center for Biological Diversity filed 58 lawsuits, an average of one every 32 days.*[40]

When awarded or settled attorney fees are multiplied by the many suits preservationist groups file against the government under the ESA, the sums the government (taxpayers) pays out become substantial. Although there are no central records where government payments of exclusionists' attorney fees in ESA suits are listed, from use of the Freedom of Information Act and record searches at several federal courthouses, the *Sacramento Bee*'s Knudson wrote:

> *During the 1990s, the government paid out $31.6 million in attorney fees for 434 environmental cases brought against federal agencies. The average award per case was more than $70,000. One long-running lawsuit in Texas involving an endangered salamander netted lawyers for the Sierra Club and other plaintiffs more than $3.5 million*

> *in taxpayer funds .... Few firms win larger fee awards than San Francisco-based Earthjustice* [the Sierra Club's legal arm]. *When Earthjustice won a coho salmon suit recently, for example, it submitted a bill for $439,053 to the Justice Department, and settled for $383,840. Most of the invoice was for 931 hours of legal work by* [an] *Earthjustice senior attorney ... at $350 an hour.*[41]

The Earthjustice Legal Defense Fund, formerly the Sierra Club Legal Defense Fund, is the nation's largest nonprofit environmental law firm.

The number of citizen suits filed by such organizations, and the amount of attorney fees they seek, has caused government lawyers and other government officials to question whether species protection is as much a motivating factor in the suits as the money. According to Elizabeth Megginson, who investigated numerous cases when she was chief counsel for the U.S. House Committee on Resources, "[t]his has become a cottage industry. Lawsuits are filed not so much to benefit species but for other reasons." And when the Sierra Club's lawyers sought $5 million in attorney fees in the salamander case in Texas, the U.S. Attorney responded with a brief, pointedly titled: "FEDERAL DEFENDANT$ OPPO$ITION TO PLAINTIFF$ MOTION ... FOR AWARD OF THEIR COMBINED CO$T OF LITIGATION." The brief stated: "The claim is excessive by any standard of fairness and reasonableness."[42]

Jamie Rappaport Clark, Director of the FWS in the second Clinton-Gore term, was a longtime environmental professional in the FWS, who in 2002, joined the National Wildlife Federation as senior vice president, and two years later became executive vice president of Defenders of Wildlife. Even Clark, while at FWS, reacted angrily when she learned that attorney fee awards to preservationist litigators in some cases were exceeding $100,000: "I believe citizens should have the opportunity to sue the government, but this has gone over the edge."[43] Maybe so, but it continues.

In late November, 2007, the Center for Biological Diversity (CBD), filed six lawsuits – the first of a grand total of 55 they plan to file, on behalf of the Mexican garter snake, the Mississippi gopher frog, and the loach minnow. The CBD, which describes itself as an endangered species advocacy group, claims that these animals were denied ESA protections including 8.7 million acres of critical habitat, a total area of 13,593 square miles, bigger than the state of Massachusetts. The suits target the Department of the Interior for interference with the ESA.

"These guys sue us all the time, and I don't doubt they would accuse this administration of political interference," Hugh Vickery of Interior told the *Christian Science Monitor*. "It's part of the whole history of the [ESA]. The provisions just aren't working. They're just a litigation magnet."[44]

For that purpose the provisions are working well, generating expense for taxpayers and revenue for exclusionist organizations. This has to do with the use – or lack thereof – of scientific evidence to support ESA listings and designations of critical habitat.

The Best Scientific Data Available

The ESA requires that both listings and designations of critical habitat be determined "solely on the basis of the best scientific ... data available."[45] But the Services, as well as the courts, have interpreted "best available" to mean any evidence whatsoever. As a result of the 46 species taken off the endangered or threatened list in the years since the ESA's enactment, 16 were removed because they should never have been listed in the first place. That is, the data relied upon by the FWS was so scientifically erroneous or deficient that the listings of those 16 species were acknowledged as mistakes. Failure to use the best scientific data available also accounts for overly broad designations of critical habitat, which, as in the Alameda whipsnake case described later, can be highly detrimental to property owners within the designated area.

Even though the ESA requires that listing determinations and critical habitat designations be based solely on the best scientific data available, the Act does not specifically require that either the data or the agency's determination be peer reviewed. As a result, so-called scientific documentation gathered by the Services is rarely subjected to scrutiny by independent scientists. And when peer review is conducted, it is often informal, ad hoc, and selective.

Where the listing of a species is initiated and advocated by exclusionist groups, which is frequently the case by reason of the citizen suit provision, their submissions of so-called scientific data to support the listing petition are often incorporated into the Services' Biological Opinions without substantial scrutiny. The result is often politicized science, that is, deficient, incomplete, or dubious science advanced to promote the group's eco-political objectives. One of many examples of this occurred in the Klamath River Basin in 2001, when contract irrigation water that had regularly been delivered to more than a thousand farmers and their predecessors for nearly a century, was abruptly shut off on orders from NOAA Fisheries.

With much of the data in NOAA Fisheries' Biological Opinion (BO) supplied by exclusionist groups and their allies, the BO concluded that continued water delivery for irrigation purposes would jeopardize ESA-listed fish. NOAA Fisheries disregarded the substantial, credible scientific data showing that continued water diversion for agricultural users would not jeopardize the fish. After a loud hue and cry from the agricultural community, Interior Secretary Gale Norton asked the National Academy of Sciences to peer review the Biological Opinions' data and conclusions. An expert scientific committee of that body determined that the Services' Biological Opinions were flawed and that the best scientific data showed that continued water diversion for irrigation would not have jeopardized the listed fish.[46]

In their zeal to protect, restore, and preserve endangered or threatened species, the crafters of the Endangered Species Act created a law that has worked against the needs and interests of people. After 35 years of command-and-control implementation and enforcement by federal agencies and preservationist litigators, the ESA's record of preserving and restoring struggling species is negligible. Instead of encouraging the cooperation of the owners of the private land that makes up 75 to 80 percent of endangered and threatened species habitat, the axis of exclusionist groups and government enforcers of the ESA have run roughshod over the very people whose personal embrace of species preservation is essential to its success.

NOTES

1. "News," U.S. Department of Interior, Office of the Secretary, May 28, 2003, http://www.doi.gov/news/030528a.htm

2. Randy T. Simmons, "Nature Undisturbed," *PERC Reports*, Property and Environment Research Center, Vol. 23, No. 1, March 2005, p. 3.

3. Michael G. Barbour, "Ecological Fragmentation in the Fifties," in *Uncommon Ground - Rethinking the Human Place in Nature*, W.W. Norton & Co, New York: 1996, William Cronon, editor, p. 233.

4. Daniel Botkin, *Discordant Harmonies, A New Ecology for the Twenty-first Century,* Oxford University Press, 1990, p. 76.

5. Barbour, *op. cit.*, p. 233.

6. Dr. Botkin was a pioneer in this field; *Discordant Harmonies, op. cit.*, pp. 115 - 120.

7. *Ibid,* pp.122, 124.

8. Jonathan Weiner, *The Beak of the Finch,* Vintage Books: 1994, p.134.

9. *Ibid,* p. 4.

10. *Ibid,* p.14.

11. *Ibid,* p. 3.

12. Botkin, *op. cit.*, pp. 42-43.

13. Randy Simmons, "Nature Undisturbed," *op. cit.*, p. 3.

14. "Navy Sonar May Trigger Lawsuit Over Whale Strandings, Deaths," *Environment News Service,* July 15, 2004.

15. Randy T. Simmons and Kimberly Frost, *Accounting for Species: The True Cost of the Endangered Species Act*, p. v, http://www.perc.org/publications/articles/esa_costs.php

16. ESA, 16 *U.S. Code 1532*, "Findings, Purposes, and Policy," Section 2(a)(3).

17. *Tulare Lake Basin Water Storage District v. United States,* 49 Fed. Cl. 313 (2001).

18. In 2006, Myers' nomination was returned to the President after 60 votes could not be secured to evoke cloture to end a Senate filibuster by Democrat members. President Bush then named him to the Ninth Circuit as a Recess Appointment (a temporary appointment). In September, 2006, the President renominated Myers to the Ninth Circuit, where, in November, while he again was awaiting Senate confirmation, the Democrats took control of both houses of Congress. In early January, 2007, Myers withdrew as a judicial nominee to the federal appellate court.

19. These included heirs to the Getty Oil fortune, the Hewlett-Packard computer fortune, and an investment partner of U.S. Senator Diane Feinstein's husband. Myron Ebell, "Environmentalist Attack Richard Pombo," *Human Events Online*, November 2, 2006, http://www.humanevents.com/article/php?id+17832

20. Kimberly Strassel, "Green Goodies, It's payback time for another left-leaning lobby," *Wall Street Journal,* June 15, 2007.

21. Robert J. Smith, "The Endangered Species Act: Shoot, Shovel, and Shut Up," Competitive Enterprise Institute; http://www.ipi.org/ipi%5CIPIPublications.nsf/PublicationLookupFullText/1C84DBE6BCD5AEE98625683A001A354

22. "Saving the Species," *Orange County Register*, 29 September 1995.

23. Ike C. Sugg, "Ecosystem Babbitt-Babble, "*The Wall Street Journal*, April 2, 1993, p. A12.

24. Mr. Cone's experience with the red-cockaded woodpecker was described by Richard L. Stroup, "Endangered Species Act: Making Innocent Species the Enemy," *Property and Environment Research Center* (PERC), April, 1995, http://www.perc.org/perc.php?id=648

25. Elizabeth Brubaker, "How not to save species," *National Post Online*, September 13, 1999, http://www.environmentprobe.org/EnviroProbe/evpress/091399a_fpost.html

26. Dean Lueck and Jeffrey A. Michael, "Preemptive Habitat Destruction under the Endangered Species Act," *The Journal of Law and Economics*, University of Chicago Press, 2003, pp. 27- 60.

27. Charles C. Mann and Mark L. Plummer, *Noah's Choice: The Future of Endangered Species*, New York: Alfred A. Knopf, 1995, as cited by Dean Lueck and Jeffrey A. Michael, "Forest Management under the Endangered Species Act," *Cardon Research Papers in Agricultural and Resource Economics*, Research paper 2004-20, November, 2004, p. 32-33; http://ag.arizona.edu/arec/pubs/workingpapers.html

28. Michael Fumento, "Endangered Species Act Deserves Extinction," (1996), www.Fumento.com

29. David Hogberg, "Shoot it or lose it," *The American Spectator*, Feb. 28, 2006.

30. ESA, 16 U.S.C. Section 1540, "Citizen Suits," Section 11 (g).

31. Bruce C. Benson, "Unnatural Bounty: Distorting the Incentives of Major Environmental Groups," *Property and Environment Research Center* (PERC), Policy Series No. 37, p. 1, July, 2006; www.perc.org

32. Dana Joel Gattuso, "Environmental Litigation Threatens Endangered Species," *National Policy Analysis No. 482*, September, 2003, National Center for Policy Research, www.ncpr.org ; citing "Endangered Species Act 'Broken' – Flood of Litigation Over Critical Habitat Hinders Species Conservation," press release, U.S. Department of Interior, May 28, 2003, and Testimony of Craig Manson, Asst. Secretary for Fish and Wildlife, Committee on Environment and Public Works, Washington, D.C., April 10, 2003; and **"Farmers, Ranchers Call for ESA Reform,"** *Environment and Energy Daily*, July 18, 2003.

33. Tom Knudson, "Litigation Central, A flood of costly lawsuits raises questions about motive," *Sacramento Bee*, April 24, 2001, http://www.sacbee.com/static/archive/news/projects/environment/20010424.html ; other Knudson articles in the series are: "Movement's prosperity comes at a high price" (April 22); "Mission adrift in a frenzy of fund raising (April 23); "Playing with fire" (April 25); and "Solutions sprouting from grass-roots efforts" (April 26).

34. Bruce C. Benson, "Unnatural Bounty: Distorting the Incentives of Major Environmental Groups," *op. cit.*

35. James R. May, "More than Ever: Trends in Environmental Citizen Suits," *Widener Law Review* 10: 1-47, 2003.

36. Knudson, "Litigation Central," *op. cit.*

37. *American Rivers v. U.S. Army Corps of Engineers*, Civil No. 03-241, U.S. District Court for the District of Columbia, Washington, D.C., July 12, 2003.

38. Court order, *American Rivers v. U.S. Army Corps of Engineers*, *ibid.*

39. Gattuso, "Environmental Litigation Threatens Endangered Species," *op. cit.*.

40. Knudson, "Litigation Central," *op. cit.*

41. *Ibid.*

42. *Ibid.*

43. *Ibid.*

44. Mark Clayton, "Politics undercut species act, suit says," *Christian Science Monitor*, November 20, 2007. http://www.csmonitor.com/2007/1120/p03s01-usgn.htm

45. ESA, 16 *U.S. Code* 1533, "Basis for Determinations," Section 4 (b).

46. See National Academies, Press Release, "Broader Approach Needed for Protection and Recovery of Fish in Klamath River Basin," Oct. 22, 2003, at http://www4.nationalacademies.org/news/nsf/isbn/0309090970?OpenDocument

CHAPTER 8

POLITICIZED BIOLOGY: A CASE STUDY

As a consequence [of the Endangered Species Act] *this nation may think it is preserving biological diversity when it is not. And worse, it risks hurting the economy by efforts to save populations that are not unique at all.*

--Alston Chase[1]

RACHEL CARSON'S ATTACK on DDT did more than imperil millions of people around the world. It also developed a schism within the science community. In the concluding paragraph of *Silent Spring* she characterized an entire era of biologists as from "the Neanderthal age of biology ...[their] concepts and practices of applied entomology ... date from that Stone Age of science," and "so primitive a science." Over the next decade, the movement she catalyzed grew more aggressive. Activist members, together with a number of biologists who viewed plant and wildlife species preservation as biology's primary concern, challenged the very heart of biology by redefining the venerable term "species." This they accomplished in 1973 with the enactment of the Endangered Species Act.

This redefinition pitted the exclusionist biologists against those who viewed the long-established scientific categories of species as critical to the continuing order and integrity of biology. Where these science-oriented biologists took pride in the improved quality of life their work yielded for people, the new breed of political biologists that came of age in the 1960s and 1970s regarded people as primarily responsible for species and habitat destruction. Although they were colleagues in science, neither in the run-up to the ESA's enactment, nor in the decades since has there been much collegiality between these two groups.

Dr. Gordon Edwards was one of those who opposed the hijacking of biology by exclusionism. As a biologist and professor at San Jose State University for 40 years, he studied and taught taxonomy, the scientific classification of plants and animals according to their natural relationships, biological systematics, and nomenclature. A major element in Dr. Edwards' career as a biologist was the definition, structure, and order of species, subspecies, and infrasubspecific categories of animals. In his chapter of the *Standard Handbook of Environmental Science, Health and Technology*, Dr. Edwards states:

> *For nearly a century scientists around the world have recognized that biological species must be "reproductively isolated" and "genetically distinctive" natural populations .... This scientific categorization of species classification bears no resemblance to the political use of the word in the Endangered Species Act. Environmental extremists have distorted the word "species" to uselessness with their "endangered species" propaganda. The "endangered species" radicals have deliberately violated every procedure and every scientific requirement that generations of scientists established regarding biological species .... Political environmentalists have spurned the legitimate scientific requirements for the recognition of "real species." Instead, they consider any loose assortment of similar individuals to be a "species," and the identity of such so-called "species" is vague, uncertain, and meaningless. The Endangered Species Act of 1973 is based on this spurious use of the word "species."[2]*

The ESA defines "species" to include "any subspecies of fish or wildlife or plants, and any distinct population segment of any species of vertebrate fish or wildlife which interbreeds when mature."[3] Those who crafted the ESA deliberately omitted the requirement that species be "reproductively isolated" and "genetically distinctive" natural populations. "Based on [this] political definition," says Edwards "the entire world would be populated by unrecognizable hordes of birds, mammals, reptiles, amphibians, insects ... and plants, with only a jumble of vague local names that would be meaningless to anyone seeking to engage in scientific study or research about any species."[4]

The ESA's creation of the term "distinct population segment," which it nowhere defines, has allowed the FWS and NOAA Fisheries to expand or contract a regulated local population by arbitrarily drawing either a large circle or a small circle around the target species. This has resulted in inconsistent and arbitrary designations of "distinct population segments" that have no relation to generally accepted biological standards. For example, rather than designating genetically identical Pacific Coast salmon as one species, as discussed in Chapter 12, NOAA Fisheries divided this biological species into several locally situated units, and treated each as a separate species. As Dr. Edwards wrote:

> *A few examples of animals that have been "listed" as "endangered species" (even though they are not species at all) are Florida panthers, Eastern timber wolf, Columbian whitetail deer, Sonoran pronghorn, Florida scrub jays, California clapper rails, Tecopa pupfish, San Francisco gartersnakes, Santa Cruz long-toed salamanders, Louisiana black bear, Del Marva fox squirrels, Indiana bats, Tipton kangaroo rats, Illinois mud turtles, Arizona jaguars, Mt. Graham red squirrels, northern spotted owls, lost river suckers ... delta smelt, Snake River snails, Colorado squawfish.* [Citing 41 Federal Register 47197, Oct. 27, 1976.] [5]

During the past 35 years there frequently have been different opinions between the two camps of scientists over not only whether a species is endangered or threatened, but even whether a particular plant or form of wildlife is a legitimate biological species to begin with.

The biologists who respect the term "species" as the disciplined product of a century of careful scientific work are a hardy group. They have neither the numbers, the law, nor the weight of political correctness on their side, yet they stand up in the name of legitimate science. Most biology majors and graduate students in the nation's colleges and universities since the early 1970s have been educated in an era dominated by the ESA's definition. With the generally liberal bent of graduate schools, few biology students have been seriously exposed to the traditional view of species, or to ideas such as those contained in Dr. Edwards' chapter on "Controversies Surrounding the Endangered Species Act" in the *Standard Handbook of Environmental Science, Health and Technology.*

With the popularity of field and marine biology, and the opportunity to work outdoors protecting and preserving endangered plants and wildlife, biology graduates have found employment opportunities with federal and state environmental regulatory agencies very attractive. But biologists who question the scientific legitimacy of the ESA's definition of species, or who suggest that returning to the true scientific definition would enable better protection of really struggling species, would stand little chance of being hired by the FWS or NOAA Fisheries. The same can be said of independent biologists whom the agencies hire for special projects or when staff is overloaded. Unless they hold politically correct biological views consistent with those of the Services' biologist-dominated bureaucracy – in other words, with the ESA's political objective – they stand little chance of gaining employment with the government. This further stacks the deck in favor of the exclusionist view, and against the more balanced approach of conservationism.

A CASE STUDY

The ongoing saga of the Preble's meadow jumping mouse, hereafter "the Preble's," is representative of what has occurred on other occasions in varying degrees over the past 35 years under the politicized biology of the ESA.

In his 1899 revision of the taxonomy (scientific classification) of North American jumping mice, naturalist E. A. Preble assigned the jumping mouse inhabiting parts of Colorado and Wyoming to one of the existing five subspecies of jumping mice – the Bear Lodge meadow jumping mouse – common also in North and South Dakota, Montana,

Nebraska, and Missouri. In 1954, wildlife biologist Phillip Krutzsch, in reviewing Preble's work, conducted comparative measurements of the skulls of the Colorado/Wyoming jumping mouse that Preble had assigned to the Bear Lodge subspecies with skulls of that subspecies.[6]   Although his measurements of the Colorado/Wyoming mouse skulls were limited to only three specimen, Krutzsch concluded that Preble had been mistaken. The Colorado/Wyoming mouse was not the same as the Bear Lodge subspecies, but was in fact a distinct subspecies itself. Krutzsch's conclusion served as the basis for official taxonomic recognition of the "Preble's meadow jumping mouse" as a new and separate subspecies of North American jumping mouse.

Nearly 50 years later, Krutzsch's conclusion became the source of high controversy throughout the west due to the diminishing numbers of the presumed subspecies while the Bear Lodge subspecies remained common and plentiful throughout the multistate region. In listing the Preble's as a "threatened" species under the ESA in 1998, the FWS found that the mouse's preferred habitat along the heavily vegetated banks of natural waterways was imperiled by degradation from agricultural, residential, commercial, and industrial development.[7]

In 2003, exclusionist organizations petitioned the FWS to designate critical habitat for the Preble's. The FWS complied, setting aside 31,000 acres along hundreds of miles of riparian waterways in eastern Colorado and southeastern Wyoming – from Colorado Springs, through Denver and Fort Collins, and up to Laramie, as the mouse's critical habitat. This designation was extremely contentious in Colorado and Wyoming, embroiling the states' governors, Denver-based Earthjustice and the Center for Native Ecosystems, builders and developers, ranchers and farmers, two President George W. Bush-appointed Interior Secretaries with differing views, the FWS, and even the Denver Museum of Nature & Science. As *Wall Street Journal* editorial writer, Stephen Moore, described it: "What we have here is arguably the most contentious dispute over the economic impact of the ESA since the famous early-'90s clash between the timber industry and the environmentalist lobby over the 'endangered' listing of the spotted owl in the Northwest."[8]

The designation of the Preble's critical habitat stymied the ability of Colorado's growing communities to provide housing, infrastructure, and necessary services to accommodate the inflow of people. Real estate developers and commercial and residential builders have suffered out-of-pocket, as well as lost-opportunity, costs in the tens of millions of dollars. Taxpayers have had to absorb major infrastructure projects to accommodate the Preble's. For example, "[o]ne water district in Colorado was recently required to build two tunnels for the mice under a man-made pond to spare the critters the inconvenience of having to scurry around it. Regulators even asked local officials if it would be feasible to grow grass in the tunnels for the mice, which was only slightly less absurd than padding the mouse thoroughfares with red carpet. The extra cost to the water project to make it mouse-friendly? More than $1 million."[9]

The Preble's also has imposed onerous conditions on homeowners in Colorado. For example, the FWS requires that local approval of new homes contain a binding covenant that the homeowners keep their cats inside at all times to restrict them from roaming and killing the Preble's mice. As a FWS biologist told a meeting of county officials and homeowners, "It may be a problem to individuals who think they have a right to let their cats roam at night."[10] Exclusionist biology thus discriminates against the cat species as well as their owners.

In Wyoming, a 2004 Economic Impact Report funded by the Governor's Office estimated various losses in Wyoming due to the Preble's critical habitat in the multimillions of dollars. With 77 percent of the Preble's protected land in Wyoming being privately owned, the rural economy of the region, in particular agriculture and ranching, has been hard hit.

With the Preble's getting so much attention, and its subspecies status originating from a small number of skull measurements, the Preble's taxonomy was ripe for revisiting. The Denver Museum of Nature and Science was especially well-situated, both biologically and geographically, to perform such research. In 2002, a Museum biology official approached Dr. Rob Roy Ramey II, Ph.D., then the Museum's Genetic Zoologist and Curator of Vertebrate Zoology, about conducting a genetic review of the Preble's mouse.

Like Gordon Edwards, Dr. Ramey epitomizes the professional desire "to keep truth in science and environmentalism." While supporting the spirit of the ESA in preserving real and struggling species, he has been outspoken in his testimony, lectures, and debates, "that much of the science that's driven [the ESA] has been sloppy." For example:

> *The truth is, there are a lot of bogus old taxonomies that date to fifty, a hundred, 200 years ago that are still on the books because they haven't been challenged. And they haven't been challenged because until the creation of the Endangered Species Act, they haven't had any legal significance. Now, with the ESA, those biological designations matter, and they matter in a huge way when it comes to policy and society and the allocation of conservation resources. But a lot of these designations are highly suspect. The Preble's is just one example.*[11]

After Ramey scoured everything he could find on the Preble's, especially the subspecies designation based on Kurtzsch's 1954 skull measurements of only three specimen, he then decided it was time for a modern review. On behalf of the Denver Museum, under whose auspices the study would be performed, Dr. Ramey sought funding to cover the costs. Because Wyoming Governor Dave Frudenthal welcomed a review of the mouse that was causing economic havoc in his state, Wyoming agreed to provide $61,000 in funding. There was one string attached, to which Dr. Ramey reluctantly agreed: if the Preble's study team concluded that the Preble's and Bear Lodge jumping mice were of the same subspecies, the report of their findings and conclusion was to be sent to the Wyoming Game and Fish Department as soon as it was completed.

Because the FWS regularly grants funding to a variety of entities engaged in scientific study of plants and wildlife, including the Denver Museum of Nature and Science, Dr. Ramey arranged a meeting with FWS' Preble's Mouse Recovery Team, based in the Service's Denver office, to solicit funding. Although the FWS would grudgingly agree to provide $20,000 for the project, Ramey observed during his presentation that most of the recovery team's biologists, including Team Leader Bruce Rosenlunt, were not sympathetic to the possibility that the Preble's status as a distinct subspecies could succumb to his study. Nonetheless, with funding for the project arranged, in the spring of 2003 the Denver Museum authorized Dr. Ramey to go forward.

His initial step called for conducting comparative DNA sequencing analysis of both the presumed Preble's subspecies and the Bear Lodge subspecies. If the DNA sequencing analysis did not show a sufficient match, the second step would be unnecessary. The DNA sequencing analysis was performed by the Museum's population geneticist, Dr. Hsui-Ping Liu, Ph.D. Based on the 99.5 percent genetic match results of this analysis, the Ramey team concluded that the Preble's was a population within the Bear Lodge meadow jumping mouse subspecies. Although a high percentage genetic match through DNA is quite persuasive biologically, Dr. Ramey recognized that the controversy surrounding the Preble's would cause his study to be closely scrutinized by those who favored the ESA's more amorphous definition of species. So long as the Preble's remained a separate, "threatened" subspecies, residential and commercial development, farming, ranching, mining and other land uses – even house cats – could continue to be prohibited or severely restricted within the designated critical habitat area. But if the Preble's was another population of the common Bear Lodge subspecies, it likely would not retain its "threatened" subspecies status under the ESA, and its critical habitat designation would be terminated.

The second step of Dr. Ramey's study called for Denver Museum Research Assistant Lance Carpenter, Ramey's colleague in numerous conservation studies, to begin the tedious process of measuring and comparing the shapes of the skulls of the Preble's and Bear Lodge mice, as Krutzsch had examined. But instead of measuring such a small number, Carpenter utilized the many specimen of the mice in storage at the Denver Museum, as well as museums in Kansas, Nebraska, and New Mexico. That way, other biologists could review and verify his measurements.

The results of Carpenter's mice-skull measurements and comparisons were consistent with the DNA findings. The Ramey team concluded that these were not two distinct subspecies of jumping mouse. Simply put, the Preble's was a less genetically diverse population of the Bear Lodge subspecies, and should be considered the same subspecies.

The Ramey report on the Preble's became public in mid-December, 2003, when Wyoming Governor Frudenthal attached it to Wyoming's petition to delist the Preble's.[12] Joined by Coloradoans for Water Conservation and Development, and later by the Governor of Colorado, the delisting petition to FWS made the case that the Preble's 1998 listing was based on "Original data in error."

Although the Ramey team's study concluded that the Preble's was not a distinct taxonomic subspecies, the public release of the rough study report before it had been subjected to peer-review and formally published in a scientific journal was not how Dr. Ramey preferred it to be made public. When he later submitted the study report as an article to *Animal Conservation*, a scientific journal of the Zoological Society of London, a peer-review panel of recognized biologists was assembled. After reviewing the study, the panel recommended that the Ramey team collect and analyze additional data to complement their DNA sequencing data, and resubmit the paper, which they did. Only after the Ramey team successfully addressed additional concerns of the panel, as well as others of the journal's editor, was the scientific article accepted for publication. The result of this rigorous process not only confirmed the conclusion that the so-called Preble's and Bear Lodge jumping mice were of the same subspecies, it actually expanded and improved the supporting scientific evidence on which that conclusion was based. But Ramey's scientific article would not be published in *Animal Conservation* for another year and a half; in the meantime, he came under a great deal of pressure, with predictable results.

The public release of Ramey's rough report with the delisting petition triggered the attack of Earthjustice and the Center for Native Ecosystems, the exclusionist groups that just the year before had petitioned the FWS to designate the Preble's critical habitat. The designation had effectively accomplished their purpose of stopping significant development, as well as farming, ranching, mining, and other productive activity in the two-state region.

In 2004, because the Ramey team's study had not yet been published in a peer-reviewed journal, the FWS obtained peer reviews of it from 14 biologists. "Of the 14 peer reviews, 5 supported the Ramey study and its conclusions ... 3 leaned toward support of the study and its conclusions ... and 6 were generally critical of the study or skeptical of its conclusions. ... However, some of these peer reviewers were also supportive of portions of the study." From these individual peer reviews, FWS preliminarily concluded that the Ramey study demonstrated that the Preble's original listing was in error, and proposed delisting the Preble's under the ESA. It solicited additional information before making its final determination.[13]

Even before this "12-Month Finding" was published, the exclusionist groups were aware of its recommendation and began escalating their attacks on Dr. Ramey. Using the sharply honed tactics of the movement, they publicly denigrated him, accusing him of being "dishonest," "doing everything possible to hijack science," branding him "a whore for industry," and a "shill for the Bush administration."[14] They weren't the only players who regarded Ramey's study as a growing threat.

There had been no mistaking the Recovery Team's unfriendliness toward his proposed Preble's study back when Ramey was seeking funding. The manifestations became outright hostile when FWS bosses found the study to justify a formal review of the Preble's threatened status. As *Rocky Mountain News* editor and columnist, Vincent Carroll, tells it:

> *Among those most irate ... was an official in the* [FWS], *whose complaints became so vocal by September 2004, according to Ramey, that* [Denver] *museum executives met with him to smooth his feathers. But he remained unappeased – or so it seems based upon a letter the museum's chief curator and another top official sent to him on Oct. 26, 2004. "Labeling Dr. Ramey as 'pro-development' is unfortunate and inaccurate, they advised. Moreover, they suggested, "to suspend all funding for continued understanding of this animal," as the federal official apparently threatened to do, "seems counter to the principles of the USFWS."* [15]

Later, a well-documented letter from U.S. Senator Wayne Allard (R-CO) to Secretary of Interior Dirk Kempthorne, requesting the Secretary's review of whether "political influence was used when determining the listing status of ... the Preble's Meadow Jumping Mouse," indicates that the "irate" FWS official was Preble's Recovery Team Leader Bruce Rosenlund.[16]

Senator Allard's letter to the Secretary also documents an email Rosenlund sent to an ally at the University of Colorado, Biology Professor Andrew Martin: "I was going to include something with the e-mail on Ramey, but I did not want to make it seem I was mad as hell. To lower my blood pressure, I wrote a letter and sent it to the recovery team. Most of the Preble's Recovery Team was also mad...." A short time later, Professor Martin responded: "Hi any chance agency or non-profit are considering funding a genetic study of [jumping mouse subspecies] that is independent of the Ramey group? ... If this is on the burner, please consider us," Martin solicited on behalf of his biology department.

Not long after Dr. Ramey's article on the Preble's appeared in *Animal Conservation* (August, 2005), a memo circulated from the Preble's Recovery Team (Denver) office: "Since the Preble's has now published and the reality of what we need to accomplish is now coming into focus, we're starting to think more seriously about this USGS study." This was shortly followed by the FWS' appointment of Dr. Tim King, Ph.D., a wildlife biologist with the U.S. Geological Survey, a sister agency of FWS, to conduct another study refuting Dr. Ramey as reported in his published article. Senator Allard's letter to Kempthorne pointed out that Dr. King has a "one-sided history of splitting into subspecies and distinct population segments."

Senator Allard's letter adds: 'It appears that FWS staff set their minds on rebutting Ramey whatever the cost .... I have reviewed correspondence between FWS staff that shows them scrambling to reallocate funds from other programs to cover the cost of King' review. These emails show willingness by staff to go to almost any lengths to provide funding for the unnecessary review." The Senator's letter then recites, with names and dates, a list of ongoing communications between Dr. King, FWS biologists, and other staff while his study was under way. It suggests a close-knit working group of FWS biologists, exclusionist organizations, biology professors and others firmly committed to maintaining the Preble's as a distinct subspecies. The outcome of Dr. King's study, meanwhile, proved no surprise to anyone.

Not only did it find that the Preble's was a distinct subspecies, but it declared that Ramey's conclusions "should be considered questionable." One biology professor who reviewed King's study said: "The Preble's jumping mouse is distinct from other jumping mice, which means that the Preble's mouse should have protection under the [ESA] and development may have to be controlled in some way in the critical habitat areas." The professor, an unabashed supporter of the ESA's politicized biology, declared that "Ramey's work reflects the Bush administration's intrusion of politics in its scientific research."[17]

Hardcore defenders of the ESA often come to resemble characters in Lewis Carroll's *Alice in Wonderland*. But the FWS' efforts to silence and discredit Dr. Ramey and his views of the ESA's political brand of biology did not stop with the production of the King study. As Senator Allard noted:

> *The FWS campaign culminated in what was supposed to be an independent panel review of Ramey and King's work. But FWS staff seems to have colluded with King and academia to influence even the review process. FWS staff had behind-the-scenes contact and communication with the panel chosen to review Ramey's work .... In addition FWS crafted an agenda for the* [Sustainable Ecosystems Institute] *meeting and passed it along to Tim King .... Apparently due to complaints from Dr. King, a panelist* [Dr. Eric Routman of San Francisco State University] *was removed from the SEI panel based on fears he would be sympathetic to the Ramey work .... The panel review on Preble's was a model of selective interpretation.*[18]

The outcome of the SEI panel review proved no surprise to anyone. It came down largely in support of the King study, finding the Preble's to be a distinct species. What is so blatant about the FWS' efforts to obliterate the Ramey study – as in "the reality of what we need to accomplish is now coming into focus"– is that, as Senator Allard's letter to Secretary Kempthorne points out, "[p]rominent on the FWS' Preble's web page is Dr. King's work and the SEI panel review. Crandall and Marshall [an article by biologists who supported Ramey's study] is nowhere to be found." Conspicuously absent from the FWS web page were: Dr. Ramey's Preble's published article in *Animal Conservation*, three other Ramey articles on the Preble's, and the scientific writings of any biologist suggesting that the Preble's was not a distinct subspecies.

For Dr. Ramey, the fear and anger reached a boiling point much closer to home. He received an email from Carron Meaney, a colleague on the Denver Museum staff, which warned Ramey that "there are a lot of people who question your approach and have concerns about working with the museum in the future. I love the DMNS, and am very concerned to watch the alienation your behavior has wrought between the museum and the biology community."[19] Not long thereafter, FWS Preble's Recovery Team Leader Rosenlunt emailed Meaney: "Carron: Thanks again for your time and effort you have devoted to the DMNS Preble's issue."[20] Yet, as the pressure mounted on Dr. Ramey, a positive comment on his Preble's study arrived – from none other than biologist Phillip Kurtzsch himself.

Then 80-year old Dr. Kurtzsch graciously wrote that the Ramey team's findings "clearly invalidate" his own findings of 1954. "The tools of today are indeed cutting-edge," wrote Dr. Kurtzsch. "Ramey should be satisfied with the in-depth and reproducible analysis he presents. I can think of other listed endangered species that could have benefited from a prior, detailed, scientific appraisal, and I thank him for his eloquent study."[21] Nevertheless, Ramey's superiors at the Denver Museum continued to entertain negative characterizations about him.

One official inquired whether anything in the background of the 27-year, highly regarded biologist could "embarrass" the Museum. Another echoed the exclusionist opinion that Ramey had been "co-opted" by developers. Growing tired of the increasingly unpleasant atmosphere at the Museum, where the value of his study's defense of science-based biology had been shunted aside for a blatantly political brand, Dr. Ramey resigned from the Museum whose name enshrines both nature and science. His great sin in the eyes of the dominant camp of biologists is that he views the ESA as a tool for achieving species conservation, whereas they see it as a means of preserving every species. He explains:

> *Think about biodiversity as a tree that's in trouble. Do we want to try and save the little twigs at the end of the big branches, or do we want to try and save the big branches? Which is going to save the tree in the long term, looking out a hundred, 500 years? If we keep running around filing lawsuits, trying to save all these little twigs, we're wasting conservation resources at the expense of the big branches. We just have to understand that we may have to lose some of the little twigs out there. That means that some groups will lose their ESA cash cows, but it's for the long-term good.*[22]

This thinking makes good sense but remains anathema to exclusionists. Their intrigues continue on other fronts.

"Data-tinkering review vowed. Ex-Interior official changed endangered species reports," read the May 10, 2007, headline in the *Sacramento*

Bee. The article, similar to others around the country, told of an Interior Department Inspector General's report finding that Julie MacDonald, former Deputy Assistant Secretary of Interior for Fish and Wildlife, had interfered with species-related decision making of FWS biologists. It quoted exclusionist groups and their allies in Congress, charging the Bush administration with failing to review MacDonald's "manipulation of scientific decisions" on endangered species. Congresswoman Lois Capps (D-Santa Barbara), in another *Alice-in-Wonderland* moment, declared MacDonald's so-called interference with FWS biologists a reflection of "the [Bush] administration's troubling tendency of dismissing conclusive scientific evidence that contradicts its political goals."

The drumbeat against MacDonald dragged on for several months. In late July, 2007, the Committee on Natural Resources of the U.S. House of Representatives, chaired by ultra-green Congressman Nick Rahall (D-W. VA.), held hearings focused on the Interior Inspector General's findings against MacDonald. It was part of the ongoing campaign against the Bush administration's environmental policies that had begun shortly after President Bush declined to sign on to the international Kyoto Protocol early in his administration. President Clinton had signed the Protocol shortly before leaving office, but the U.S. Senate overwhelmingly rejected it, with members of both parties concerned that it would negatively impact the U.S. economy.

The Clinton-Gore administration, with Bruce Babbitt as Secretary of Interior, had been unabashedly exclusionist in its environmental agenda. For example, it had added millions of acres to "wilderness" areas and greatly expanded "roadless" areas. Under the Antiquities Act, the administration created national monuments involving tens of thousands of acres. The 25 million acres put off-limits on behalf of the northern spotted owl decimated the timber industry. The Bush administration, in contrast, is more conservationist, encouraging the prudent use of the nation's natural resources and showing more restraint toward the ESA-enabled "splitting" of subspecies into smaller units.

Julie MacDonald found herself the target of a campaign advanced by an axis of organizations like Earthjustice and the Center for Biological Diversity, the Union of Concerned Scientists, representing government scientists, including FWS and NOAA Fisheries biologists, eco-political members of Congress, and others. Earlier, perhaps coincidentally about the same time Dr. Ramey and his Preble's study were under heavy attack, an anonymous complaint had been filed with the Department of Interior's Office of Inspector General alleging that Ms. MacDonald had been involved in "unethical and illegal activities." Specifically, the complainants were upset because she had "rejected staff scientists' recommendations to protect imperiled animal and plants under the ESA at least six times in the past three years."[23]

The complaint charged that MacDonald had "bullied, insulted, and harassed the professional staff of [FWS] to change documents and alter biological reporting regarding the Endangered Species Program."[24] Much was made over MacDonald's efforts to exercise oversight and rein in FWS biologists' institutional attitude of "we're the scientists – we alone decide species science."

By education, Ms. MacDonald is a civil engineer with a master's degree in management. Her first federal service was as a hydraulic engineer with the Bureau of Reclamation. In 1987 she moved to California and to the policy side of government, working as a Republican staff consultant to the California Legislature and senior staff to a California Senate Minority Leader. She later served in different high-level positions in the administration of California Governor Pete Wilson, who appointed her Deputy Secretary for Legislative Affairs of the California Resources Agency. There she is credited with gaining bipartisan support for new provisions of California's Endangered Species Act. In 2002 she returned to Washington as senior advisor to Assistant Interior Secretary and Chief of the FWS, Craig Manson, the official who in 2001 declared the ESA "broken." In 2004, Interior Secretary Gale Norton promoted MacDonald to Deputy Assistant Secretary for Fish and Wildlife.

One of the six species on which Ms. MacDonald was accused of tampering was the Preble's meadow jumping mouse. According to the Inspector General's Report, based on conversations with biologists within FWS, "[t]he zoologist's study [Dr. Ramey's study] claimed that the Preble's mouse was not a species unto itself and was part of a more common species of mouse ... based on this information, MacDonald wanted to delist the species from the endangered list." When the Preble's Mouse Recovery Team contracted with Sustainable Ecosystems Institute (SEI) to organize "an independent review panel" to determine which study was most sound, "MacDonald wanted to hire an outside consultant other than SEI." Based on her impressions of SEI, she privately predicted what soon would come true, that SEI's report would state that "the Preble's mouse is a distinct species." [25]

"MacDonald is more interested in political views than in getting it right," one FWS biologist supervisor told the Inspector General's investigator. This comment deserves some attention because it reflects an inherent flaw in the thinking of the biologist-bureaucracy of the FWS, and of many in government. There is vast difference between a department executive making a "political" decision, and the making of a "policy" decision. While purely political decision making is improper, policy-based decision making is not only appropriate, but what voters intended and expected when they elected George W. Bush, rather than Al Gore, as president. Gore's well-known views of how the ESA should be implemented align more closely with the FWS' biologist staff. Thus, the policy decisions of Bush's Secretary of Interior, the Assistant Secretaries, and the Deputy Assistant Secretaries are expected to be in line with, and to advance the views of, the president for whom they work.

When executive branch bureaucrats like FWS biologists hold a contrary policy viewpoint to that of the Chief Executive, they take the attitude: "Mr. President, we were here before you came, and we will be here after you leave. If you don't like the way we're performing our jobs, you'll have to monitor our every move. And with our numbers, our protected civil service status, our friends in Congress, and in the press, be assured that won't be easy and we won't go along quietly."

As a policy-oriented veteran in government service, and having read numerous proposed species listing decisions written by FWS biologists, Ms. MacDonald was cognizant of their practice of "splitting" subspecies into multiple units. With each of the species on which MacDonald challenged the biologists' decisions, including the Preble's, she reflected the administration's more conservative, less activist policies. Rather than engaging in political usurpation of science, she confronted and sought to limit biologists' capacity to play games with science. If government biologists are allowed, in the name of science, to embrace the approach of splitting subspecies, while top-level department executives are prohibited from vetting their decisions because they are not scientists, then the biologists will have effectively usurped the Chief Executive's prerogative to set and implement environmental policy. That was the dominant mindset Ms. MacDonald understood and challenged.

The ESA states that listings of endangered or threatened species are to be based solely on the best scientific data available. In written testimony to the Committee on Resources hearing concerning Ms. MacDonald, Dr. Ramey stated the importance of distinguishing science from nonscience:

> *The fundamental distinction between science and non-science is the criterion of falsifiability. In other words, all hypotheses must be testable. When clear-cut criteria are laid out in advance of data collection and all information considered (the scientific method), then there is less room for bias through selective interpretation of the information .... If ESA decisions are not made in such an open and transparent way, then the moral authority of the ESA is compromised .... I write today because there does appear to be a "Crisis in Confidence"* [the words of Committee Chair Rahall in a pre-hearing press statement] *with some of the "science' used in* [ESA] *decisions .... There can also be serious consequences for those who dare to ask questions about information used in some ESA decisions ... In the case of the Preble's mouse ... the record will ultimately show that special interest groups, individuals, and academics with vested financial interests, and some* [FWS] *staff, have managed to maintain an invalid subspecies as an ESA-listing by obfuscation, intimidation, and ignoring contrary evidence.*[26]

Dr. Ramey had resigned his position with the Denver Museum of Nature and Science under orchestrated pressure by biologists who did not want their pet subspecies overturned. FWS biologists who feared losing their lock on species decision making orchestrated the resignation of Julie MacDonald from Interior, as Ms. MacDonald's letter to Interior Secretary Dirk Kempthorne reveals:

> *[A]t no point was I provided a formal opportunity to respond to the allegations contained in the* [Inspector General's] *Report. I was*

never formally provided an official copy of the full report, the redacted report, or the executive summary, prior to the report being leaked [to the press] nor after it was leaked .... [While] the Interior Conduct Accountability Board provides a process for reviewing the IG report ... [w]hen the Accountability Board met I was not allowed to be present nor to be a part of the presentation or discussion, nor was I informed of their recommendation if there was one .... The reality is that I was accused and judgment was rendered, with absolutely no opportunity to defend myself or correct the record .... It is incomprehensible to me why it would be in the interest of the Interior Department or of any department to allow spurious charges against executive staff not only to remain unchallenged but also to be leaked to the press and others, apparently with the sole purpose of destroying my professional and personal reputation and providing a platform to unfairly criticize the President. This has been a difficult experience for me. As a result of the refusal to address my responses and documentation ... [t]he inaccuracies included in the report have been widely reported, all over the world.[27]

On November 1, 2007, FWS announced its decision on the status of the Preble's meadow jumping mouse. Was the Preble's of the same subspecies as the Bear Lodge meadow jumping mouse, and thus neither endangered nor threatened in the multistate region, as Dr. Ramey contended, with support from Phillip Kurtzsch? Or was it a distinct and separate subspecies in Colorado and Wyoming that need ESA protection, as Dr. King and the SEI panel countered. It came as little surprise that the FWS sided with its hand-picked experts that the Preble's was a distinct subspecies.

But what is surprising – and downright bizarre – is FWS' further decision to delist the Preble's in Wyoming, but to continue its ESA-protected status in Colorado. How is that possible from the scientific standpoint that is supposed to govern such decision? As Dr. Edwards and others have pointed out, scientifically it isn't possible. The FWS made a purely political decision, effectively "splitting" the Preble's subspecies into the further subspecies of *"Colorado* Preble's meadow jumping mouse."[28]

Colorado's Senator Allard suggested the absurdity of the FWS decision with this comment: "I have a difficult time comprehending how a mouse could nest along Colorado's northern border and wake up one morning listed as an 'endangered species,' cross over into Wyoming to forage for food, and no longer be listed …. [He] called the decision a cave-in to "environmental extremists who plan on using this decision to extort private property owners and prevent the responsible growth of Colorado's economy."[29] This is what happens when politicized science trumps real science. It's been going on for 35 years, with few attempts to calculate the cost.

NOTES

1. *Great Falls Tribune,* July 30, 1991.

2. Edwards, "The Definition of Biological Species: Controversies Surrounding the Endangered Species," *Standard Handbook of Environmental Science, Health and Technology*, McGraw-Hill, 2000, pp. 20.58 - 20.59.

3. ESA, 16 *U.S. Code* 1532, "Definitions," Section 3 (16).

4. Edwards, *Standard Handbook of Environmental Science, Health and Technology, op. cit.*, p. 20.60.

5. *Ibid.*, citing 41 *Federal Register* 47197, Oct. 27, 1976.

6. "Skull measurements are more useful for positive identification." Final Rule Listing the Preble's meadow jumping mouse as a Threatened Species, 63 *Federal Register* 26517, May 13, 1998.

7. *Ibid.*

8. Stephen Moore, "Of Mice and Men," *Wall Street Journal*, March 23, 2006, http://www.opinion-journal.com/cc/?id=110008128

9. "Cats are a target in Preble's mouse preservation," *The Associated Press*, January 22, 1999.

10. *Ibid.*

11. David Holthouse, "Building a Better Mousetrap," *Westword*, January 20, 2005, http://www.westword.com/2005-01-20/news/building-a-better-mousetrap/

12. "Research Shows Preble's is Common Species of Mouse," Office of Governor Dave Frudenthal of Wyoming, December 18, 2003, http://www.citizenreviewonline.org/jan2004/rodents.htm

13. 12-Month Finding on a Petition to Delist the Preble's Meadow Jumping Mouse, 70 *Federal Register* 5404, February 2, 2005.

14. David Holthouse, "Building a Better Mousetrap," *op. cit.*; Stephen Moore, "Of Mice and Men," *op. cit.*

15. Vincent Carroll, "On Point: The mouse that roared," *Rocky Mountain News*, April 5, 2006, http://www.rockymountainnews.com/drmn/opinion_columnists/article/0,2777,DRMN_23972_459583 0,00.html

16. Senator Wayne Allard letter to Interior Secretary Dirk Kempthorne, July 30, 2007.

17. "Tiny Mouse Stands In Way of U.S. Government," *Associated Press*, as reported on foxnews.com, January 30, 2006.

18. Senator Allard letter to Kempthorne, *op.cit.*

19. Vincent Carroll, *Rocky Mountain News*, *op. cit.*

20. Senator Allard letter to Kempthorne, *op. cit.*

21. David Holthouse, "Building a Better Mousetrap," *op. cit.*

22. *Ibid.*

23. "Bush Appointee Said to Reject Advice on Endangered Species," *Washington Post*, October 30, 2006.

24. Report of Investigation of Julie MacDonald, Deputy Assistant Secretary, Fish, Wildlife and Parks; Office of Inspector General, Department of Interior. This report of DOI's Inspector General appears to bear no date; it is believed to have issued in late spring, 2007

25. *Ibid.*, p. 9.

26. Written testimony of Rob Roy Ramey, Ph.D., Committee on Natural Resources, United States House of Representatives, July 31, 2007.

27. Julie MacDonald letter to Interior Secretary Kempthorne, May 6, 2007.

28. "Seeing double – Mouse saga takes another bizarre turn," *The Gazette* (Colorado Springs), editorial, Sunday, November 4, 2007, http://www.gazette.com/opinion/wyoming_29303_article.html/mouse_colorado.html

29. *Ibid.*

CHAPTER 9

THE REAL COSTS

COST-BENEFIT ANALYSIS (CBA) is the process by which the benefits derived from a project can be compared with the costs expended to achieve those benefits. CBA can be utilized with conceptual or prospective projects, to determine whether going forward would be practical, or with projects already under way, to decide whether continuation of a project is economically worthwhile – that is, that the net benefits meet the expectations of the decision maker. Although used in the private sector much earlier, government projects did not begin to use CBA until the federal Flood Control Act of 1936.

This federal statute required the U.S. Army Corps of Engineers to carry out waterway system improvement projects "if the benefits to whomsoever they may accrue are in excess of estimated costs." The legislative mandate of the use of CBA – albeit an elementary version by today's standards – forced the Corps of Engineers to formulate a systematic approach to measuring benefits and costs. Initially conducted from an engineer's perspective, it wasn't until the 1950s that economists entered the process and began to apply a more rigorous, uniformed method for measuring benefits and costs. Since then, governments at all levels have relied on CBA to determine the feasibility and/or efficiency of public works projects and other government-implemented programs. One monumental government program, however, has been entirely excluded from the scrutiny of cost-benefit analysis: the Endangered Species Act of 1973.

The ESA authorizes the Secretary of Interior to list a species as endangered or threatened solely on the basis of the best scientific data available.[1] Deliberately omitted from this listing criteria was any reference to the economic costs of listing a species, or the grant of any discretion to the Secretary to balance or even compare a listing's overall benefit to society against the costs involved. Although later amendment of the Act required the Secretary of Interior to undertake an economic impact analysis before designating critical habitat for the species, the loosely worded language of the new provision allowed the Secretary (or his designee, usually the FWS) to side-step the actual conduct of an economic impact analysis. It wasn't until the court decision in the Alameda whipsnake case that the Act's economic impact analysis became mandated. Why does the ESA spurn such a commonsense tool as cost-benefit analysis in the economically haphazard arena of public policy? The answer comes from the philosophy of modern exclusionism.

As explained by the imminent Harvard biologist, E. O. Wilson, one of the 20th century's foremost champions for saving every species, "every scrap of biological diversity is priceless, to be learned and cherished, and never to be surrendered without a struggle."[2] Nearly a half-century earlier the naturalist, Aldo Leopold, provided a similar explanation: "if the [living world], in the course of eons has built something we like but do not understand, then who but a fool would discard seemingly useless parts? To keep every cog in the wheel is the first precaution of intelligent tinkering."[3]

The ESA does not permit the use of cost-benefit analysis because those who crafted the law, and those who continue to animate it, still passionately believe in the balance of nature – that is, that every member of every plant and wildlife species in the world has intrinsic value that is priceless, beyond man's ability to quantify or his right to impair. According to this thinking:

> *No creature exists in a vacuum. All living things are part of a complex, delicately balanced network .... The removal of a single species within an ecosystem can set off a chain reaction affecting many*

other species. It has been estimated, for example, that a disappearing plant can take with it up to 30 other species, including insects, higher animals, and even other plants.[4]

As the Sierra Club affirms: "The human impact, from prehistory to the present time and projected into the next several decades, threatens to be the greatest extinction spasm since the end of the Mesozoic era 65 million years ago," quoting E. O. Wilson.[5] "There is no way to estimate the health, economic and spiritual costs of this massive loss of life."[6]

This view of the natural world, while attractive on a purely emotional level, is impractical and even dysfunctional as the controlling regime for the federal government's implementation and enforcement of a major statutory program. Without cost-benefit analysis as a tool for measuring the economic cost and biological effectiveness of species protection and restoration programs, the American taxpayers are placed in the untenably compromised position of living under, and paying for, a virtually unaccountable law.

There are two categories of parties that incur the economic costs generated by the implementation and enforcement of the Endangered Species Act: the regulator and the regulated. The regulator is, of course, the federal government. But because the government pays its bills primarily from tax revenues, it is really the American taxpayers who, for three and a half decades, have paid – and continue to pay – the costs of the ESA.

The "regulated" are the property owners, large and small. The presence on their property of a plant or wildlife species listed as endangered or threatened under the ESA restricts or even prohibits the use of their land. Either way, it is the American people who incur the economic costs. So, how much does it cost the taxpayers each year for our government to implement and enforce the ESA? As with much about the ESA, the government supplies no clear or comprehensible answer.

Although the ESA became law in 1973, it wasn't until 1988, a full 15 years later, that Congress recognized its fiscal responsibility to provide the American people a means for determining how much the ESA was actually costing them. However, because the results of a full and thorough accounting of the government's ESA-related expenditures could turn the taxpaying public against the "whatever the cost" approach, Congress tiptoed to the task.

By amendment, Congress directed that, beginning in 1989, the Secretary of Interior, through the Fish and Wildlife Service, compile and publish in an annual report, a "species-by-species" accounting of "all reasonably identifiable Federal expenditures" made to implement the Act. These reports would also include "all reasonably identifiable" expenditures made by those states receiving species-conservation grants from the FWS.[7]

Before preparing the first report, FWS staff met with the staffs of the House and Senate policy committees that had crafted the amendment, to get a sense of what the words "all reasonably identifiable" expenditures meant. Was the report to provide a full and thorough accounting of costs attributed to the ESA, as the Act's critics wanted, or would a partial and minimal accounting of ESA expenditures, as the preservationist lobby intended, do? As stated in every FWS report since the first, "the service determined [from the meetings with congressional staff] that [while] a good faith effort was expected ... [n]o extensive or extraordinary measures to develop exceptionally precise data were sought."[8]

From its first report in 1989, and continuing in every annual report that followed, the FWS regarded certain words in the amendment as providing convenient loopholes in its reporting requirement. Repeatedly, the FWS declined to list known ESA-related expenditures because they were either not reasonably identifiable – a highly subjective determination – or because they did not benefit one specific species, but may have benefited two or more. This mindset gives renewed credence to the old bureaucratic excuse: "close enough for government work." Regrettably, as a tool for shining light on the ESA's true economic costs, the FWS annual report has amounted to, as Randy Simmons and Kimberly Frost put it, "little more than a bureaucratic effort to keep Congress minimally happy."[9]

On this basis, FWS reported ESA-related expenditures for the first nine years as follows:

Year	Expenditures	Number of Listed Species
1989	$ 43.7 Million	554
1990	$ 102.3	591
1991	$ 176.8	639
1992	$ 291.5	728
1993	$ 222.2	809
1994	$ 244.6	914
1995	$ 297.6	957
1996	$ 285.7	963
1997	$ 300.9	1,111[10]

During these years, many who urged stricter scrutiny of the ESA, including some members of Congress, grew increasingly suspicious that FWS' annual expenditure reports failed to provide a complete or accurate picture of what the government actually spent to implement the ESA. Periodic articles quoted FWS biologists and other government sources estimating substantially higher costs for protecting some species than FWS was reporting.[11] Further, ESA-responsible agencies testifying before a congressional committee indicated much higher expenditures than those in the FWS reports.

Yet, the voluminous annual reports, with information from 20 federal agencies, each with different reporting approaches, based on varying interpretations of what a "reasonably identifiable" or species-specific expenditure was, and covering hundreds (and annually increasing) listings of different species, were just some of the obfuscatory factors that made the annual reports difficult to track, compare, or understand. When combined with the year-to-year inconsistencies in the states' ESA cost-reporting, for which there was no uniform criteria, and which came to FWS on a purely voluntary basis, determining how much money the federal government was actually spending on the ESA proved impossible. This largely explains why, during these years, there were no published independent accounting reviews or economics articles shedding light on the meager content or methodology of FWS' annual reports.

In 1998, the FWS failed to publish an ESA Expenditures Report. It failed to do so in 1999 and again in 2000. ESA critics in Congress, such as Members Donald Young (R-AK), Chair of the powerful House Resources Committee, and Richard Pombo (R-CA), Chair of the Congressional Western Caucus,[12] as well as business and public interest organizations tracking the ESA, clamored for Interior Secretary Bruce Babbitt, and his Assistant Secretary for Fish and Wildlife Jamie Rappaport Clark to provide the reports for the missing years. Not until early 2004, during the Bush administration, did the FWS produce *Three-Year Summary of Federal and State Endangered Species Expenditures, Fiscal Years 1998-2000*,[13] a report it described as "the most comprehensive" ESA-expenditure account yet published. As it revealed:

Year	Expenditures	Number of Listed Species
1998	$ 454.3 Million	1,166
1999	$ 514	1,202
2000	$ 610	1,235

The publication of this report also highlighted the absurdity this on-going scenario had become. The ESA had been in operation for almost 30 years, and for the past decade the FWS had expended untold taxpayer resources presumably reporting what the government was spending on the Act's implementation. Yet, it could not be said with any sense of certainty whether the ESA was costing Americans merely several hundred millions of dollars every year, as FWS reported, or whether the ESA's yearly implementation costs were really in the multibillion dollar range, as ESA critics suspected. At this point, with no future prospect of more complete or accurate cost information being provided by the federal government, Pacific Legal Foundation decided to take action.[14]

It commissioned the nonprofit Property and Environment Research Center (PERC) in Bozeman, Montana,[15] to examine the three-year, "most comprehensive" ESA-cost report just issued by FWS, and determine whether it provided a generally accurate picture of annual ESA expenditures. PERC decided that the most effective way to answer that question was by identifying known direct ESA costs that were left out of the report.

As a second question, PERC was asked to offer a general monetary range of government spending to implement the ESA: were annual ESA expenditures several hundred million dollars, or several billion dollars? In disclaiming its ability to arrive at anything more accurate than an estimate or approximation of ESA costs, PERC noted the two types of audits the government would have to perform to gain a more complete picture of its ESA-implementation costs: "One audit would be a program audit that identified the various government programs that spend money to implement the [ESA] and evaluated their effectiveness. The second audit would scrutinize those programs' expenditures. These kinds of audits have not been conducted at the national or state levels."[16]

In April, 2004, Pacific Legal Foundation and PERC released the study, entitled *Accounting for Species: The True Costs of the Endangered Species Act.* Its findings are remarkable:

1) Because the ESA's annual expenditure reporting provision requires the listing of expenditures on a "species by species basis," the 20 federal agencies with ESA responsibilities included in the report do not list administrative expenses such as employee salaries, operations, maintenance and other services that clearly carry substantial price-tags.[17] These sizeable expenditures are not listed "because they generally cannot be attributed to the conservation of a specific species. Thus, none of these expenses are identified, even though we know they are occurring."[18]

In addition, and for the same reason, the substantial costs of law enforcement, agency consultations, species recovery coordination, and litigation (including Department of Justice enforcement litigation) are not listed in the report.[19]

2) Although the Act calls for the reporting of ESA-related "expenditures," instead of listing actual expenditures the FWS encouraged agencies with ESA responsibilities to merely "estimate" their costs. Because estimating costs well after the task is performed allows careless, selective,

and even deliberate rounding-off of the real numbers, analysis shows that actual expenditures are normally greater than estimated costs. "In sum, the data in the report cannot accurately reflect the total cost of conserving listed species."[20]

3) Even though the report includes data from 19 federal agencies in addition to the FWS, there are many other agencies with significant ESA costs that were totally missing from the report. For example, the only estimated ESA-related expenditures that the Department of Energy reported was for the Bonneville Power Administration; yet, the Department's other power generators – the Southeastern, Southwestern, and Western Area Power Administrations – submitted no estimated costs, even though they, like Bonneville, spend substantial sums protecting the numerous listed species in their regions.

The same occurred with the Department of Interior's Minerals Management Service and Office of Surface Mining. There is no mention of them in the report, even though they also deal with endangered species. As well, numerous agencies within the Department of Agriculture that have ESA responsibilities do not show up on the report. And there are others.[21]

4) Because the reporting provision calls for listing expenditures on a "species by species basis," funds that benefit, or may benefit multiple species simultaneously are not listed in the report. For example, the FWS' total budget for fish-protection programs in 1998 was nearly $71 million. The presumed beneficiaries of these expenditures were both endangered and threatened fish species, as well as nonlisted species. Yet, because this limitation made it impossible to identify how much of the $71 million was spent on specific listed species (as opposed to all other fish), the $71 million of expenditures was conveniently omitted from the report.[22]

5) Nor does the report include those taxpayer funds the government expends to protect endangered or threatened species in foreign countries. During the reporting period, FWS listed 517 foreign endangered species and 41 foreign threatened species. The study cites examples that range from African elephants and crocodiles to Australian rat-kangaroos and the Corsican swallowtail butterfly. American taxpayer funds help enforce rules against international trade in endangered species, provide financial assistance to foreign wildlife law enforcement agencies, allow international

collaboration in habitat conservation and joint research projects, and other species protection efforts. Yet, the several million dollars annually spent for these purposes are not listed in the report.[23]

6) Although the ESA requires states receiving species conservation grants to report their ESA expenditures to the FWS for listing in its annual report, because the Secretary of Interior never established standardized reporting procedures, the few states that reported expenditures directly to FWS did so irregularly and voluntary. In fact, the states' expenditure information that FWS included in the three-year report was collected through the International Association of Fish and Wildlife Agencies; FWS simply incorporated the Association's $115 million figure with no attempt at verification. "Thus," notes PERC, "it is highly unlikely that the $115 million the states voluntarily reported spending in 2000 is a complete account of the ESA costs actually incurred by the states."[24]

7) Although FWS is required to report expenditures "that are appropriated [by Congress] for conservation of endangered and threatened species,"[25] the states and local governments spend large amounts of their taxpayers' dollars (not federal dollars) implementing a variety of species conservation programs. PERC provided the following as examples, but there are many such programs throughout the country: a San Diego Habitat Conservation Plan (HCP) with an estimated cost of $650 million; a Riverside County, California, HCP estimated to have cost $45 million; and a Balcones Canyonlands HCP, in Travis County, Texas, estimated to cost $160 million. Yet, major ESA expenditures such as these, while costing state and local taxpayers multimillions of dollars, did not receive even a footnote in FWS' report.[26]

In addition to these findings, PERC examined a 2002 General Accounting Office (GAO) study to quantify the federal costs of salmon preservation efforts in the Columbia and Snake River basins in Oregon, Washington, and Idaho for the five-year period, 1997 - 2001.[27] According to the GAO study, the federal government spent $1.505 billion in taxpayer dollars, or about $301 million per year, on salmon-construction, research, and monitoring projects, spawning-ground surveys, agency consultations, and other ESA-required activities.[28]

However, in an independent PERC review of the GAO's study, it was determined through direct communications with the federal agencies involved, that the costs of those salmon preservation efforts over the five-year period were significantly higher than what the GAO study stated – $2.879 billion, or $575.5 million per year.[29] "But even if one accepts the GAO numbers as accurate," PERC explains, "it becomes obvious that the expenditure estimates provided by the FWS in its ESA cost reports for the years 1997 through 2000 cannot be accurate since the expenditures just on salmon preservation efforts alone total more than the amount that the FWS claims was spent on *all ESA-listed species* in 1997, 1998, and 1999, and close to all that was spent on *all ESA-listed species* in 2000."[30]

The PERC Study demonstrated conclusively that the FWS' three-year ESA expenditure report – and by reasonable extension all its previous reports – had grossly understated the vast taxpayer dollars that the federal government was spending to implement the ESA. At the same time, it totally ignored the huge sums that state and local governments were expending for ESA implementation. With this, PERC had effectively answered the first question.

In preparing to offer an approximation of how much was being spent by the federal government – again, the taxpayers – on ESA implementation, PERC carefully reviewed testimony given at a hearing conducted by the House Resources Committee in 1996. The purpose of the hearing was to examine the ESA-implementation expenditures of five federal agencies. Of the 20 agencies with ESA responsibilities that regularly reported to FWS, only the Fish and Wildlife Service, the Environmental Security Agency, the Army Corps of Engineers, NOAA Fisheries Service, and the Bonneville Power Administration were called to testify. Their representatives stated under oath that their combined ESA expenditures for fiscal year 1996 would amount to at least $560 million.

What is so remarkable about this combined expenditure figure from only five agencies is that, when FWS published its fiscal year 1996 expenditures report, it showed that the total ESA expenditures for all agencies and states was only $287.7 million – indeed, just about 50 percent of what the five agencies alone told the House Committee their 1996 costs would be. PERC concluded that "[t]his testimony, if accurate, confirms suspicions that the FWS' efforts to quantify ESA-implementation costs grossly underestimate them."[31] But the implications of this House Resources Committee testimony do not stop with 1996.

If the 1996 50 percent underestimate shown above is extended to FWS' 2000 report, "then the reported [2000] expenditures of $610 million are no more than half of what was actually spent .... Thus, a more accurate estimate would be at least $1.2 billion. And recall that only one-fourth of the 20 federal agencies that reported [ESA] costs for 2000 ... testified before the Resources Committee .... Conceivably, the total [ESA] cost could be four times the $610 million, or $2.4 billion in 2000."[32] PERC concluded its study with this statement:

> *The Fish and Wildlife Service's Three-Year Summary of Federal and State Endangered Species Expenditures, Fiscal Years 1998-2000 is a gross underestimate of the actual cost of implementing the* [ESA.] *The report fails to account for expenditures not identifiable with specific species on the federal and state levels. Efforts to conserve threatened and endangered species at the local level are not adequately accounted for.... It is safe to say that the most recent expenditures figure of $610 million in 2000 is far below the actual price tag of the ESA. The true costs are probably four times that — not in the millions, but in the billions.*[33]

The PERC Study is highly significant, not only for what it says about FWS' gross understatement of ESA costs in past reports (1989 - 2000), but for the inference that the ESA expenditures listed in FWS reports since the PERC Study, the 2001 - 2003 reports, are likewise deficient. Comparing expenditures from one year to the next has been a persistent challenge, with each of the reports containing this disclaimer: "Due to differences in reporting methods, this report cannot be easily compared to prior expenditure reports."[34] FWS reports for the post-PERC Study years show the following:

Year	Expenditures	Number of Listed Species
2001	$ 2.442 Billion	1,272
2002	$ 1.192	1,285
2003	$ 1.201	1,335

What immediately stands out is that 2001's $2.442 billion in reported ESA-implementation expenditures is four times greater than 2000's $610 million in costs. With only 35 additional species listed during this 12-month period, what accounts for the enormous increase in ESA expenditures? The answer is that, "[b]eginning with this report [2001], we [FWS] have sought to more fully identify other Act-related expenditures by asking for expenditures not identifiable to specific individual species .... These costs are included in this report for the first time as 'Other ESA Expenses.'"[35]

Of the $2.442 billion reportedly spent on federally funded species conservation programs in 2001, 68 percent of it – a whopping $1.665 billion – was "other ESA expenses," that is, general ESA expenditures not attributable to a specific species.[36] Because the inclusion of these other actual ESA expenses makes the 2001 report at least somewhat more accurate and credible, the obvious question is, why didn't the FWS make these expenditures a regular part of its earlier annual reporting of ESA's costs? Indeed, if it had, the annual reports would have been significantly more understandable, honest, and informative. But apparently those objectives were not the FWS' primary concerns.

However, in 2002, and again in 2003, for reasons left unexplained, FWS again modified its reporting methodology. The result was a substantial shrinkage in the category of "other ESA expenses," which caused a drastic drop in total reported ESA expenditures for those years – $1.192 billion in 2002, and $1.201 billion in 2003 – even though the number of listed species increased by 63. Nonetheless, those figures are substantially higher than the $610 million reported for 2000.

Despite FWS' continuing game of "hide-the-ball," it is possible to come to a rough estimate of how much the taxpayers are annually paying for the government to implement and enforce the ESA. The PERC Study found that FWS grossly underestimated ESA expenditures by as much as 50 percent. Even if, to be more than fair and generous, a 25 percent "underestimate factor" is applied to FWS' $2.442 billion expenditure report (2001), a conservative estimate of the federal government's ESA costs in 2001 would be nothing less than $3 billion.[37] And when the multimillions of dollars state and local governments expend on species conservation programs is heaped on top of the $3 billion in federally funded programs,

American taxpayers could easily be paying upward of $3.5 billion in ESA-implementation costs – *annually*.

Besides the ESA's direct economic costs incurred by taxpayers who underwrite the government's role as regulator, the other segment of Americans that bears ESA-imposed economic costs are the regulated. These are the individual and business owners of the private land on which 75 - 80 percent of all listed species have their habitat. Not only do property owners pay their tax share of the billions governments spend on species preservation and recovery programs, but they pay again, and substantially, just for the privilege of using, or attempting to use, their own land.

It is important to recognize that for private property owners, whether individual or corporate, ESA-generated economic costs means one thing – financial losses. As a result of the "whatever the cost" approach enunciated in *TVA v. Hill*, and the exclusionists' aversion to cost-benefit analysis, there is no national estimate of the economic losses private property owners sustain from the ESA.

Property owners who have a listed species on, or in the vicinity of their property suffer substantial economic losses just from the listing alone. If it is determined that a listed species – even one temporarily visiting or passing through or over the property – was harassed, harmed, pursued, hunted, shot, wounded, killed, trapped, captured, collected, or the focus of an attempt of any of these acts, the property owner can be prosecuted in criminal or civil proceedings. A criminal conviction, usually for a large, deliberate, or repeated harm, can result in jail, fines, probationary conditions, orders of restitution, and mitigation. A civil judgment can result in a less culpable violator being heavily fined, and ordered to pay restitution and mitigation costs. When even common and normal activities such as hiking or allowing dogs (or in Colorado – cats chasing the Preble's mouse) to run loose on one's land can result in a finding of "harm" or "harassment" of a species, the potential for criminal and civil penalties severely restrains a property owner's use of his land, and thereby effectively diminishes its economic value. But it is the designation of critical habitat on private property that imposes the greatest economic losses for property owners.

Once the FWS designates critical habitat, or indicates its intention to designate, as with the Perdido Key beach mouse, the property owner enters a federal bureaucratic process that can be enormously expensive, drawn out over many months or even years, and filled with frustration and disappointment. The most effective measurements of critical habitat-caused economic loss are the out-of-pocket losses incurred in the permit application process, and property use losses, also known as opportunity costs, caused by severe use restrictions.

For the individual property owner, the out-of-pocket loss meter begins to run when he submits an application to FWS or NOAA Fisheries for a permit to build on or otherwise modify land designated as critical habitat for a listed species. Out-of-pocket costs incurred in the permit process include the fees of environmental consultants to conduct biological studies and surveys to anticipate or address the concerns of FWS; the engineering and reengineering costs of project plans to satisfy the Service's specifications and requirements; the expense of preparing a Habitat Conservation Plan; the substantial funds required to purchase comparable and replacement habitat elsewhere; fees for attorney services in negotiations, drafting legal documents, or for litigation costs in administrative proceedings, or court action; and the cost of special FWS-required construction materials, such as road or driveway surfaces.

Property use losses, or opportunity costs, include the reduced economic profit that would have accrued from a commercial enterprise or development project, as a result of FWS-imposed land use restrictions, alterations, or denials. Even disregarding the mental anguish that often accompanies the application process, out-of-pocket losses and lost opportunity costs for the individual property owner can add up to tens of thousands of dollars.

For example, it would have cost Robert Morris a minimum of $27,000 to prepare the Habitat Conservation Plan required by NOAA Fisheries for considering his application to cut the five large trees on his half-acre parcel. Not only did this amount to more than the trees were worth as timber, but Mr. Morris also would have had to purchase comparable "shade" property elsewhere to mitigate removal of the shade trees on his property. In addition, the attorney fees for negotiating and preparing a legally binding "Implementing Agreement" would have significantly increased the total cost of the HCP. Recognizing that his out-of-pocket costs would far exceed the value of the trees as timber, Mr. Morris decided to go no further.

Yet, public disclosure of NOAA Fisheries' prohibitively expensive HCP had the effect of shrinking the market value of his parcel to $500.

In the early 1990s, a senior citizen by the name of Margaret Rector was another victim of ESA critical habitat designation. Although she received significant media attention at the time, she would have given anything just to be allowed to go into retirement as she had planned for many years. But that was not to be. Here is her story as told by Dan Byfield of Stewards of the Range.[38] His editorial commentary has been retained because it so effectively articulates the human costs of the ESA:

> *As Congressman Billy Tauzin from Louisiana* [now retired] *likes to say: "The Fifth Amendment to our Constitution does not say 'Nor shall private property be taken for public use, without just compensation,' except where there is an endangered species."*
>
> *Such a great percentage of Americans today have all been brainwashed to believe protecting the environment is so important that our civil rights can be abridged. Tell that to Margaret Rector who used to own 15 acres of land just outside Austin, Texas.*
>
> *In 1992, she received a letter from the U.S. Fish and Wildlife Service informing her that she had prime habitat for the Golden-cheeked Warbler, an endangered species, and that she could not use or develop her land without first obtaining a permit. Try as she did, she could not afford the process of obtaining a permit without which FWS would not issue the permit. The value of Margaret's land went from over $900,000 in 1992 to $30,380 in 1993.*
>
> *Margaret was not given compensation for the loss of her land. Her constitutional rights were totally trampled and she eventually had to sell the land at a tremendous loss never realizing its full potential for her retirement years. Yet, Margaret was told she had to "sacrifice" her life savings and her land for the benefit of the birds. There are so many stories like Margaret's in this country today. More people need to hear those stories. If they did, maybe their guilt for the environment would change to anger towards the government and those who wish to*

destroy what made this a great nation – the guiding principles of our Constitution.[39]

The opportunity losses imposed by excessive critical habitat requirements are multiplied millions of times over when the property owner is a home builder, developer of large commercial projects, agriculture producer, timber company, mineral extraction company, and the like. Losses for property owners on this scale run into the multibillions of dollars. Yet, because of their business need to maintain a positive working relationship with one of several government agencies that holds the fate of future land development projects in its hands, research reveals no public reports by commercial developers or other business enterprises or industry associations that document the out-of-pocket or opportunity losses these property owners incur as a result of FWS' designation of critical habitat. Press reports, however, frequently quote FWS estimates of opportunity losses. For example: "Economic analysis says between $18 million to $51 million needed to protect [Alabama] beach mouse."[40] "Study: [Oregon] Plover habitat economic impact will be up to $645 million."[41] "[C]ritical habitat for vernal pool species ... could cost the local economy ... $992 million statewide."[42]

Consider the FWS' 2003 proposed designation of critical habitat for the California gnatcatcher.[43] This designation removed from anticipated development 495,795 acres in Los Angeles, Orange, Riverside, San Bernardino, San Diego, and Ventura Counties – one of the largest centers of population growth and economic activity in the entire country.

Dr. David Sunding is the co-director for the Center for Sustainable Resource Development in the College of Natural Resources, and a Cooperative Extension economist in the Department of Agriculture and Resource Economics at the University of California, Berkeley. During the Clinton Administration, he served as senior economist at the White House Council of Economic Advisors. In an extensive study prepared for the California Resource Management Institute, Sunding estimated and projected the private economic losses that FWS' proposed California gnatcatcher critical habitat designation would generate in the six county region between 2003 and 2020. He explained: "Critical habitat designation has three basic impacts: it increases out-of-pocket expenses to the developer, it delays completion of the activity, and it reduces the output [meaning houses or commercial buildings] of the project."[44]

After inputting the detailed demographic data that supported the anticipated economic growth of the region over the next 17 years, Dr. Sunding overlayed the impact factors. From this he projected that the FWS' designation of nearly 496,000 acres of added gnatcatcher critical habitat would bar the construction of new houses over the 17-year period in the amount of $4.6 billion in economic losses; it would further eliminate $185 million in associated nonresidential construction projects; and it would wipe off the drawing boards $124 million in accompanying public infrastructure projects. Altogether, the negative economic impact or financial losses from the gnatcatcher's critical habitat designation totaled more than $5 billion.[45] "On a per-acre basis, critical habitat designation [losses] for the gnatcatcher will range from $400,000 to $150,000 per acre and average $150,000 per acre over the seventeen-year period," PERC's Dr. Simmons noted.[46]

Further, one can reasonably speculate that had Dr. Sunding's methodology been utilized to project the economic losses that would result from FWS' designation of 406,708 acres in Alameda, San Joaquin, Contra Costa, and Santa Clara Counties as Alameda whipsnake habitat, the losses also would have been in the billions of dollars. Like the gnatcatcher habitat designation in southern California, the majority of the whipsnake's designated habitat was privately owned land that was largely anticipated to accommodate new homes in the Bay Area, where home prices were already sky-high and increasing annually.[47]

In addition, the University of California, Berkeley, that owns land for future expansion within the whipsnake's designated habitat, estimated its long-term development losses at more than $100 million, while the mining business sector also estimated $100 million in losses. Letters and testimony submitted at FWS hearings suggested that costly economic impacts also would hit the Pacific Gas and Electric Company and numerous private landowners. As well, public sector property owners such as the Lawrence Livermore National Laboratory, the California Department of Parks and Recreation, and four others all anticipated substantial financial losses. But, the opportunity losses brought on by expanding acreage of designated critical habitat impacts more than just home builders, commercial developers, and public agencies.

According to Dr. Sunding, consumers feel the effects of declining buildable acreage most. "When the price of output [such as new homes] is affected by [critical habitat designation], economic impacts are borne disproportionately by consumers." But Sunding is not referring to the normal business practice of passing on to consumers the higher costs of production. Fast-growing population centers and regions of economic growth require homes and jobs to sustain themselves. With thousands of fewer acres for new home development, the housing supply tightens, driving up the prices of existing homes, while decreasing the availability of homes affordable to middle-income consumers. These home buyers are forced to settle in more distant communities where housing is cheaper. The region's demographic composition is thereby impacted for years to come, as only high-income families can afford to live in the area, while more modest-income families cannot. This causes a rippling effect: longer driving distances to work, higher gasoline, car maintenance, and auto insurance bills, longer workday and distance separations from school-age children, and greater environmental impacts due to increased stop-and-go driving. "In fact," according to the Sundig study, "consumers ... bear the brunt of the economic costs of habitat designation."[48]

In addition to the billions in economic losses ESA listings and critical habitat designations impose, other regulatory tools such as species recovery plans can inflict profound and long-lasting economic consequences on the people who live, do business, and work in the species-affected area. Take, for example, the enormous economic losses catalyzed by the government's excessive logging restrictions to protect the northern spotted owl in the forests of Oregon, Washington, and northern California. The northern spotted owl also makes for an instructive, though disturbing, story of how the exclusionists use the ESA to elevate the species above the interests of humans. It is a story worth telling.

Following a 1987 status review of the northern spotted owl (NSO), the FWS concluded that the species did not warrant listing. However, during litigation filed by the National Audubon Society and the Sierra Club, it was learned that FWS really had declined to list the species because of the significant economic impact its listing likely would have on the timber regions of the Pacific Northwest. Because listings under the ESA are to be based on the scientific, not economic considerations, the federal court ordered FWS to "reconsider" its decision not to list, and in 1990, amid much controversy, the FWS duly listed the NSO as a threatened species.

A year later, after rejecting an "owl recovery plan" proposed by the U.S. Forest Service, U.S. District Judge William Dwyer ordered a halt to more than 75 percent of planned timber sales from the Pacific Northwest national forests until such time as the Forest Service developed a final owl protection plan suitable to him. Rejecting arguments of the severe economic consequences that would come to the entire region from a termination of timber sales, Judge Dwyer upheld the exclusionist challengers' position completely. In 1992, he again rejected a Forest Service plan that would have set aside 5.9 million acres in the three states for the owl's recovery.

Over the next two years, exclusionist groups lobbied the Clinton-Gore Administration, with Bruce Babbitt as Secretary of Interior, to impose severe forest restrictions to insure the NSO's recovery. When Clinton's "Northwest Forest Plan" was accepted by Judge Dwyer in 1994, 19 national forests and eight Bureau of Land Management districts – a total of 24.5 million acres of national forestland – were put off-limits to timber harvesting. Its effect was to allow harvesting of only one-fourth of the trees being cut when the litigation had begun in the late 1980s.

With only timber companies operating on state and private forestland able to harvest, the Northwest Forest Plan's set-aside of over 24 million acres for owl recovery caused an 80 percent drop in overall timber harvests.[49] However, with groups persistently filing lawsuits to block individual harvest plans on state and private forestland, the reduction in timber harvests far exceeded 80 percent.

Jason F. Shogren is the Thomas Strock Distinguished Professor of Natural Resource Conservation and Management and Professor of Economics at the University of Wyoming. He has calculated that a forced reduction in timber harvests is an opportunity cost that can result in sizeable economic losses to the region. The Northwest Forest Plan was intended to bring about just such a forced reduction. Professor Shogren writes:

> One study estimated that an owl recovery plan that increased the [species'] survival odds to 91 percent for a population of about

1,600 to 2,400 owl pairs would decrease [the region's] *economic welfare by $33 billion (1990 dollars), with a disproportionate share of the losses borne by the regional producers of intermediate wood products, a relatively small segment of the population.* [The study estimated the cost to improve the odds of survival to 92 percent from 91 percent to be $3.8 million.] *If the recovery plan tried to push a goal of 95 percent survival odds, costs increased to $46 billion.*[50]

Thus, the estimated opportunity losses likely from the Northwest Forest Plan's owl recovery ranged from a low of $33 billion to a high of $46 billion. Those estimated billions of dollars in opportunity losses were borne out by mill closures and job losses. As Matthew Harrison observes, "Since 1989, 424 lumber mills have closed in the Pacific Northwest alone."[51] According to renowned Northwest forest industry historian and consultant, Paul Ehringer, since 1990, more than 27,000 loggers and mill workers have lost jobs.[52] Furthermore, as logging communities across the Northwest lost direct timber-related jobs, the jobs of thousands of other working people, private and public, providing goods and services to those communities also dried up. Other casualties of the Northwest timber-harvesting moratorium for owl recovery were the numerous logging counties, their employees, and their residents.

As mills closed and loggers cut loose, the federal government received smaller tax revenues from the sale of national forest timber. In turn, this sharply reduced the dollars the federal government returned to the counties where the mills were located. The drastic reduction of these funds to timber-dependent counties amounted to tens of millions of dollars in lost income, lost services, and ancillary business and commercial activity to county residents. At the same time, local school districts lost funding for operating costs.[53] Social consequences also proved severe.

As more logging families lost their incomes and became unable to pay their debts, the pressures within families increased, leading to alcohol and drug abuse, drunk driving arrests, school dropouts, domestic violence, and family breakups.[54] Testifying in 1998 before a congressional oversight hearing evaluating the impact of the owl recovery plan on Pacific Northwest forests, northern California congressman Wally Herger stated:

Since the listing of the northern spotted owl, 36 mills in my district alone have been forced to close their doors .... Th[e] dramatic loss of jobs has forced many community members on the welfare rolls. A professor at the University of California at Berkeley estimated the unemployment compensation resulting from the implementation of the President's plan for the spotted owl increased by over $745 million dollars .... Siskiyou County reported that in some years, 23 of 29 schools in the county have 50 percent or more of their children receiving meals for needy children. This is a tragedy. These people don't want welfare. They want to work.[55]

The timber-harvesting moratorium also hurt consumers. Of the 10 billion board feet of timber that grows in the Pacific Northwest, the owl recovery plans insured that only 500 million board feet would be harvested annually. "As industries lose money from the reduction of logs the difference will be passed on to consumers," Steven Zika wrote. "In January 1993 the price of 1,000 board feet of plywood was $243. The price rose to $353 in September 1993 for the same quantity of plywood."[56] "Lumber prices have jumped 82 percent since September and are likely to continue to soar with the arrival of spring, when building increases and the demand for lumber picks up."[57] And so they did.

"Lumber prices have nearly doubled since the 1991 ban was imposed," environmental author, Gregg Easterbrook, wrote in 1995, "adding roughly $5,000 to the price of a new home. This increase is regressive, hitting the working class much harder than the elite environmentalist class."[58] There are yet other losses attributable to the owl recovery efforts that began in the 1980s and culminated with the Northwest Forest Plan.

In the years when timber families and the companies that employed them were stewards of the forests, their routine practice of removing dead and dying trees, and thinning and clearing dried underbrush from the forest floor limited wildfire consumption to relatively minor acreage. The accumulation of this highly combustible, kindling-like material enables wildfires to start easier, burn hotter, spread faster, and climb higher up the trunks of healthy trees, devouring them. In the years since the excessive owl recovery efforts drove these people from the forests, and continuing today, millions of forest acres – the very owl habitat that exclusionist groups, liberal politicians, and government bureaucrats claim to care about – have been consumed by some of the hottest and wide-ranging wildfires in U.S. history. For example, wildfire conflagrations consumed six million acres of the nation's federal forests during the summer of 2002 alone, not to mention the vast state and private forest destroyed.[59]

Of the 10-billion board feet of timber growing in the Pacific Northwest's national forests, two billion board feet are destroyed each year by wildfires, and also by insects and disease.[60] This wasteful consumption of forests, compared with sustainable, productive timber-harvesting practices, is the direct result of the ill-advised and extreme owl recovery plans urged by elitist groups, and implemented by their allies in government. The plan also failed to do the owls much good.

In May, 2004, a demographic assessment showed the northern spotted owl's status in Washington declining at a faster pace than ever.[61] That news came 14 years after the northern spotted owl was listed as a threatened species, 10 years after the Northwest Forest Plan set aside 24.5-million acres of federal forestland for spotted owl recovery, and billions of dollars in economic costs were imposed by government officials – with thousands of human lives turned upside-down.

In a classic repudiation of the balance-of-nature cult so beloved of exclusionists, forestry officials now attribute the owl's rapid decline – 30 percent in Oregon over the past decade, 50 percent or more in parts of Washington – to competition from the barred owl. Migrating from the Great Plains to the West, the larger and more aggressive barred owls prey on the smaller owls' food, take over their nesting areas, mate with them, and even have been known to kill them. "Their numbers are exploding, displacing spotted owls .... The spotted-owl decline already is as significant as one might have expected in 50 years," said Oregon's Robert Anthony of the Interagency Regional Monitoring Program.[62]

It turns out that while spotted owls are finicky eaters, barred owls consume a wider variety of prey, including crayfish, skunks and even weasels. They need not scour as much forest for food and pack closer together, as many as four pairs of barred owls for each spotted owl. The barred owls reproduce faster, feed at night, and hunt around the clock. "It's like they don't sleep," [biologist Scott] Graham says. "They're kind of superbirds, [biologist David] Weins adds."[63]

But because the ESA requires continuing efforts to preserve the listed northern spotted owl, even though the barred owl – not timber harvesting – presents the most serious threat to its continued existence, in April, 2007, the Bush administration proposed shooting 576 barred owls in 18 experimental areas.[64] Yet, there are a number of disappointed participants in the spotted owl's large and costly habitat plan that don't believe that shooting barred owls will stop the spotted owl's decline. "Unless you are prepared to remove barred owls forever, I don't think it's realistic," says original Forest Service spotted owl researcher, Eric Forsman. "All species eventually go extinct …. That certainly could be the worst-case scenario."[65]

In light of the continuing and rapid decline of the spotted owl, notwithstanding the federal government's protection of millions of acres of forestland as its habitat for 14 years, one might think that the organizations that filed the lawsuits, stopped timber harvesting, influenced the excessive Northwest Forest Plan, and halted wildfire-suppression programs would be embarrassed by the full range of harm they have caused. Unfortunately, exclusionists seem immune to the consequences of their ideas and actions.

As only one example, the Seattle Audubon Society, represented by the Washington Forest Law Center, went to court against the Weyerhaeuser Company, and in 2007 succeeded in stopping timber harvesting in 50,000 acres of state and private – not federal – forestlands in southwest Washington claimed to be spotted owl habitat.[66] With the spotted owl population drastically in decline from the invasion by the barred owl, such obstructive legal actions affirm ESA critics' view that the real agenda is not to preserve species, but to halt business production, eliminate jobs, and exclude people from the forests.

Greenpeace founder Patrick Moore, veteran of the *Rainbow Warrior*, came to the same conclusion about a movement he left as extremist. "They are anti-business. All large corporations are depicted as inherently driven by greed and corruption. … The liberal democratic, market-based model is rejected even though no viable alternative is proposed to provide for the material needs of six billion people."[67]

The handful of species mentioned in the previous pages of this chapter have generated economic losses estimated in the billions of dollars. Yet the sizeable costs of attempting to protect and recover those few species are but a fraction of the true costs of implementing the ESA. As of February,

2007, there were 1,310 species of plants and wildlife listed as endangered or threatened under the ESA; 278 others were candidates for listing. A full 482 of those listed species have millions of acres of mostly private land designated as their critical habitat. No fewer than 671 listed species have approved habitat conservation plans, and 1,071 species also have recovery plans. Whether as taxpayers, property owners, consumers, or employees, Americans bear billions upon billions of dollars in economic costs every year due to implementation of the ESA.

Those who bear these costs, along with all Americans, are entitled to ask a crucial question: what biological benefits has the ESA actually produced?

NOTES:

1. ESA, 16 *U.S. Code* 1533, "Basis for Determination," Section 4 (b)(1)(A).

2. E. O. Wilson, *The Diversity of Life,* Belknap Press of Harvard University Press, Cambridge, Mass., 1992, p. 32.

3. Aldo Leopold, *A Sand County Almanac*, Oxford University Press, 1949, p. 177.

4. Alaska Department of Fish & Game, Division of Wildlife Conservation, http://www.wc.adfg. state.ak.us/index.cfm?adfg=endangered.why

5. E. O. Wilson, *The Biophilia Hypothesis*, Island Press, Washington, D.C., 1993, p. 37.

6. The Sierra Club of New York, http://www.newyork.sierraclub.org/conservation/esa/esal.html

7. ESA, 16 *U.S. Code* 1544, "Annual Cost Analysis by the Fish and Wildlife Service," Section 18 (2).

8. As an example, see *Report of Endangered Species Expenditures, Fiscal Year 1996*, pp. 1-2 of 201 pages, www.fws.gov/endangered/expenditures/Fy_1996.pdf

9. Randy T. Simmons and Kimberly Frost, *Accounting for Species: The True Costs of the Endangered Species Act*, p. 1, Property and Environment Research Center, Bozeman, Montana; 2004, www.perc.org/ pdf/esa_costs.pdf

10. *Federal and State Endangered and Threatened Species Expenditures, Fiscal Year 1998*, p. 7; http://www. fws.gov/endangered/expenditures/reports/FY_1998.pdf

11. For example: "Federal agencies have spent more than $3.3 billion in the past two decades to help Columbia River Basin salmon and steelhead runs recover...the General Accounting Office says." "Agency pegs Northwest salmon costs," *MSNBC*, Aug. 27, 2002, www.msnbc.com/news/799728. asp?0bl=_0 ;"Protecting the endangered arroyo toad in California could cost $1 billion over the next

ten years, the federal government says." "$1 billion price tag of saving rare toad," *The Daily News*, March, 2005, www.dailynews.cpm/Stories/0,1413,200-20943-2759431,00.html

12. An organization of members of Congress that works on issues of concern to the West, such as Endangered Species Act reform.

13. The report can be found at http://www.fws.gov/endangered/expenditures/19982000.html

14. Founded in 1973, Pacific Legal Foundation is a public interest legal organization that works in the federal and state courts around the country, including the U.S. Supreme Court, in defense of the individual's right to own and reasonably use private property, and to advocate a balanced approach in the implementation and enforcement of the nation's environmental laws, among other legal areas.

15. PERC is one of the country's leading research organizations in applying property rights to environmental issues. PERC Senior Associate, Randy T. Simmons, Ph.D., the lead author of the project, is head of the political science department at Utah State University. Dr. Simmons has written extensively on the Endangered Species Act. Kimberly Frost, who provided research and writing assistance on this project, was a graduate student at Utah State University; www.perc.org .

16. Simmons and Frost, *Accounting for Species: The True Costs of the Endangered Species Act, op. cit*, p. 2.

17. Several thousand employees with ESA implementation and enforcement responsibilities worked at the FWS and NOAA Fisheries Service in the years 1998 – 2000; hundreds more worked at the other 18 reporting federal agencies with ESA responsibilities.

18. Simmons and Frost, *Accounting for Species: The True Costs of the Endangered Species Act, op. cit.,* pp. 4-5.

19. *Ibid.,* p. 6.

20. *Ibid.*

21. *Ibid.,* p.5.

22. *Ibid.*

23. *Ibid.,* p. 6.

24. *Ibid.,* pp. iii and 8.

25. *Ibid.,* p. 8, quoting notes of the congressional committee that drafted the reporting provision.

26. *Ibid.,* p. 9.

27. General Accounting Office, 2002. *Columbia River Basin Salmon and Steelhead: Federal Agencies' Recovery Responsibilities, Expenditures and Actions.* GAO-02-612; http://www.gao.gov/cgi-bin/getrpt?GAO-02-612

28. *Columbia River Basin Salmon and Steelhead: Federal Agencies' Recovery Responsibilities, Expenditures and Actions,* 2002, p. 4.

29. Clay Landry, *The Wrong Way to Restore Salmon,* 2003, http://www.perc.org/perc.php?id=232

30. Simmons and Frost, *Accounting for Species: The True Costs of the Endangered Species Act, op. cit.,* p. 8.

31. *Ibid.,* p. 6.

32. *Ibid.,* p. 7.

33. *Ibid.,* p. 16.

34. FWS 2001 ESA Expenditure Report, p.iii, http://www.fws.gov/endangered/expenditures/reports/2001/Expenditure Report_Jan05.pdf

35. *Ibid.*, p. iv.

36. *Ibid.*, p. iii.

37. $2.442 billion x .25 = $610 million + $2.442 billion = $3 billion.

38. Dan Byfield, "Protect the Environment Through Pride Patriotism," *Stewards of the Range Publications,* http://www.stewards.us/publications/frameset_publications.htm

39. *Ibid.*

40. *Press-Register*, (Mobile, Alabama) August 10, 2006.

41. *Associated Press*, August, 2005.

42. "Aiding vernal pool species would be costly, U.S. says," *Sacramento Bee*, July 14, 2005.

43. 68 Federal Register 20228.

44. David L. Sunding, Ph.D*., Economic Impacts on Critical Habitat Designation for the Coastal California Gnatcatcher*. California Research Management Institute, August, 2003, p. ii, http://www.calresources.org/CRMICHGnatcatcherAnalysis.pdf

45. *Ibid.*

46. Simmons and Frost, *op. cit.*, p.17, note 10.

47. The 2003 median resale home-price in Santa Clara County alone was $565,000.

48. David L. Sunding, Aaron Swoboda, and David Zilberman, *The Economic Costs of Critical Habitat Designation: Framework and Application to the Case of California Vernal Pools*, California Research Management Institute, February 2003, p. 43. http://www.calresources.org/admin/files/crmichreport.pdf

49. Jeanne Brokaw, *Mother Jones*, Nov/Dec. 1996, Vol. 21, Issue 6, p. 15.

50. Shogren, "Economics and the Endangered Species Act," http://umich.edu/~esupdate/library/97.01-02/shogren.html , citing Clare Montgomery, G Brown, Jr., and M. Darius, 1994,"The Marginal Cost of Species Preservation: The Northern Spotted Owl," *Journal of Environmental Economics and Management* 26: 111-128.

51. Matthew Harrison, "Casualties of Modernity: Logging Companies Strive to Replace Their Aging Workforce," *Timberline Magazine*, July 1, 2006; http://www.timberlinemag.com/articledatabase/view.asp?articleID=2003

52. Susan Gordon, "Details scant on federal plan for spotted owl," *The News Tribune*, August 10, 2005; http://www.wflc.org/inthenews/nso/art8.10.05tnt/view

53. "Owls or Schools," *Seattle Press-Intelligencer*, September 3, 2001.

54. Thomas Lambert and Robert J. Smith, "The Endangered Species Act: Time for a Change," *Policy Study*, No. 119, Center for the Study of American Business, St. Louis, MO, March 1994.

55. Committee on Resources, House of Representatives, Subcommittee on Forest and Forest Health, 105th Congress, No. 105 - 79, March 19, 1998; http://commdocs.house.gov/committees/resources/hii47909.000/hii7909_0.HTM

56. Steven J. Zika, "Return to responsible timber management," *The Oregonian*, Feb. 13, 2007.

57. "Timber, Owl, and Logging," http://www.american.edu/TED/TIMOWL.HTM

58. Gregg Easterbrook, "The Spotted Owl Scam;" from Chapter 13 – "Case Study: The Spotted Owl," *A Moment on the Earth: The Coming Age of Environmental Optimism*, Viking Press, 1995. http://www.olypen.com/solidarity/spotted/htm

59. "Environmental 'Magna Carta' law under fire," *The Christian Science Monitor*, November 7, 2002.

60. Steven J. Zika, "Return to responsible timber management," *The Oregonian*, Feb. 13, 2007.

61. "Endangered spotted owl dying off at fast pace," *The Seattle Times*, May 12, 2004.

62. "Prospects bleak for spotted owl," *The Seattle Times* (from the Associated Press), August 10, 2005.

63. "So much for saving the spotted owl," *The Oregonian*, July 29, 2007.

64. "Changes in plan to protect owl raise concerns about NW forests," *The Seattle Times*, April 27, 2007.

65. "So much for saving the spotted owl," *op. cit.*

66. "Group wants logging ban to protect owl," *The Seattle Post-Intelligencer*, November 14, 2006; "Spotted-owl count down despite huge cost to communities," *The Chronicle* (Centralia, WA.), August 6, 2007; "So much for saving the spotted owl," *The Oregonian*, July 29, 2007.

67. Moore, "Environmentalism in the 21st Century," *Greenspirit*, http://www.greenspirit.com/21st_century.cfm?msid=29&page=1

CHAPTER 10

NEGLIGIBLE BENEFITS

OFFICIAL FWS DATA through July, 2007, indicated that 1,355 plant and wildlife species in the United States[1] have been listed as endangered or threatened under the ESA since 1973.[2] 1,309 of those were listed species, while 46 were delisted species.

ESA regulations state that a listed species may be delisted if (1) the biological data originally supporting the listing was in error, (2) the species has become extinct, or (3) the species has recovered.[3] Although the ESA's biological benefits are best demonstrated by the number of species the Act can be credited with recovering, which will be examined later, brief consideration of species delisted due to "original data in error" and those gone "extinct" will be useful in understanding the FWS' dubious practices in implementing the ESA. It also will offer the reader some idea of the types of species that are typically listed under the ESA.

The FWS' "Delisting Report," which also contains the Service's reasons for delisting each of the 46 species,4 reveals that 16 of the 46 were later removed from the list because of "original data in error." In other words, despite the ESA's mandate that only the best science available shall inform the listing of a species, the data the FWS relied on in listing the species turned out to be wrong.

For example, the Florida population of the pine barrens treefrog was listed as endangered in 1977 because biological surveys conducted by the FWS found only 500 of the frogs living in seven small areas of Okaloosa County. However, over the next couple of years several other significant populations were discovered in neighboring counties, as well as more in Okaloosa County. By 1980, numerous populations of the treefrog had been found in several other Florida counties. Finally, in 1983, FWS delisted the pine barrens treefrog, acknowledging "[o]riginal data in error," and conceding that this treefrog species was never endangered or threatened.[5]

Another species delisted because of error was the Arizona agave, a succulent plant listed in 1984. In 2006, a full 22 years later, FWS removed the species from the protected list, with this acknowledgment that the plant never was a true species:

> [B]ased on a thorough review of all available data ... this plant ... does not meet the definition of a species under the Act. Evidence collected subsequent to the listing indicates that plants attributed to Agave arizonica do not constitute a distinct species but rather are individuals that have resulted from recent and sporadic instances of hybridization between two species.[6]

Other species delisted because of error include the cuneate bidens, the Lloyd's hedgehog cactus, the Tumamoc globeberry, and the McKittrick pennyroyal – and those are their common names. Although FWS claims that its listing of these species was out of extra caution and urgency for their possible endangerment, this category of delistings – revealing a 36 percent listing "error" rate – raises concerns of integrity.

Of the remaining 30 delisted species, nine were delisted because they became extinct. One such species was the Amistad gambusia, a small fish whose only natural habitat was a single stream known as Goodenough Spring, in Val Verde County, Texas. When waters from the newly constructed Amistad Reservoir on the Rio Grande River inundated Goodenough Spring in 1968, the population was extirpated. Just before the Amistad Reservoir was filled, however, specimen of the fish were collected by an ichthyology professor. In 1980, FWS listed the species as endangered based on the meager number of captive descendants of the specimen collected in 1968. Within a few years, however, hybridization and predation eliminated the captive population as well. When a 1987 search for natural populations of Amistad gambusia revealed what FWS had known for 20 years, the Service declared the species officially "Extinct."[7]

The Santa Barbara song sparrow was known in the 1950s to inhabit only the 640 acres of Santa Barbara Island, part of the Channel Islands National Monument off the coast of Los Angeles. After a devastating fire destroyed most of the island in 1959, none of the birds was ever seen again. Nonetheless, this subspecies of song sparrow was listed as endangered under the ESA in 1973. In 1983, FWS delisted the species as extinct.[8]

The Sampson's pearlymussel was last observed in the 1930s in limited areas of the Wabash River in Illinois and Indiana, and the Ohio River near Cincinnati. Nonetheless, it was listed as endangered in 1976. Finally, in 1984, FWS delisted the species as extinct.[9]

Two fish species – the longjaw cisco and the blue pike – both inhabitants of the Great Lakes region, declined drastically in the late 1950s due in large part to overfishing, and hybridization with other fish species. Both were known to have disappeared completely by 1967. Still, they were listed as endangered under the ESA in 1973 and 10 years later delisted as extinct.[10]

In the 1950s, the only habitat of the dusky seaside sparrow was Florida's Merritt Island and the nearby marshes of the upper St. Johns River. In 1958, with the construction of mosquito control impoundments, drainage canals, highways, and other development, the species' population decreased drastically. It was listed as endangered under an ESA predecessor statute in 1967 and grandfathered under the ESA in 1973. In 1979, the six surviving male sparrows were brought into captivity, but when no females could be found for them to mate, the species became extinct and was delisted in 1990.[11]

The Mariana mallard and the Guam broadbill, duck species endemic to the Northern Mariana Islands,[12] were listed as endangered in 1977 and 1984, respectively, because excessive hunting severely diminished their numbers. However, with no sightings of the Mariana mallard after 1979, or of the Guam broadbill after 1984, both species were delisted as extinct in 2004.[13]

The Tecopa pupfish was discovered by an ichthyologist in 1948 in "outflow streams of two springs, north and south Tecopa Hot Springs – 10 yards apart on the east side of the road leading north from Tecopa, California." Diminishing numbers caused by rechanneling of the streams and predation by two introduced exotic fish species led to listing of the pupfish as endangered in 1970 under an ESA predecessor statute. When a 1972 search for the fish in the springs where it was discovered came up empty, the species was presumed extinct. Finally, 10 years later, FWS delisted the Tecopa pupfish as extinct under the ESA.[14]

Although these nine species were declared extinct under the Endangered Species Act of 1973, neither the Act nor a predecessor statute played any role in protecting them from their total demise. However, these few species extinctions do expose the myth of the chronic and declining health of the natural world. Despite the incessant, scare-mongering claims and reports that human activities are driving plant and wildlife species to extinction in vast numbers, the truth is that only these nine have been declared extinct since the ESA became law 35 years ago. Six of the nine were known by FWS to be extinct even before the ESA became law, while three others were known to be extirpated as long as 20 years ago – although the FWS did not choose to delist them until more recently.

Only two of the nine species became extinct due to direct human activity; three of the nine became extinct from accidental or natural causes. Indeed, two of the nine were set in motion toward extinction by the hunting practices of island inhabitants halfway around the world from the U.S. And, with the exception of the two fish species endemic to the Great Lakes, the seven other extinct species were highly localized and known primarily to a narrow field of biologists. At the time of their delisting, neither the common names nor the photos of those seven species were familiar to but a handful of people.

According to the FWS' Delisting Report,[15] the remaining 21 of the 46 delisted species were removed from protected status because they were "Recovered." It is this delisting category that should best answer the question: has the ESA, over its 35-year lifetime, provided the American public sufficient biological benefits to justify the tens of billions of dollars in costs they have paid or incurred for its implementation?

Under the ESA, a species is considered "recovered" when, due to its improved status, it is no longer in need of listing as endangered or threatened. However, before one accepts the FWS' conclusion that an ESA-listed species has recovered, two caveats should be considered. First, the question is not merely whether the species recovered following the ESA's enactment in 1973, but whether the ESA's operation was primarily responsible for the species' recovery. If the species recovered for reasons other than the operation of the ESA, then the recovery cannot be regarded as a biological benefit of the ESA.

The second caveat is this: FWS biologists have a vested bureaucratic – sometimes even personal – interest in attributing recovery of a species to the ESA. It should be remembered that most of the people employed by FWS, NOAA Fisheries, and the Army Corps of Engineers, especially the wildlife and marine biologists and other personnel who work in the field, do so because preserving wildlife is what they have chosen as their life's vocation. The same can be said for the independent (nonstaff) biologists who seek contract work with, and are consistently hired by, those agencies whenever their employee staffs are otherwise busy, or where the nonstaff biologist is considered to possess special expertise with a particular species. Naturally, both staff and independent biologists working to implement the ESA want their work to be effective, and to be credited. As a result, FWS biologists' determinations about a species' recovery status, including attributing recovery to the ESA, contains a highly subjective element that can color whether, and to what extent, the ESA is responsible for the recovery, or has provided a biological benefit to the American public.

One of several species demonstrating the validity of these caveats is the Hoover's woolly-star.[16] The annual herb with gray fuzzy stems and tiny pale-blue flowers is prolific up and down California's Central Valley following the winter rainy season. However, in 1986, while the Valley was undergoing drought conditions, FWS biologists who had neglected to do their presurvey homework on the woolly-star, including recognition of its positive response to rain, hastily searched for the plant in limited and unproductive locations. Their meager findings of woolly-stars led to the species being listed as threatened. However, when the rains finally came, woolly-stars popped up all over their normal range.

Thirteen years later, in 2003, the FWS reluctantly recognized its original listing survey deficiencies, and delisted the species, giving as the reasons: "Recovered & Original data in error (New information discovered)." The truth is, "Original data in error" was the only legitimate reason; the "Recovered" portion was little more than a lame excuse for the FWS' inadequate presurvey preparation. As the Service's Final Report on Delisting stated: "Hoover's woolly-star is no longer a threatened species .... This determination is based on the discovery of new populations .... Beginning in 1990, recovery efforts for this species succeeded in locating additional populations, discovering through research that [Hoover's woolly-star] is more resilient and less vulnerable to disturbance than previously known."[17] Typically, the FWS carefully couched its language to give the impression that the finding of additional woolly-stars was the result of recovery efforts, when, in fact, the species never stood in need of recovery.

As attorney Emma Suarez wrote of the Service's reason for delisting Hoover's woolly-star:

> *Most of the public ... is unfamiliar with ... [how the FWS works], so it may be worthwhile illustrating the point .... The delisting decision, published on October 7, tries to explain why the plant no longer needs the protections afforded by the ESA. What we discover, though, is that the plant should have never been listed in the first place because it was never in peril .... What the Service now realizes – after a decade of managing, monitoring, and imposing regulatory burdens on landowners up and down the San Joaquin Valley – is that the plant is everywhere, and that the threats to its habitat were illusory.*[18]

In research for this chapter on February 5, 2007, the author observed FWS' website "Delisting Report" for the Hoover's woolly-star[19] as stating: "Recovered & Original data in error (New information discovered.)" But upon another review just one month later (March 7, 2007), that same Delisting Report had been revised to state only "Recovered." Clearly, the FWS wanted to credit the ESA with the wooly-star's recovery, when in fact the species was never in jeopardy, but listed through FWS data error.

This under-cover-of-darkness revision raises the serious question: what other ESA data has been or is being quietly "revised" after the fact? The woolly-star is by no means an isolated case.

"Species populations are commonly undercounted at the time of listing, or species are listed that are thought to be distinct populations, but they are later determined not to be distinct at all,"[20] note Simmons and Frost. The FWS' 2005 delisting of the Eggerts sunflower as "Recovered & Original data in error (New information discovered)" marks another example of how the FWS performed inadequate prelisting surveys, and then claimed that the species was recovered because numerous plants were later discovered that the Service had failed to locate initially.[21] The Eggert's sunflower was really delisted because its listing was due to original data error.

Consider also the Tinian monarch, a forest bird endemic to Tinian, three islands north of Guam in the western Pacific. Only 38 square miles and inhabited by about 3,500 people, Tinian is part of the Commonwealth of the Northern Mariana Islands, which, because of its political union with the United States, is subject to laws like the ESA.

No actual surveys of the monarch's status were taken at the time of its listing under an ESA predecessor statute in 1970. The listing decision was based on a lone ornithologist's dubious post-World War II report that there were only 40 to 50 monarchs on Tinian. The bird's population was assumed to be critically low due primarily to the destruction of native forests by pre-World War II agricultural practices and by military activities during the war. In the late 1970s, however, another ornithologist estimated monarchs to number in the tens of thousands, and a 2000 study reported more than 55,000 monarchs on Tinian. The FWS delisted the Tinian monarch in 2004, as "Recovered."[22] Yet, once again, the ESA played no role. Because there was never any hard evidence that the monarch population on Tinian had actually declined as a result of the war, it has been suggested that the Tinian monarch's delisting should be attributed to "Original Data in Error," rather than "Recovered."[23]

Yet, even though the monarch's listing was questionable to begin with, and the species was delisted in 2004, the FWS has expressed continuing concern for "the potential threat of an accidental introduction of the brown treesnake." While the treesnake is not known to exist on Tinian, because the FWS believes its presence would be disastrous for the monarch and other species, the Service is working with other federal departments, the Government of Guam, the Commonwealth of the Northern Mariana Islands, and the State of Hawaii to control the brown treesnake around transport centers. For example, United States Navy personnel continuously inspect all cargo originating in Guam prior to loading and again before off-loading in Tinian, looking for brown treesnakes. The FWS also has funded construction of a brown treesnake barrier and quarantine yard at the commercial port on Tinian.[24] It remains highly doubtful that the American public would consider the protection of a plentiful bird from a potential threat of an accidental introduction of a predator snake to an island located closer to China than to the United States as a valuable biological benefit of the ESA.

In 1995, the FWS delisted three species of kangaroos – the red kangaroo, the western gray kangaroo, and the eastern gray kangaroo – all inhabitants of mainland Australia. Having originally listed the kangaroos in 1974 out of concern over the importation of kangaroo skins and other body parts from Australia, the FWS' 1984 plan to delist the three kangaroo species was delayed when the Australian government advised that a drought had substantially reduced their populations. The rains returned in the mid-1980s, and by 1990 it was reported that there were 7.5 million red kangaroos, 1.7 million western gray kangaroos, and 4.7 million eastern gray kangaroos throughout Australia.

When the FWS later renewed its plan to delist the three Australian kangaroo species, substantial opposition came from animal-rights groups like the Humane Society of the United States, and Greenpeace USA, decrying the Australian government's sanctioned slaughter of 5.2 million kangaroos in 1992. The Center for International Environmental Law even accused President George H. W. Bush of "a political action [that] is not justified by biological decision." It took the FWS thousands of dollars in staff resources – even sending teams of biologists to the Australian outback to monitor kangaroos, and nearly 20 agonized pages to declare the three kangaroo species delisted. Despite the fact that the ESA had nothing whatsoever to do with recovering the species, the FWS' reason for delisting the kangaroos was "Recovered."[25]

The Palau fantail flycatcher, the Palau ground dove, and the Palau owl are each inhabitants of the Republic of Palau.[26] Although, like the Tinian monarch, survey information following the end of World War II was un-reliable, it was believed that the islands inhabited by the three species were severely damaged as a result of military activity, and thus the birds' habitats were in jeopardy. On this basis, the three species were listed for protection under an ESA predecessor statute in 1970. However, even before their listing, each species was naturally and rapidly increasing in numbers, so much so that the FWS considered it unnecessary to establish a recovery or management plan for them. In 1985, FWS delisted all three Palau species as "Recovered," although the ESA played no role in that status.[27]

In fulfilling its lead wildlife protection responsibilities under the ESA, the FWS in 1994 delisted the gray whale as "Recovered."[28] However, be-cause the protection and recovery of marine mammals and anadromous fish species are the enforcement responsibilities of the National Marine Fisheries Service (now NOAA Fisheries) in the Department of Commerce, the FWS' delisting of the gray whale was primarily an administrative func-tion. Even though the gray whale was declared recovered under the ESA, it was NOAA Fisheries, operating under the Marine Mammal Protection Act, that oversaw the gray whale's recovery.[29]

In fact, as Michael Fumento notes, "[r]ather than a success story at-tributable to the Endangered Species Act, the gray whale's numbers have been growing steadily since the turn of the [20th] century, largely due to the declining commercial value of whale products. According to estimates compiled by Steven Reilly of the National Marine Fisheries Service, the gray whale population grew from about 2,000 in the late 19th century to 10,000 in the 1940s, and to about 15,000 by the time it was listed under the ESA. The current [1993] estimate is a little over 21,000."[30]

Much the same occurred with FWS' delisting of the Columbian white-tailed deer in 2003 as "Recovered."[31] The FWS' Final Rule on Delisting makes clear its recognition that Oregon's state endangered species act, as implemented by the Oregon Department of Fish and Wildlife, was fully responsible for the recovery of this subspecies. The ESA was relevant only as a monitoring tool, with the FWS performing only an administra-tive role.[32]

The question of whether the ESA is primarily responsible for a recov-ery came up vividly with the delisting of the American alligator.[33] During the 1950s and 1960s, with the popularity of alligator skin-covered wearing apparel and other items, as well as other alligator products, commercial demand led to overharvesting. The resulting reductions in populations caused the U.S. Department of Interior in 1967 to declare the American alligator an endangered species (under an ESA predecessor statute) in all of its habitat states. Yet in 1987, when the FWS issued its Final Rule delisting all alligator populations because the species was "Recovered," the FWS credited a statute other than the ESA with stopping the alligator's decline and setting it back on the path to recovery: "This problem [the overharvesting or "taking" of alligators for commercial purposes] was reversed primarily through a more effective protective mechanism brought about by the Lacey Act Amendment of 1969,[34] which prohibited interstate commerce in illegally taken reptiles and their parts and products. This law provided Federal authority for dealing effectively with illegal activities in the market place."[35] Congress' 1969 amendments also increased the maximum criminal penalty to $10,000 and one year's imprisonment, per offense, and expanded civil penalties to apply to negligent violations, including those who "in the exercise of due care should" have known they were violating the law.

The fact is, the alligator's recovery was already well under way by the time the ESA became law in December, 1973. So quickly were alligators propagating in Louisiana, for example, that early in 1974 the state's governor petitioned the Secretary of Interior, requesting that alligator populations in certain of his parishes be delisted under the ESA altogether. The Louisiana governor's petition

> *was found by the Director* [of FWS] *to present substantial information warranting a review of the status of the alligator throughout its range. ... This review produced evidence that the American alligator is making encouraging gains in populations over much of its known historical range and that significant losses of populations have occurred only in geographically peripheral and ... ecologically marginal areas. Population levels in parts of South Carolina, Georgia, Florida, Louisiana, and Texas are high, and in many areas over these regions are considered to be ecologically secure.*[36]

Although the FWS monitored the alligator's numerical status within its habitat states, and performed other administrative functions relevant to the progress of the species, the ESA played no actual role in recovering the alligator.

Nor did the ESA contribute to the recovery of the Arctic peregrine falcon, the American peregrine falcon, or the brown pelican. According to the FWS' 1985 delisting of the brown pelican, the recovery was attributed exclusively to the 1972 ban of DDT.[37] Similarly, in its 1994 delisting of the Arctic peregrine falcon,[38] and the 1999 delisting of the American peregrine falcon,[39] the FWS was unreserved in attributing those recoveries to the banning of DDT.

In only 5 of the 21 species that FWS delisted as recovered has the ESA played a significant role in the recovery. The Robbins cinquefoil, a perennial herb endemic to two small, distinct areas of land (less than 10 total acres at an elevation of approximately 5,000 feet) in the White Mountains of New Hampshire, grows in a cold, harsh climate that has always made its survival problematic. It was listed as endangered in 1980 because overzealous specimen collecting and trampling by hikers was directly jeopardizing its survival. FWS biologists, together with White Mountain Forest Service personnel, implemented a recovery plan that included construction of a scree wall, signs to alert the public to stay on the trail, the placement of education posters about the plant, and relocation of other trails to avoid disturbance to the plant. As a result of these infrastructure efforts, the plant increased in numbers, and in 2002, the Robbins cinquefoil was delisted as "Recovered."[40]

Historically, the Aleutian Canada goose was endemic to some 190 of the Aleutian Islands that lie off the western point of the Alaskan Peninsula. The decline of this species began in the mid-18th century when Arctic foxes (and to a lesser extent, red foxes) were introduced to the Aleutians for the purpose of developing a fur industry. When the goose's numbers were already low, hunting and the alteration of habitat on its migration and wintering range in California put the species at risk of extinction. By the time it was listed as an endangered species in 1967 under an ESA-predecessor statute, its only known breeding ground had been reduced to one small, isolated island at the western edge of the archipelago.

The FWS' 1979 formal recovery plan consisted of four activities: the removal of Arctic and red foxes on the goose's historic nesting islands; the release of captive-reared and wild, translocated family groups of geese to fox-free islands; protection of the goose throughout its range from hunting and disease; and finally, protection and management of the goose's migration and wintering habitat. These steps proved effective, and in 1989, when some 6,300 geese were counted, the species' status was reduced to threatened. By 2000, the Aleutian Canada goose had increased its numbers to more than 33,000, and in 2001, FWS delisted the species as recovered.[41]

The gray wolf – Minnesota Distinct Population Segment (primarily Minnesota) and the gray wolf – Western Great Lakes Distinct Population Segment (primarily Michigan's Upper Peninsula and Wisconsin) were delisted as "Recovered" on the FWS Delisting Report as of February 28, 2007. Although the gray wolf (*Canis lupus*) is a single species, the ESA authorizes the FWS to create "Distinct Population Segments" of a species when seeking to protect portions of the same species living in different regions of the country.[42]

The wolf has had a hate-love relationship with Americans that dates back before the formal founding of the country. So despised was the wolf in earlier times that European settlers in the midwest attempted to eliminate them entirely, and nearly did. In 1817, Congress passed a wolf bounty law covering the Northwest Territory, and bounties on wolves became the norm. Indeed, the ninth law that the Michigan Legislature enacted in its first legislative session (1838) was a wolf bounty, which remained in effect until 1960. Wisconsin's wolf bounty law, enacted in 1865, remained until 1957, by which time the wolf had been totally extirpated in the state. Minnesota did not repeal its wolf bounty law until 1965.

The FWS' recovery plan for the gray wolf contained two criteria. One was to maintain and protect Minnesota's remnant wolf population, to enable it to increase in numbers, stock quality, and disbursement throughout its historic range in the state. Aiding in this goal was the ESA's prohibition against the "take" of a listed species, which includes the infliction of physical or psychological harm. This potential criminal violation essentially stopped the deliberate killing and harming of wolves. As the FWS and Minnesota Department of Natural Resources implemented and enforced this measure, gray wolf numbers in Minnesota increased from fewer than 1,000 in 1974, to approximately 1,600 in 1988-89, to some 2,400 in 1997-98, to around 3,020 wolves in 485 packs in 2005-06, disbursed throughout 40 percent of the state.

The FWS' second criterion for the wolf's recovery required the reestablishment of at least one viable gray wolf population within its historical eastern range, outside of Minnesota, that would contain not fewer than 200 members for at least five consecutive years. Through the efforts of FWS, and the Departments of Natural Resources of Wisconsin and Michigan, combined wolf numbers in Wisconsin and Michigan's Upper Peninsula increased from virtually zero in 1976, to 34 in 1988-89 (the initial group was the result of translocation of wild gray wolves from other regions), to approximately 320 in 1997-98, to some 900 by 2005-06. With both criteria achieved, the Minnesota and the Western Great Lakes Distinct Population Segments of gray wolf were delisted as "Recovered" in 2007.[43]

One final high-profile species was delisted as recovered in July, 2007 – the bald eagle. Listed in 1967 under an ESA predecessor statute, the bald eagle's recovery is one of the ESA's true success stories. Although, as with the two falcon species and the brown pelican discussed earlier, FWS attributes the eagle's recovery largely to the banning of DDT, no recovery plans have received more attention, effort, or funding from the federal government than that of the bald eagle. According to the FWS Bald Eagle Expenditure Report of July 25, 2007, federal funds expended for eagle recovery between 1989 and 2006 amounted to more than $230 million. Since 1999 alone, when President Clinton himself announced that the eagle was recovered – although it took eight more years and a court order for the FWS officially to delist the species – the FWS has spent nearly $100 million on the eagle's recovery. However, recognizing how grossly understated the FWS' annual ESA cost reports to Congress have been, the actual amount the federal government has spent on eagle recovery efforts since the ESA's 1973 enactment may range closer to $400 million. In addition, charitable foundations and private biologists have contributed immensely to eagle nesting programs and tracking techniques, and have been instrumental in the bald eagle's recovery.

So, exactly what biological benefits have the American people received for the billions of dollars spent or incurred over 35 years as a result of the ESA? Of the 1,355 plants and wildlife species listed as endangered or threatened, only 5 – that is, 37/100ths of one percent – have been "recovered," more or less, as a result of the operation of the ESA. Even if the FWS' more generous number of 21 recovered species were accepted without question, that still would be only a 1.5 percent recovery rate over 35 years.

But what of the claim that the real biological benefits of the ESA are not only the species recovered by the ESA, but the 1,309 endangered and threatened species that continue to be protected under the Act? What would have happened to them – and what would happen to them – without the continued protection of the ESA? Before briefly addressing that question, it is useful to have some understanding of the composition of those 1,309 species.

According to the FWS,[44] 744 are plant species (which includes flowering plants, conifers and cycads, ferns and lilies, and lichens), while 566 are wildlife species (which includes mammals, birds, reptiles, amphibians, fish, clams, snails, insects, arachnids, and crustaceans). Numerous wildlife species have been on the ESA's protected list for more than 30 years, while a great many have been under ESA protection for more than 20 years. Among the 713 protected flowering plant species or subspecies, for example, there are 13 commonly known as "Alani," 28 called "Haha," 13 labeled as "Lo'ulu," and 109 with "no common name." These are known only by their scientific names.

In a 2003 - 2004 progress report to Congress relative to the recovery status of the 1,309 species listed under the ESA, the FWS reported 42 percent as "uncertain," 22 percent were "declining," 27 percent were "stable," while only six percent were "improving." Three percent were either "extinct" or "found only in captivity."[45]

From a cost-benefit perspective, the hard reality of the ESA after 35 years looks like this: on the "cost" side, tens of billions of dollars expended or incurred by the American people to implement and enforce the Endangered Species Act; on the "benefit" side, less than one percent "recovered" and only six percent of the 1,309 currently listed species "improving." Only those who "argue that it is impossible, if not repugnant, to put a price tag on saving an endangered species"[46] have no problem with that record.

This is the statute, it should be noted, that Interior Secretary Bruce Babbit hailed as "the most innovative, wide-reaching and successful environmental law" of the past quarter century, and which the United States

Supreme Court in *TVA v. Hill* said was "the most comprehensive leg-islation for the preservation of endangered species ever enacted by any nation." The Center for Biological Diversity called the ESA "the most important environmental law in history," and for the Endangered Species Coalition it is "the crown jewel of our nation's environmental laws."

In light of the ESA's costs and benefits, as shown in this chapter, these plaudits must be based on intentions alone. While 19 species may have been delisted by FWS as "recovered" in the ESA's 35 years – and that's a "stretch" – only five were recovered as a result of the ESA. This dismal recovery record is only outdone by its misery record in the treatment of human beings.

NOTES:

1. This number also includes species in U.S. territories, in small republics affiliated with the U.S. and subject to certain laws like the ESA, as well as species indigenous to other countries, but whose skins, feathers, or other body parts are commercially sold or traded in or through the U.S.

2. FWS, http://ecos.fws.gov/tess_public/Boxscore.do

3. 50 *Code of Federal Regulations* 424.

4. FWS, http://ecos.fws.gov/tess_public/DelistingReport.do

5. 48 *Federal Register* 52740, November 22, 1983.

6. 71 *Federal Register* 35195, June 19, 2006.

7. 52 *Federal Register* 46083, December 4, 1987.

8. 48 *Federal Register* 46336, October 12, 1983.

9. 49 *Federal Register* 1057, January 9, 1984.

10. 48 *Federal Register* 39941, September 2, 1983.

11. 55 *Federal Register*, December 12, 1990.

12. The North Mariana Islands are a commonwealth within a political union with the United States, and thus subject to some U.S. laws, including the Endangered Species Act.

13. 69 *Federal Register* 8116, February 23, 2004.

14. 47 *Federal Register* 2317, January 15, 1982.

15. FWS, http://ecos.fws.gov/tess_public/DelistingReport.do

16. See "Woolly-star, Hoover's (Eriastrum hoover)," http://ecos.fws.gov/tess_public/DelistingReport.do

17. 68 *Federal Register* 57829, October 7, 2003.

18. Emma Suarez, "Act to Protect Species in Need of Huge Reform," *The Fresno Bee*, December 19, 2003. At the time this article was published, Ms. Suarez was an attorney with Pacific Legal Foundation. http://www.pacificlegal.org/?mvcTask=opinion&id=442&PHPSESSID=b2e94084951c741 9e3daefae8e5cac7e

19. FWS, http://ecos.fws.gov/tess_public/DelistingReport.do

20. Simmons and Frost, *Accounting for Species: The True Costs of the Endangered Species Act, op. cit.,* p. 15; citing Lambert and Smith, "The Endangered Species Act: Time for a Change," *Policy Study*, No. 119, Center for the Study of American Business, March 1994.

21. 70 *Federal Register* 48482, August 18, 2005.

22. 69 *Federal Register* 56367, September 21, 2004.

23. Alexander F. Annett, "Reforming the Endangered Species Act to Protect Species and Property Rights," *Backgrounder #1234*, The Heritage Foundation, November 13, 1998, http://www.heritage. org/Research/EnergyandEnvironment/BG1234.cfm

24. *Report to Congress on the Recovery of Threatened and Endangered Species, Fiscal Year 2003-2004*, U.S. Fish and Wildlife Service, p. 17.

25. 60 *Federal Register* 12887, March 9, 1995.

26. Palau is situated on an archipelago in the North Pacific Ocean, 500 miles southeast of the Philippines. Under a 1994 Compact between Palau and the United States, the ESA controls issues of species protection and recovery.

27. 50 *Federal Register* 37192, September 12, 1985.

28. Only the eastern North Pacific ("California") population of gray whale was declared recovered; the western North Pacific ("Korean") population remained as "endangered."

29. 59 *Federal Register* 31094, June 16, 1994; 56 *Federal Register* 58869, November 22, 1991.

30. Michael Fumento, "How to Save Endangered Species: As Costs Soar, Markets May be the Best Tool," *Investor's Business Daily*, January 8, 1993.

31. The delisting applied to only the Douglas County Distinct Population Segment of the deer, while the Columbia River Distinct Population Segment remained as endangered.

32. 68 *Federal Register* 43647, July 24, 2003.

33. Florida, Louisiana, and Texas contain the majority of American alligator habitat, nearly 12 million acres, or 80 percent of the U.S. total, but South Carolina, Georgia, Alabama, Arkansas, Mississippi, North Carolina, and Oklahoma also have alligator populations.

34. For more information on the Lacey Act, and its several amendments, see http://www.animal-law.info/articles/arus16publlr27.htm

35. Final Rule in Delisting American alligator, *52 Federal Register* 21059, at 21061, June 4, 1987.

36. Rule Reclassifying the American Alligator to Threatened, 42 *Federal Register* 2071 -2072, January 10, 1977.

37. 50 *Federal Register* 4938, February 4, 1985.

38. 59 *Federal Register* 50796, October 5, 1994.

39. 64 *Federal Register*, August 25, 1999.

40. 67 *Federal Register* 54968, August 27, 2002.

41. 54 *Federal Register* 15643, March 20, 2001.

42. ESA, 16 *U.S. Code* 1532, "Definitions," Section 3 (16).

43. 72 *Federal Register* 6051, February 8, 2007.

44. FWS, http://ecos.fws.gov/tess_public/Boxscore.do

45. *Report to Congress on the Recovery of Threatened and Endangered Species, Fiscal Year 2003-2004*, p. 21 http://www.fws.gov/endangered/recovery/recovery_report_2004.pdf

46. Don L. Coursey, "The Revealed Demand For a Public Good: Evidence from Endangered and Threatened Species," *NYU Environmental Law Journal* (1998), http://www.nyu.edu/pages/elj/html/archives/6nyuelj411t.html

PART THREE

THE HUMAN
MISERY INDEX

CHAPTER 11

DEATHS AND ENDANGERED HEALTH

FOR 35 YEARS the ESA has been implemented and enforced – in the words of the U.S. Supreme Court – at "whatever the cost." The harsh, unbending operation of the Act has cost numerous human lives and put human health and safety at risk. Yet, rarely does the mainstream media report these deaths or life-threatening incidents as having any connection to the ESA.

Government agencies such as the FWS, NOAA Fisheries, and the U.S. Forest Service steadfastly stonewall reports that the ESA caused or contributed to human deaths or threatened health and safety. The media-astute exclusionist organizations, with their ample financial resources, utilize aggressive media consultants, internet publications, and mass mailings to turn accounts of the ESA hurting people on their heads. For example, the website of the National Environmental Trust declares stories of ESA-inflicted harm as "apocryphal stories and anecdotes," many of them "pure fiction or, at best, half-truths."[1]

Never shy about stretching the truth, these groups deny or downplay ESA culpability by attributing its dire consequences to any conceivable cause other than the ESA. As a result, many people remain in the dark as to the ESA's true record. That record is evident in the real-life accounts that follow, although they are but a sampling of those that could be told.

HURRICANE KATRINA AND SAVING SHRIMP AND CRABS IN LAKE PONTCHARTRAIN

> [Hurricane] *Betsy made ... landfall on September 9* [1965] *over Grand Isle, Louisiana, at just 1 mph below Category 5 strength. The hurricane moved up the Mississippi River, causing the river to rise ten feet at New Orleans. A storm surge moved into Lake Pontchartrain and overtopped and breeched levees, flooding much of the city, including the 9th Ward. More than 160,000 homes were flooded along the Mississippi, and Betsy became the first storm in United States history to exceed $1 billion in damages.*[2]

Not long after Hurricane Betsy's massive damage in southeastern Louisiana, including 58 deaths, Congress approved, and President Lyndon Johnson signed, the Flood Control Act of 1965. Among other flood-control improvements around the nation, this act authorized the Army Corps of Engineers to design and construct the Lake Pontchartrain Hurricane Barrier Project. Lying north of the city of New Orleans, Lake Pontchartrain had risen almost 10 feet when Betsy's powerful storm-surge drove water from the Gulf of Mexico into the lake through two narrow passages named the Rigolets and the Chef Menteur Pass.

The model that the Army Corps chose for the Lake Pontchartrain Hurricane Barrier Project was the massive storm gates that had been built to protect the coast of the Netherlands from North Sea surges.

> *Fully one-half of The Netherlands lies below seal level .... In 1953, hundreds of miles of dikes along rivers gave way in a violent storm and the flooding killed nearly 2,000 people .... After the catastrophe, the Dutch government vowed "never again" .... In their most ambitious project, the Dutch built three giant sea walls, called storm surge barriers, to protect the fragile inlets and dikes. The barriers remain open in normal weather – but during a storm surge* 63

hydraulic-powered sluice gates, each 20 feet tall, keep the rising waters out.[3]

The Lake Pontchartrain Barrier Project was to include similar hydraulically powered gates that could be shut as a Category-3 hurricane approached New Orleans, thereby preventing the raging storm surges from barreling into the lake. The gates would be opened as soon as the danger from the storm surge had dissipated. Not long after the Army Corps made public its plan, an exclusionist group known as Save Our Wetlands, supported by similar national organizations, raised environmental concerns and sparked opposition to the plan in New Orleans.

In late 1977, nearly 12 years following congressional and presidential approval and annual funding of the barrier gates project, and with the Army Corps having engineered and cleared sites for its construction,[4] Save Our Wetlands and allies petitioned a federal court in New Orleans for an injunction to stop the project on grounds that the Army Corps' environmental impact report was deficient. The court granted the injunction based on the petitioners' argument that the closed barrier gates would harm shellfish and other aquatic life in Lake Pontchartrain by diminishing the natural flow of Gulf waters into the lake. Although there were several grounds for appeal – one was that the huge gates would remain closed for only a few days – the Army Corps chose not to appeal the injunction.

In 1985, due largely to persistent litigation and pressure,[5] the Army Corps abandoned the Lake Pontchartrain Hurricane Barrier Project. As an alternative, the Corps implemented a plan that was not objectionable to the exclusionist community; it consisted of little more than raising the numerous miles of levees surrounding New Orleans by about three feet, at a cost of more than $1 billion.

Much has been reported about the many lives lost and vast damage caused when Hurricane Katrina slammed into the southeastern Louisiana and Mississippi coasts on the morning of August 29, 2005. However, although "[s]ome parts of New Orleans were flooded by Hurricane Katrina's precipitation and overtopping of levees ... the major source of flood waters appears to have been the floodwall breaches of the Lake Pontchartrain and Vicinity Project," that is, the precise location that the shelved barrier gate project would have protected.[6] The 135 mph storm surge into Lake

Pontchartrain pounded and in a matter of hours destroyed several levees on Lake Pontchartrain. Within 48 hours after Katrina passed, waters entering from Lake Pontchartrain's broken levees inundated 80 percent of the city, some areas by as much as 15 feet. Three-quarters of the 1,570 people in Louisiana who died from Katrina were residents of New Orleans.

"If we had built the barriers, New Orleans would not be flooded," said Joseph Towers, retired chief counsel for the Army Corps' New Orleans District at the time the barrier gates project was moving forward, in a 2005 *Los Angeles Times* interview.

"My feeling was that saving human lives was more important than saving a percentage of shrimp and crab in Lake Pontchartrain. I told my staff at the time that this judge had condemned the city. Some people said I was being a little dramatic."[7] The *Times* article also noted that "[t]he principal members of [Save Our Wetlands], several of whom lived in the flooded areas of the city, could not be reached for comment."

Sometimes after the *Los Angeles Times* article ran, Save Our Wetlands put a piece on its website condemning the newspaper for "violating basic journalistic ethics," criticizing Joseph Towers for "stirring up a hornet's nest of hatred and genocide against Save Our Wetlands," and accusing the Army Corps of "illegal and criminal acts." The Save Our Wetlands website article is worth reading if for no other purpose than to observe how the organization views and treats any who would disagree with its exclusionist approach.[8]

THE FEATHER RIVER LEVEE AND THE LONGHORN ELDERBERRY BEETLE

The northern half of California's Central Valley is home to several rivers, including the Feather, the Bear, the Yuba, the Sacramento, and the San Joaquin, each with its own sloughs and secondary streams. Beginning in the 1870s, an extensive system of levees was constructed along these waterways to protect the adjacent, highly favored farming land from frequent flooding. Later, these levees also served to channel northern California water to aqueducts that facilitated its flow to the Central Valley and on to more arid southern California. Over the decades since, while there have been periodic levee breaks resulting in costly flooding of surrounding areas, the 1,600-mile system of northern Central Valley levees, for the most part, has performed its flood control function as well as rural levees built in the 19th century could be expected. But aging levees require continuous monitoring and ongoing maintenance.

While the State of California owns the levees, under state law, the daily monitoring and routine maintenance responsibilities are carried out by locally elected reclamation district boards, that impose annual levee maintenance assessments on district property owners to fund the monitoring, maintenance, and other general district expenses. In more rural areas, these districts have limited staff and resources. When serious levee problems, including emergencies arise, the funding for repairs is supposed to come from the state, with the major work performed under the supervision of the Army Corps of Engineers. However, in practice, it is the local reclamation district people who work with the Army Corps to respond to levee repair issues, and with the FWS whenever an ESA-listed species is involved.

In 1986, high river levels due to heavy rainfall contributed to a levee rupture along the Feather River in the community of Arboga, near Olivehurst, north of the state capital, Sacramento. After staunching the leak, Reclamation District 784 decided to launch a major effort to restore the Feather River's levees within its district. According to Yuba County Supervisor, Brent Hastey: "[t]his work [was] not new construction or betterment, but simply major maintenance to existing levees."[9] However, rather than allowing RD 784 to commence the needed levee restoration work immediately, FWS required the district to perform an environmental assessment of the levees.

This study identified 43 clumps of elderberry bushes, made up of 1,538 stems, that would be disturbed by the proposed levee restoration work. The elderberry bush is habitat for the ESA-listed insect species known as the North Valley longhorn elderberry beetle. In addition, the FWS informed RD 784 that before any levee restoration could begin, the district had to mitigate the damage its work would cause to the 1,538 elderberry bush stems. The FWS demanded that the district purchase a 76-acre mitigation site, which, at then-going land prices, amounted to nearly $2 million in unanticipated costs to the district. As Supervisor Hastey testified to the House Resources Committee:

There were identified 43 clumps of elderberry bushes. And when an elderberry bush is checked on by the Fish and Wildlife Service, they go through the process of measuring every stem. And every stem that is over one inch is required to be mitigated. They identified 1,538 stems on elderberry bushes. To mitigate it, they ripped out 76 acres of prime ... peaches that were in production and planted 76 acres [of elderberry bushes] at a cost of $1.9 million. They planted the elderberry bushes' stems at a 5-to-1 ratio .... It came to a cost of $55,800 per bush to mitigate for these stems for an Elderberry Beetle ... And when you talk to ... the Corps of Engineers, we would ask the Corps: "Why are we doing this?" And the Corps would say, "Because it's not worth fighting with Fish and Wildlife over this. It is just better to go spend the $2 million." And we would rip our hair out, and we would build mitigation-sites instead of fixing levees that protect people's lives.[10]

In 1990, while the process that Supervisor Hastey described was under way, the Corps of Engineers conducted a separate study of RD 784's Feather River levees. The Corps reported that the district's proposed repairs should be performed as expeditiously as possible, stating, "Loss of life is expected under existing conditions, without remedial repairs, for major flood events." Yet, FWS paid no heed to the warning of its sister agency. Nearly seven more years passed with RD 734 working to comply – and pay for – all of FWS' ESA-based demands. No actual levee restoration work had yet begun.

Then, on January 2, 1997, after unusually warm rains and melting snow swelled the rivers of northern California, the Feather River levee burst at the very Arboga site that RD 734 had feared and the Corps had referenced in its 1990 report. Claire Royal, a retired elementary school teacher, Marian Anderson, a grandmother married to the local levee manager, and Bill Nakagawa, a World War II veteran, died when the floodwaters inundated their community. The waters flooded 25 square miles, much of it prime agricultural land on which farm families depended, drove 32,000 people from their homes, and drowned 600 head of livestock. Ironically, the North Valley longhorn elderberry beetles that had lived in the elderberry bushes along the Feather River levee also were washed away.

Yet, despite indisputable evidence that the decade-long delay in levee restoration that led to these tragic consequences was due to the ESA, the exclusionists denied the obvious conclusion. Typical was the testimony of Walter Cook before the House Resources Committee in April, 1997:

> *I am a retired attorney, and I own a walnut orchard which is located adjacent to the Feather River levee which broke on January 2, 1997. Much of my orchard was washed away. The remainder is covered by about six to eight feet of sand. My house, shop, and mobile home were disintegrated. Most of my equipment is hidden under the sand in unknown, scattered locations ....*
>
> [Nonetheless], *we need to change our outlook on the natural world. The destruction of my orchard is not the fault of nature. The flood was caused by the refusal of we humans to accept the natural world the way it is. And our pitiful attempts to force the river to go where it would not go, blaming other species, which we are about to destroy forever, is not the answer.*
>
> *Despite our greed and arrogance, what right do we have to satisfy our own desires by driving other creatures to extinction? Humans can build faulty levees and dams that don't work, but we cannot create even one of nature's most insignificant bugs or rodents. Rather than doing everything we can to destroy the earth, we must learn to live with and protect the paradise we were given.[11]*

THE THIRTY MILE FIRE – WHERE FISH WERE PROTECTED AND FIREFIGHTERS DIED

For most of the 21 firefighters who became trapped in a narrow canyon in the Okanogan National Forest near Winthrop, Washington, on July 10, 2001, the Thirty Mile Fire will forever be a harrowing and tragic memory. Assigned initially to do mop-up work on the remnants of a nearly extinguished fire, 14 of the firefighters became trapped when exceptionally warm temperatures generated winds that caused stands of mature trees, suffering from months of drought, to explode into flames. Within a few hours, the fire expanded from roughly 100 acres to 2,500 acres.

On July 29, 2001, the *Seattle Times* published a lengthy article describing the fire fighters' valiant efforts to battle and survive the Thirty Mile Fire. The account that follows, including the quotes and notes of firefighters, is drawn from this compelling article, unless otherwise specified.[12]

Dispatch logs and later interviews with firefighters at the scene indicate that the elite fire-fighting crew, called "Hot Shots," that had contained the previous evening's 100-acre blaze, retired for a rest-break at around 4:30 a.m. At that time, the local U.S. Forest Service office was called to schedule a helicopter that would scoop water from the nearby Chewuch River and douse the dying embers to begin at first light, about 5:30 a.m. The dispatch office advised that the helicopter could not be there until 10 a.m.[13]

The crew-boss for the arriving 21 firefighters who were replacing the Hot Shot crew, 24-year Forest Service firefighter, Ellreese Daniels, and the mission's crew-boss trainee, veteran Forest Service firefighter, Pete Kampen, briefed their squad leaders on how the mop-up work would be approached, including helicopter water-drops beginning at 10 a.m. At 10:22 a.m., although the helicopter had not yet arrived, the 21 firefighters began their mop-up assignment. With the night dew drying from the rising temperature, spot fires were beginning to crop up from the reviving embers; it was evident that this could become more than a mop-up action.

When the helicopter had not arrived by noon, Kampen radioed the dispatch office to voice his exasperation. Dispatchers responded by offering him a 300-gallon dump from a small air tanker, which Kampen declined because the canyon was too narrow for the plane to maneuver; he would wait for the helicopter that could fly lower and drop its loads with more precision. He was given no other information about the helicopter.

At 12:52 p.m., the original Hot Shot crew that had earlier knocked down the fire returned, and together with the 21 firefighters, worked quickly to put down the growing fire. They were making progress when a spot fire erupted in spruce trees in front of the fire line. After working the fire for a time in the 102-degree temperature, on top of the heat generated by their protective gear, the crews had to pull back for a rest and lunch break. Where was the helicopter?

At about 2 p.m., a fire manager arrived and urged the crews to step up their efforts before the fire jumped the road, surged up the canyon wall, and crossed into Canada, where it would likely burn for several weeks. All hands rushed back to the challenge. Still, no word on the helicopter.

At about 3 p.m., a call went out for hand crews to attack some small spot fires burning a short distance up the road. Pete Kampen and Ellreese Daniels responded, and so did another team headed by eight-year fire-fighter, Tom Craven, whose work ethic and positive attitude gained respect among the crew. When he called to his team: "Let's do it," members Karen Fitzpatrick, Devin Weaver, and Jessica Johnson jumped to the order.

The teams attacked different spot fires along the road, some 50 - 75 feet apart. Suddenly, "without warning, the smoke column tumbled. The sky went dark and red. It hailed embers, red bouncing off hardhats, the vans, the road .... Now Kampen was scared. 'Get back in the van, *now*,' he ordered the six firefighters with him." From the spotter plane above came the order: "Everybody pull out."

There was only one road in and out of the Chewuch River Canyon. The first van down the road was the Hot Shot crew. By the time Kampen's team scrambled into their van, the flames were crossing the road. He bar-reled through the invading flames just as the road became impassable. The time was 3:58 p.m.

At the last moment, recognizing that the road was now impenetra-ble, crew-boss Daniels, with the remaining crew members, turned his van around, and the 14 trapped firefighters headed back up the canyon, look-ing for the widest spot in the road with no trees. That was where a slope of rocks rose on one side of the road. They exited the van, each looking for the safest place: Daniels and eight others chose locations on the road; Craven and four others hiked a ways up the slope, looking for a flat spot with no shrubbery to burn. Although crew-boss Daniels later stated that he called out to those on the slope that it was not the best place, none of the five – perhaps not hearing him – came down.

One crew member recorded his observations and thoughts in a small notebook, which the *Seattle Times* reporters included in their story:

> *The wind rips through the canyon, I watch the top of trees sway-ing violently from the high winds that the fire is creating. It's chang-ing and twisting all around us.'* Still, for a time, there appeared the

possibility that the fire might push to the north, missing them. But, at about 5:24 p.m., the fire 'fell back on itself and pushed straight at them .... Daniels barked to pull out their fire shelters .... The fire washed over them. A sound like a jet. A locomotive. A tidal wave. A scream.'

When the roaring flames had passed over them and it was safe to emerge from their protective shelters, Daniels ordered a head count. The 10 who deployed on the road survived. Four of the five that had deployed their fire shelters on the rocky slope did not answer the call: Tom Craven, 30, father of two young children; Karen Fitzpatrick, 18, a month out of high school and three weeks out of fire school; Devon Weaver, 21, an electrical engineering student who finished firefighter school six weeks before; and Jessica Johnson, 19, a college student who knew even in high school that she wanted to fight wildfires. Each had been asphyxiated by the fire's superheated air. The fifth member who sat down on the rocks survived, but suffered severe burns.

Within hours of the fire's passing, word began circulating among the firefighters that the reason the helicopter was not deployed at a time when it could have changed the entire course of the day was that the Chewuch River contained ESA-listed Chinook salmon, steelhead, and bull trout. Local Forest Service managers were reluctant to authorize scooping water from the river for fear of taking some of the fish. Two days later, the *Associated Press* confirmed that account, quoting the environmental officer for the Okanogan and Wenatchee National Forests as saying that "environmental concerns caused crucial delays in dispatching the helicopter .... [B]ecause there are endangered species in the Chewuch River, they [local Forest Service managers] wanted to get permission from the district in order to dip into the river."[14]

Fox News reported that the delay in deploying the helicopter – about five hours from its expected 10 a.m. drop time – was caused when the Okanogan dispatch office could not reach anyone at the district office with authority to approve the helicopter scooping water from the river. "Two former USFS firefighters familiar with the Thirty Mile Fire told *Fox News* that getting permission to dip into the Chewuch caused the delays that led to the death of their colleagues .... The first load of helicopter water was dumped on the fire at 3 p.m., but the fire was by then out of control."[15]

Over the four and a half years since the fire, family members of the deceased firefighters have demanded that the Forest Service itself, and those in its ranks, be held accountable for managerial errors and regulation violations that appear to have occurred as the 21 firefighters fought and struggled to survive the Thirty Mile Fire.[16] But instead of facing up to the real cause of that tragic day, in December, 2006, the Forest Service, through the U.S. Attorney for the Eastern District of Washington, took a step unprecedented in federal forest firefighting history: charging crew-boss, Ellreese Daniels, with four counts of "involuntary manslaughter," for conduct "that was grossly negligent ... in wanton and reckless disregard for human life."[17]

This scapegoating of one veteran Forest Service firefighter does a disservice to the young firefighters who died. Neither Daniels' conviction nor a plea bargain forcing his retirement from the Forest Service will prevent a similar tragedy in the future. The real culprit in the Okanogan National Forest on July 10, 2001, was not a person, but the nonnegotiable anti-people proposition advanced by exclusionists, and accepted by many in government, that species come first and people come last. As Mr. Daniels later lamented: "If we'd had the water when we asked for it, none of this would have happened."[18] His trial has been set for January 15, 2008.

The Forest Service never admitted that dithering over whether they should scoop water from a river containing ESA-protected fish was the reason for the five-hour delay in dropping water when it would have made a difference. It was as if the ESA was so sacrosanct that even its misinterpretations by local Forest Service managers should not be officially discussed for fear the public might wake up and demand that people's lives and safety receive priority.

As one commentator noted, "The Forest Service's shameless revisionism about the Thirty Mile Fire shows that it's still more interested in blowing smokescreens than in clearing them up. Last month [referring to May, 2002], the agency released a final report so full of blacked-out redactions that it looked like the authors had used pages to clean a charcoal grill."[19]

But this was hardly an isolated case.

ESA Suit Bars Firefighting Tools and Costs Lives

In 1910, after a thousand wildfires came together and consumed three million acres of national forests in Idaho and Montana, killing 85 people, Congress declared war on wildfires as an enemy that was destroying the nation's forests. For the next 80 years Congress funded and encouraged the Forest Service to suppress every forest fire as aggressively as possible. "Forest Service camps and offices echoed with tales of fires fought and fires defeated until the culture became that of warriors. Specialized fire fighting crews became hot shots and smokejumpers."[20]

Later, in the 1950s, the Forest Service began deploying airplanes and helicopters to drop chemical fire retardants on fires, while on the ground, bulldozers played an increasingly significant role in creating fire breaks and performing other critical fire suppression functions during and in advance of wildfires.

As a result of the Forest Service's aggressive fire-fighting approach, annual national forest acreage destroyed by wildfires diminished from 40 to 50 million acres in the early 1930s to about 5 million acres in the 1970s. "From 1994 to 2001, the Forest Service fought, on average, over 10,000 wildfires per year on national forests."[21]

However, with the emergence of the modern environmental movement in the early 1960s, and its growing public influence during the next three decades, both Congress and presidential administrations began to view the national forests differently. As the early conflict between the exclusionism of John Muir's "pristine wilderness," and the conservation of Gifford Pinchot's "prudent use of forest resources," was replayed at century's end, commercial logging replaced wildfires as the primary enemy of the nation's forests.

As timber companies shut down in response to government policies to protect species under the ESA,[22] thousands of logging families that had cared for the forests as their homes left to find other work. The exclusionist ideology greatly expanded the "wilderness" areas where humans were unwelcome, and also "roadless" areas. Indeed, the government closed hundreds of miles of national forest roads long used by firefighters to quickly reach isolated wildfires. Agencies terminated salvage timber sales, also called "post-fire logging" – the mutually beneficial practice of allowing timber companies to sell for profit fire-killed trees (that would become future fire-starting fuel) in return for cutting and removing them from the forest. Exclusionists demanded, and got, a reduction in the use of prescribed burns to clear away accumulating kindling-like undergrowth on the forest floor, on the grounds that the practice harmed protected species of plants and wildlife.

These policies caused the national forests to become overgrown, over-fueled, and inaccessible. As a result, wildfires took a remarkable jump.

When 1994 wildfires destroyed 3 million acres and killed 14 fire-fighters, many called for timber-thinning in these overgrown areas; but the Natural Resources Defense Council (NRDC) opposed these plans as being a mere "pretext for accelerated logging." .... The General Accounting Office warned in 1999 of the dangerous accumulation of fuel, but environmentalist pressures continued to prevent humans from "managing" environments that greens preferred to keep "pristine." In a recent Wall Street Journal article, Robert H. Nelson surveyed the resulting damages and body counts. In 2000, 8.4 million acres went up in smoke. In 2002, 6.9 million more acres were reduce to ashes, as were 800 homes, in firestorms that also took the lives of 23 more firefighters, and cost $1.7 billion. Now [referring to the 2003 devastating fires in Southern California], *three-quarters of a million acres of California are gone, and with them, over 3,500 homes, $2 billion, and 22 more human lives* [civilian] . *And all this doesn't count the impact on* [species]. [23]

Having made a vast contribution to this explosive wildfire danger, one might think that exclusionists would be less bold in further advancing such ill-founded positions. But their politics often turn common sense on its head. In October, 2003, during what would be the most devastating fire season in California history, a preservationist group known as Forest Service Employees for Environmental Ethics (FSEEE) filed "the first-ever lawsuit challenging the Forest Service's firefighting mission and practices."[24] With membership primarily consisting of retired Forest Service employees of the exclusionist persuasion, FSEEE advocates the "let-it-burn" approach to our national forests. According to the organization's executive director, fighting wildfires is like "putting fans on the coast of Florida to blow hurricanes away, or trying to prevent earthquakes."[25]

Claiming, among other things, that chemical fire retardants and bulldozers kill and destroy the habitat of ESA-listed fish and other forest species, FSEEE asked the federal court to stop the Forest Service and its firefighters from using aerially applied chemical retardants and bulldozers. FSEEE also asked the court to order the Forest Service to comply with the ESA requirement that it "consult" with the appropriate Service – the NOAA Fisheries as to anadromous fish species or FWS for all other fish species – prior to fighting each wildfire to insure that the chemical retardants, and the bulldozers' lug-tracks and blades, do not harm an ESA-listed species or its habitat in the course of fighting the fire.

The Forest Service responded that to avoid aerially applied chemical retardants from reaching forest waterways, it had three years earlier adopted "Guidelines"[26] instructing its pilots to shut off their sprayers or cease drops within 300 feet of known rivers and streams. As a result, only minuscule amounts of retardant might fall in or near forest waterways. To FSEEE's complaint that it did not consult with the Services prior to fighting wildfires, the Forest Service pointed out to the court that, because the ESA's "consultation" process involves conducting surveys, writing reports, and meetings, the Service could not aggressively or effectively respond to several thousand wildfires around the country each year if it had to initiate consultation for each one. Its firefighters must be able to reach the fire line and commence operations within a matter of hours. This was especially true in the expanded wilderness and roadless areas, where aerial-application of fire retardants was firefighters' primary, if not only, weapon.

The human-hands-off approach to wildfires in the national forests is the most bizarre aspect of a movement filled with contradictions. Professing to care about protection of the forests and the species, while simultaneously opposing the suppression of fires that destroy both the forests and the species – not to mention the numerous people killed each year by wildfires – is difficult to comprehend from a commonsense or scientific perspective. For a group that uses "Environmental Ethics" in its name, it is especially perplexing. Yet, in an unprecedented decision, the court granted FSEEE's injunction, barring Forest Service use of aerially applied chemical fire retardants and bulldozers in fighting wildfires in the national forests unless approved through consultation with the proper Service. As part of the consultation process, the court ordered the Forest Service to analyze the environmental impact of fire retardants that might kill endangered fish.

Although the Forest Service initially filed a Notice of Appeal in the Ninth Circuit Court of Appeals, it dismissed the appeal in September, 2006 – which suggested it would comply with the court's order. However, prior to the court's given deadline for consultation, including analyzing the environmental impacts of fire retardants, the head of the Forest Service, without giving a reason, ordered the consultation not to occur. When FSEEE asked the court to hold the Forest Service chief in contempt of court for his disobedience, its executive director hinted at the probable reason: "I think they have to take a hard look at their 100-year war against wildfire and explore alternatives that will allow us to live with fire, and that is what they don't want us to do."

It is likely that the Bush administration, as the policy-making arm of the government, does not want a judge setting policy on whether and how the Forest Service should fight wildfires, and that is where the Administration sees FSEEE's contempt action going. At this writing, little is known of how forest fires in the vast wilderness and roadless areas will be fought in the future, or how protected forest species will survive the "let-it-burn" approach.

WHO GETS SCARCE WATER IN A DROUGHT?
WHY THE SILVERY MINNOW, OF COURSE

The Rio Grande silvery minnow is a small fish that lives in the Rio Grande basin. It was listed as an endangered species under the ESA in 1994. In recent years, there have been drought conditions in the Rio Grande basin, making water that the species relies upon for its survival scarce.

Situated near the upper section of the Rio Grande River lies New Mexico's largest city, Albuquerque, with more than 500,000 residents. Since the 1960s, the city has planned for and spent millions of taxpayer dollars to obtain contract water rights from sources north of the Rio Grande basin to assure its existing and anticipated populations an adequate supply of water.

The U.S. Bureau of Reclamation operates the San Juan Chama Project, a water reclamation project on the Upper Colorado River Basin in New Mexico. Its purpose is to store and distribute water in this arid region for agricultural, municipal, industrial, and domestic uses, with the secondary purpose of providing recreation and wildlife benefits. Although run by the Bureau of Reclamation, the entire cost of the San Juan Chama Project has been paid for through the contracts by the water users themselves. Waters accumulated in the San Juan Chama Project are distributed pursuant to contract.

This water is collected and stored in Heron Reservoir and distributed to the contract-holders, including the City of Albuquerque. Under the contract, the amount of water distributed is dependent upon the water flow in a given year: where there is a water shortage, all contract-holders share equally in the shortage and must reduce their usage accordingly; where there is sufficient or excess water, all users are entitled to its beneficial use, with unused water stored to protect against water shortages in drought years.

The year 2002 was a time of drought in the Rio Grande basin. This triggered the ESA's consultation process between the Bureau of Reclamation and the FWS regarding the silvery minnow. The consultation resulted in a Biological Opinion prepared by government fish biologists that recommended relocating the minnow population to upstream portions of the Rio Grande which would not dry out – thus protecting the population not only in 2002, but in subsequent drought years as well.

It is important to note here that the water stored in Heron Reservoir is imported from the San Juan Chama Project; thus, flows from the Heron to contract water users are not those that are naturally occurring in the Rio Grande where the minnows live, but the result of long-term planning, construction, and funding by the water users primarily for human usage.

Later in 2002, a coalition of exclusionist groups, including Defenders of Wildlife, Forest Guardians, the National Audubon Society, and the Sierra Club, filed suit in federal court, challenging the compromise Biological Opinion, and demanding, as a remedy, that water from the Heron Reservoir be released into the Rio Grande for the minnow.

In an order that ignored Albuquerque's nearly half-century of planning and funding, that abandoned the law of contract, and that disregarded the Biological Opinion's well-thought-out compromise to save the silvery minnow and protect humans' vital access to water, the District Court ruled that Albuquerque's water in the Heron Reservoir must be tapped and diverted to the Rio Grande, to increase its flow for the benefit of the minnows. The court's ruling was despite the fact that the water collected and stored in the Heron Reservoir was not water that naturally would have flowed into the Rio Grande, and thus would not have benefited the minnow in any case. The federal appellate court affirmed the ruling, declaring that the government's first duty was to the fish, and therefore, it must divert water contractually obligated to Albuquerque's residents for the benefit of the silvery minnow, citing the Supreme Court's "whatever the cost" language in *TVA. v. Hill*.[27]

With drought conditions persisting and the court's opinion ordering the water that Albuquerque residents were counting on delivered instead to the silvery minnow, a potential water crisis emerged. So serious was the potential danger to the people of Albuquerque that in November, 2003, in an action unprecedented for the ESA, the U.S. House and Senate enacted special legislation accepting the compromise Biological Opinion that the exclusionist groups had successfully knocked out in their lawsuit. Although the rains returned not long thereafter, relieving the immediate crisis for both people and fish, the harsh operation of the ESA posed a clear threat to the health and safety of the people living in this arid region. Had the drought continued, people may have died while the fish may have survived.

IF A PROTECTED SPECIES ATTACKS, DROP YOUR GUN AND RUN

John Shuler and his wife purchased a piece of ranch property near Dupuyer, Montana, in 1986, and began raising sheep. In mid-August, 1989, the Shulers found the first dead sheep, mauled by grizzly bears, a species listed as "threatened" under the ESA since 1975.

The grizzly bear, or brown bear, one of the so-called charismatic species for which the ESA was originally enacted, stands as an example of the ESA's selective application. There are an estimated 53,000 grizzly bears in North America: 30,000 of them in Alaska, and more than 21,000 in Canada, with another 2,000-plus in Montana and other northwestern states. These are not the numbers of a species whose survival is actually threatened. But the FWS, pushed by exclusionists, continues to promote the bear's expansion into states with increasing human populations.

Pursuant to ESA regulations, the Shulers called in the FWS to remove the bears from their property, but the Service's several attempts with traps, helicopters, and "aversive conditioning" proved unsuccessful. By early September, bears had killed several of the Shulers' sheep, valued at $1,200.

One night in September, Mr. Shuler spotted a bear from his living room window. Barefoot and in his underwear, he ran outside with his gun. About 30 feet from the house, three bears were running through his flock. He fired over them and the bears scampered away. Just then, a fourth bear charged out of the darkness. When it was only a few strides away, it reared up on its hind legs and let out a fierce bellow. Fearing for his personal safety, Shuler shot the bear, and it fell back. Although he presumed the bear was dead, due to the darkness he chose not to investigate further. However, when he went outside the next morning, the bear reared up again and came toward him. Shuler shot the bear again, causing it to fall. When the bear got up again, Shuler shot it a third time, killing it. He then called and informed FWS that he had shot and killed a grizzly bear.

The Department of the Interior initially fined Shuler $7,000 for "taking" an endangered species in violation of the ESA. He appealed the Department's finding and penalty, arguing that he shot the bear under the ESA's "self-defense" provision. The Department's appeal judge found that Shuler was not actually defending himself, but was defending his sheep, and had "purposefully placed himself in the zone of immediate danger of a bear attack." As such, he "was blameworthy to some degree in bringing about the occasion for the need to use deadly force." The judge did, however, reduce the fine to $4,000.

Shuler then appealed to the Department's Ad Hoc Appeals Board, which upheld the judge's ruling, finding that Shuler's dog, having gone on point when the bear reared, had "provoked the bear." It increased the fine to $5,000.

Finally, in March, 1998, some nine years after he shot the bear in what he believed was a life-threatening situation, the U.S. District Court for Montana vacated Mr. Shuler's conviction and fine.[28] So intent was the FWS on enforcing the ESA to protect the grizzly bears, that instead of giving Shuler the benefit of any reasonable doubt, it sought to teach him and other human residents of Montana which species had priority under the ESA.

NOTES:

1. National Environmental Trust, *The Assault on the Endangered Species Act,* "Chapter 4: ESA Horror Stories and Urban Legends," 2005, p. 69, http://www.net.org/esa/

2. *Hurricane Resources: Historical Records of the U.S. Army Corps of Engineers' Response to Recent Hurricanes.* http://www.hq.usace.army.mil/history/Hurricane_files/Hurricane.htm

3. "How the Dutch Mastered the North Sea," *All Things Considered, National Public Radio,* September 14, 2005; (includes photos), http://www.npr.org/templates/story//story.php?storyId=4847805

4. "1976 GAO Report describing the progress of the Lake Pontchartrain and Vicinity, Louisiana Hurricane Protection Project," which began following Hurricane Betsy, August 31, 1976, http://www.hq.usace.army.mil/history/Hurricane_files/Hurricane.htm

5. Save Our Wetlands' website boasts; "While politicians talk, SOWL sues! SOWL has been in-volved in countless lawsuits involving Lake Ponchartrain (sic) on every subject, [including] New Orleans Mosquito Control Drainage schemes in wetlands of New Orleans East [and] Corps of Engineers Hurricane Barrier Project ... SOWL has always fought bitterly against the United States Army Corps of Engineers." http://www.saveourwetlands.org/history.html

6. *New Orleans Levees and Floodwalls: Hurricane Damage Protection,* CRS Report for Congress, September 6, 2005, http://www.fas.org/sgp/crs/misc/RS22238.pdf

7. *Times* staff writers Ralph Vartabedian and Peter Pae, "Katrina's Aftermath: A Barrier That Could Have Been," *Los Angeles Times,* p. A10, September 9, 2005.

8. "Response to the *L.A. Times* Article, 'A Barrier That Could Have Been,'" Save Our Wetlands, http://saveourwetlands.org/response2latimes.html

9. Testimony to Committee on Resources, House of Representatives, April 10, 1997, p. 10 (of inter-net copy), http://commdocs.house.gov/committees/resources/hii40915.000/hii40915_0.HTM

10. *Ibid.*

11. Testimony to Committee on Resources, *op. cit.*, p. 37 (of internet copy).

12. Reporters Chris Solomon and Craig Welch, "Firefighters who were there tell the story of the deadly Thirty Mile blaze," *Seattle Times,* Sunday, July 10, 2001, p. A1.

13. "The Thirty Mile Fire burns in the Okanogan -Wenatchee National Forest," *Associated Press*, July 13, 2001.

14. *Ibid.*

15. Reporter William La Jeunesse, "Endangered Species Act May Be Responsible for the Deaths of Four Fire Fighters," *Fox News with Britt Hume*, aired July 31, 2001.

16. Solomon and Welch, "Rules broken to fatal effect in July 10 wildfire," *Seattle Times*, September 23, 2001.

17. Criminal Complaint, *United States of America v. Ellreese N. Daniels*, Case No. MJ 06-308, filed December 19, 2006.

18. "Rules broken to fatal effect in July 10 wildfire," *op.cit.*

19. Syndicated columnist, Michelle Malkin, "The Forest Service smokescreen," *Insight*, June 21, 2002, http://www.jewishworldreview.com/michelle/malkin062102.asp

20. "Forest Fire – a Snapshot History," *History Link* (made possible by the Washington Forest Protection Association), http://www.historylink.org/essays/printer_friendly/index.cfm?file_id=5496

21. *Forest Service Employees for Environmental Ethics v. U.S. Forest Service*, U.S. District Court, District of Montana, CV 03-165-M-DWM, Complaint for Declaratory and Injunctive Relief, pp. 5,6.

22. See discussion on the northern spotted owl, Chapter 9, "What the ESA Really Costs."

23. Robert James Bidinotto, "Earth to California: thank environmentalism for your wildfires," *Center for the Defense of Free Enterprise*, November 7, 2003, http://www.cdfe.org/earth_to_california.htm

24. *Forest Service Employees for Environmental Ethics v. U.S. Forest Service, op. cit.*

25. "Group to sue over firefighting," *Missoulian.com News Online*, Missoula, Montana, October 13, 2003, http://www.missoulian.com/articles/2003/10/13/news/local/news02.txt

26. "Guidelines for Aerial Application of Fire Retardants and Foams in Aquatic Environments," April 20, 2000, http://www.fs.fed.us/fire/retardant/index.html

27. *Rio Grande Silvery Minnow et al v. Keys*, United States Court of Appeals, Tenth Circuit, No. 02-2254, June 12, 2003, http://www.kscourts.org/ca10/cases/2003/06/022254.htm

28. *Shuler v. FWS*, Case No. 96-110-GF-PGH, March 17, 1998. See Ike C. Sugg, "Rule of law: If a grizzly attacks, drop your gun," *The Wall Street Journal*, June 23, 1993.

CHAPTER 12

DESTROYED LIVELIHOODS, DAMAGED BUSINESSES

THE LOSS OF 30,000 jobs and much of the Pacific Northwest's timber industry caused by government programs and policies to preserve the northern spotted owl ranks as a classic example of the ESA's destructive impact, but far from the only one. Those that follow are but a few of the many accounts.

THE KLAMATH FISH THAT BROUGHT 1,400 FARM FAMILIES TO THEIR KNEES

It was May, 2001. Gordon and Sandra Kandra looked despairingly at the land they had farmed for nearly 40 years – the same land Gordon's immigrant grandfather began farming when he came to the Klamath River basin in 1916. What they saw looked much like the desolate dryland farm Gordon's grandfather had left in South Dakota.

At the beginning of the 20th century, after California's and Oregon's legislatures relinquished lands in their border-straddling counties to the federal government, Congress and President Theodore Roosevelt enacted the Reclamation Act of 1902. Among other things, this Act authorized the construction of the Klamath Project to drain and reclaim marshlands, build dams for water storage, provide irrigation for agriculture, and control flooding.

Over the next several years, the Klamath Project's engineers constructed seven dams in the Klamath River basin. The lakes the dams created were initially filled by waters drained from surrounding marshlands – a reclamation process that steadily made available more arable public land. Replenished seasonally from surrounding mountain snowpack and rain, the waters in the lakes, when the construction was complete, would travel through a network of nearly 700 miles of canals and ditches to contract water users via 40 pumping stations.

In 1917, the reclaimed public lands were opened for homesteading. Each homesteader entered into a contract with the U.S. Bureau of Reclamation in which he agreed to pay for, and the government agreed to provide, irrigation water. Under these contracts, the water users, and their successors, also repaid the government for constructing, operating, and maintaining the Klamath Project's infrastructure. Gordon Kandra's grandfather was among the early homesteaders lured to the Klamath basin by the government's promise of irrigation water.

The Lower Klamath Lake is situated along the Pacific Flyway, the ancient north-south migration route for millions of ducks and geese. In 1908 President Roosevelt designated the lake region as the nation's first federal wildlife refuge for waterfowl. Each year in spring, and again in fall, hordes of migratory waterfowl stop over in the farmers' agricultural fields for weeks at a time to feed and rest on their journey between Alaska and the southern end of South America, and back. Over the years, the farmers of the Klamath River basin have become accustomed to annually donating thousands of dollars in free food (crops) and lodging to these thundering flocks, as well as to numerous land species. Steve Kandra's "Sharing the Land: Wildlife and agriculture sharing the land can be spectacular and burdensome," is a beautifully written documentation of this biannual procession.[1]

By the 1980s, the reclamation efforts of the Klamath Project had converted three-quarters of the Klamath basin's marshlands into farmland.

Some 1,400 farm families were growing alfalfa, potatoes, onions, wheat, barley, hay, and raising cattle, on 220,000 acres. These families were paying for and receiving 550,000 acre-feet of water annually from the Bureau of Reclamation.

The Lost River sucker fish and the shortnosed sucker fish were documented in 1879 to inhabit Upper Klamath Lake and its tributaries. Because their numbers had been declining for several decades, FWS listed the two fish as endangered in 1988. FWS attributed their decline to the construction and operation of the Klamath Project, stating:

> *Dams, draining of marshes, diversion of rivers and dredging of lakes have reduced the range and numbers of both species by more than 95 percent. Remaining populations are composed of older individuals with little or no successful recruitment for many years. Both species are jeopardized by continued loss of habitat, hybridization with more common closely related species, competition and predation by exotic species, and insularization of remaining habitat.*[2]

Following the listing of the two sucker fish, both the FWS and Bureau of Reclamation tried to balance the irrigation needs of the farmers with the water needs of the fish. The balancing act worked reasonably well in years of adequate rainfall and snowpack. But in the months preceding the April irrigation season in 2001, a drought struck the Klamath River basin hard. As April approached, NOAA Fisheries issued a Biological Opinion warning that the spring run of the threatened coho salmon would be jeopardized unless the Bureau of Reclamation doubled the water it planned to release into the river. FWS issued a similar Biological Opinion relative to the sucker fish in Upper Klamath Lake.

In late March, the Oregon Natural Resources Council (ONRC) filed an ESA-based lawsuit, asking a federal court to order the Bureau of Reclamation to shut off all contract irrigation water to the farmers, and to instead release it for the benefit of the two sucker fish species and the coho salmon. The court obliged, ruling that the Bureau had violated the ESA by not effectively consulting with the Services. Given no alternative, and much to the shock of Klamath farmers and agriculture-support businesses, on April 6, 2001, the Bureau of Reclamation abruptly announced that it was shutting off the spigot: there would be no irrigation water released through the Klamath Project in 2001. This marked the first time in the Klamath Project's near 100-year history that the government abandoned the contract water users.

Without the water the government had promised, what Gordon Kandra and his wife saw on that day in May, 2001, was a winter grain crop that had quickly dried up and blown away, taking with it their sole source of income and the value of their farmland – their primary family asset.

For most of the region's 1,400 farm families, the income generated from the current year's crops is prerequisite to their financial capacity to plant the following year. The government's shut off of water drove down the value of land from as much as $2,500 per acre to $50 per acre, and severely impaired farmers' ability to borrow against their land. As the *Oregonian* observed, "[c]ollective losses in the Klamath Basin, if they encompass the decline in value of land turned barren for lack of water, could top $500 million."[3] A number of farm families filed bankruptcy, and two farmers were reported to have committed suicide due to their dire financial condition caused by the cutoff of irrigation water.

"This is an epic tragedy, the remaking of the *Grapes of Wrath*," wildlife photographer Larry Turner said. "The Endangered Species Act has an overbite that doesn't factor in people …. They're destroying a civilization, one that government encouraged us to set up in the first place," declared Paul Christy, 83, a farmer who in World War II had flown cover for General George Patton's North Africa campaign. "After 50 years, they're jerking the rug out from under us."[4]

As the century-old agricultural communities of the Klamath River basin suffered severe social and economic distress from the government's diversion of their contract irrigation water to the fish, exclusionist organizations continued to argue, consistent with their principles, "that farmers should never have been in the 'dry' Klamath valley in the first place." In her column, "Rural Cleansing," *Wall Street Journal* editorial writer, Kimberley A. Strassel, wrote:

> *That is what's really happening in Klamath – call it rural cleansing … the goal of many environmental groups – from the Sierra Club to the Oregon Natural Resources Council – is no longer to protect*

nature. It's to expunge humans from the countryside .... The strategy of these environmental groups is nearly always the same: to sue or lobby the government into declaring rural areas off-limits to people who live and work there. The tools for doing this include the Endangered Species Act .... In some cases owners lose their property outright. More often, the environmentalists' goal is to have restrictions placed on the land that either render it unusable or persuade owners to leave on their own accord .... Environmental groups have spoken openly of their desire to concentrate people into cities, turning everything outside city limits into a giant park.[5]

Strassel's article illustrates the old adage about policy coming down to whose ox is gored. For people in urban areas, the ESA enjoys the reputation of a law that saves animals. Yet, for people living, working, and owning property in the nation's rural regions and smaller communities, the ESA has an entirely different image. Rural residents and businesspeople view themselves as economic and social victims of "rural cleansing." They are victims of an oppressive statute that, more often than not, is enforced in an excessively intrusive and unreasonable manner by federal bureaucrats in turn leveraged by hardcore environmental activists.

For example, if residents of a large population center, say New York City or Los Angeles, were to receive notice from the U.S. Fish and Wildlife Service that, to assure sufficient water for an ESA-protected fish inhabiting the river that supplies water to households and commercial users, a rationing plan was being imposed limiting each address to three gallons of water per day, a loud hue and cry would go up. Nearly all would complain about how oppressive and unfair it is to put the needs of fish above the needs of people. The communities, surrounding areas, and many members of Congress (as compared with the few members who represent rural regions) might finally recognize the need to reform the ESA to insure that when serious conflicts between the needs of people and wildlife species occur, people receive higher priority. However, FWS' selective implementation of the ESA has insured that such conflicts in large population areas rarely occur. Albuquerque's residents were among few to even come close to having their ox gored in this manner.

Meanwhile, despite their disappointment and frustration, the communities of the Klamath River basin rallied. On June 16, 2001, six members of Congress on the House Resources Committee held a field hearing at the Klamath County Fairgrounds in Klamath Falls, Oregon, at which 1,500 people attended. Out of that hearing came calls for the FWS' and NOAA Fisheries' Biological Opinions compelling more water for the fish to be peer-reviewed by an independent group of scientists. The National Academy of Science accepted Interior Secretary Gale Norton's request for its review of the science behind the Services' 2001 water-distribution decisions.

After months of careful review, in late 2001 an independent panel of 12 scientists assembled by the National Academy of Science reached a stunning result: "In allowing professional judgment to override site-specific evidence in some cases during 2001 ... the [Services] accepted a high risk of error in proposing actions that the available evidence indicated to be of doubtful utility." What the panel was saying here was that the Services' decision to take water from the farmers and give it to the fish was dictated more by a professional bias in favor of enforcing the ESA "whatever the cost" than by sound analysis of the on-site scientific evidence. The panel's report concluded that:

> there is no substantial scientific foundation at this time for changing the operation of the Klamath Project to maintain higher water levels in Upper Klamath Lake for the endangered sucker populations or higher flows in the Klamath River's main stem for the threatened coho salmon population .... Thus, the committee finds no substantial scientific evidence supporting changes in the operating practices ... over the past 10 years." [6]

The implications of the National Academy's report relative to the ESA are beyond remarkable. First, not only were the economic and social convulsions inflicted on the 1,400 farm families and all residents of the Klamath River basin by the government's cutoff of irrigation water unnecessary, but neither the two endangered species of sucker fish nor the threatened coho salmon ultimately received any observable benefits as a result of receiving the additional water in 2001.

The second implication of the National Academy's report goes to the very heart of the ESA itself. The government agencies shut off the farmers' water and gave it to the fish in furtherance of the ESA's unbending mandate that wildlife species must be preserved at all costs. The National Academy's independent panel of scientists, on the other hand, were not operating under the ESA's mandate; they were asked to review the quality of the science behind the Services' Biological Opinions that called for the fish to get the water. And there lies the ESA's primary fault: it cooks the science to fulfill its mandate, instead of letting good science dictate what is in the best interest of people and species. And as this case shows, it also is erratic and unreliable in its impact on wildlife.

The Klamath Project was shut down for farmers so endangered fish could have the water. Yet, the ESA rendered those same farmers' fields unavailable for millions of migrating waterfowl and other wildlife species. "On my farm, I [usually] have 30 or 40 miles of exposed water," says Steve Kandra. "Usually, you can find a duck every other couple yards. Last year [2001], there were no birds or other creatures to be seen. The greatest travesty of all was the ultimate impact the shutoff had on wildlife."[7]

AS MUCH AS A HALF BILLION DOLLARS IN JOBS AND BUSINESS LOST TO A BIRD

The western snowy plover is a tiny bird that breeds, among other places, on sandy beaches in California, Oregon, and Washington between March and September. It was listed as a threatened species under the ESA in 1993. There is substantial scientific data indicating that the coastal plover is genetically identical to the healthy inland plover that inhabits the foothills east of the Pacific coastal mountains. Because they are the same species, and thus their combined numbers are substantial, it has been argued that the coastal snowy plover is not, as a scientific matter, a "threatened" species under the ESA.[8]

While the ESA's listing process is flawed and vulnerable to manipulation of scientific data-gathering, it is the FWS that impacts people's livelihood with its designation of critical habitat and recovery plans. Once critical habitat is designated, activities that might cause or increase human-associated disturbance of the species are forbidden, subjecting violators to stringent penalties. Just walking on the beach, for example, could result in a fine of $50,000 and jail time should a plover's nesting grounds be accidentally damaged.

In 1999, the FWS designated 29 critical habitat areas for the snowy plover that directly impacted 20,000 acres of west coast beaches in communities such as Coos Bay, Oregon, and Monterey, Pismo Beach, Morrow Bay, Lompoc, and Coronado, California. Between Memorial Day and Labor Day, these beach communities become crowded with tourists and beachgoers, patronizing the restaurants, motels, service stations, beach shops, fishing boat rentals, and other vendors, in turn generating numerous jobs, as well as tax revenues to the local communities.

In order to restrict human activity in critical habitat areas, the FWS' practice is to find some basis for attributing the species' diminished status to disturbances by people. Sometimes this requires a real stretch. For instance, with regard to the plover, FWS found that "European beachgrass ... [a] non-native plant ... introduced to the west coast around 1898 to stabilize dunes" was primarily responsible for loss of plover breeding grounds. And even though most plover nest destruction is caused by predatory mammals and other birds, FWS attributed that predation to people by finding that "urban/agricultural areas" attract crows and ravens, and the "accumulation of trash at beaches attracts" skunks, raccoons, gulls, and the "introduced eastern red fox."[9] Presumably, if those entrepreneurial Europeans of yesteryear had not brought their beachgrass to the Pacific coast to stabilize the dunes, or if people had not created communities or farmed rural lands, there would be no crows or ravens to destroy plover nests; and if people were not allowed to visit the beaches, there would be no trash to attract skunks, raccoons, gulls, and red fox.

On the assumption that people were responsible for disturbing the plover's nesting process, the FWS' list of "prohibited activities" on these beaches included walking, jogging, clam-digging, sunbathing, picnicking, kite flying, beach cleaning, horseback riding, hang gliding, motorized vehicle use, and camping – every year during spring and summer. Because beachgoers and visitors to these areas could no longer enjoy beach recreation or even walking on the beach, businesses and their employees have suffered significant financial losses and even their livelihoods. Yet, in designating critical habitat for the plover on these beaches, FWS once again ran roughshod over the ESA's only provision designed to consider people.

That provision requires the FWS to evaluate the economic and social impact of the proposed designation on people living and working in the area, in comparison to the potential benefit to the species. Instead of performing these evaluations, the FWS summarily concluded that the designation of these beaches as critical habitat for the plover would have no additional economic or social effect on people.

In 2002, entities that had suffered, or potentially would suffer, economic losses from FWS' closures or restrictions on the beaches filed suit to force the FWS to conduct the evaluations required by the ESA.[10] One year later, the court found that the FWS had indeed failed to conduct the required evaluations. But instead of setting aside FWS' unlawful critical habitat restrictions because of the failed evaluations, the court left FWS' onerous "prohibited activities" restrictions in place until the FWS performed the evaluations – a bizarre ruling influenced by the *TVA v. Hill* decision that species were to be preserved "whatever the cost." In this fashion, the FWS was able to continue causing significant economic distress, despite the ESA's clear mandate that the evaluations were to be conducted *before* critical habitat restrictions were put in place.

Finally, in August, 2005, seven years after FWS imposed plover critical habitat restrictions, the FWS issued its real economic evaluation, estimating that these human-use restrictions would result in depressed business and employment losses of between $273 million and $645 million over the next 20 years. Yet, as economically severe as these losses are, John Griffith, the Coos County Commissioner whose lawsuit compelled FWS' belated economic study, took issue with the figures as grossly understated. He pointed out that local and Oregon state government reports had estimated the 1999 losses from closing beaches on one small spit of Coos Bay alone was $430,000 – for just eight months.[11]

POLITICIZED SALMON DECIMATE THE PACIFIC FISHING INDUSTRY AND MANY JOBS

Perhaps no question within the biological debate is more hotly contested than why hatchery-spawned salmon are not treated as the full and legitimate members of the Pacific salmon species they are. Exclusionists regard artificially propagated salmon as unwelcome interlopers or, even worse, as look-alike assassins of so-called "wild" salmon populations.

All species of Pacific Coast salmon are anadromous fish, meaning they are spawned and spend the early months of their lives in freshwater streams, rivers, or lakes. Usually within their first year, they migrate to the open ocean where they spend the next one to three years. When their genetically coded alarm clock rings, the salmon instinctively locate the mouth of the waterway from which they entered the ocean and begin their grueling upstream return to the river or lake where they were spawned. Upon arrival, they spawn and die shortly thereafter.

The five Pacific Coast salmon species that inhabited the coastal waters of Washington, Oregon, and northern California in the early 1870s were native fish, natural descendants of fish that had inhabited those same waters from ancient times. In 1874, naturalist Livingston Stone observed that the spring run of chinook salmon on the upper Sacramento River were "much depleted" and he recommended the use of artificial propagation to revitalize the run.[12] Stone's recommendation for creating fish hatcheries was accepted by the federal government, and he became the original manager of the government's first hatchery. Thus began a program of federal, state, and privately operated hatcheries that over the course of the next 100 years released virtually billions of hatchery-spawned fish into the anadromous cycle.

Naturally, the fish artificially propagated in hatcheries and the native salmon of the same species got together and bred, which is understandable, considering that their DNA makeup is identical. Except for the hatchery salmon's missing antipode fin, a nonessential appendage that is clipped by the hatchery to provide a means of distinguishing it from fish spawned in the wild, it is near impossible even for fish biologists to differentiate the two. As a result of their continuous breeding over the past century, there are no longer – and this has been true for decades – any pure "native" salmon. The offspring of hatchery-spawned salmon and the once-native salmon came to be called, for lack of a more descriptive term, "wild" or "natural" salmon. But in truth, all Pacific salmon today are the descendants of generations of artificially propagated fish.

Fish hatcheries and artificial propagation as a means of revitalizing wild salmon runs are anathema to exclusionists. They loathe hatchery fish because, as they see it, these artificially spawned fish eliminated the natural purity of original native salmon. They also condemn hatcheries because the continuous replenishment process, in their view, is accelerating the decline and eventual extinction of wild salmon populations. From their viewpoint, the constant infusion of artificially propagated fish allows the timber, agriculture, hydroelectric generation, and other industries to feel less guilty about their ongoing degradation of freshwater habitat.[13]

Fish biologists at NOAA Fisheries generally have little use for hatchery-spawned salmon, claiming them to be behaviorally inferior to wild fish, and therefore less able to survive once they enter the ocean. They also view the larger numbers of hatchery-spawned salmon as competition for the wild salmon. Because of this view, NOAA Fisheries' practice in determining which of the numerous Pacific Coast salmon runs to list as endangered or threatened is to count only the meager numbers of wild fish, and exclude the plentiful hatchery-spawned fish from the count. (The missing fin is how the counters recognize which returning fish not to count.) Were the numerous hatchery fish counted, far fewer salmon runs would be listed as endangered under the ESA, and that is a result the exclusionist community, together with their allies in NOAA Fisheries, do not want. The presence of only ESA-listed species enables the government, and by extension the exclusionist movement, to regulate, and in time reduce, Americans' use of their land.

This issue of whether hatchery fish should be counted when making the ESA listing determination came before a federal court in Oregon in 2001. In its decision, the court ruled that because so-called wild salmon and hatchery-spawned salmon were the same fish – that is, their genetic makeup, their DNA, were identical – for purposes of the ESA, NOAA Fisheries could not arbitrarily count the one, but exclude the other: either all the fish should be counted, or none of the fish should be counted.[14]

Yet, even though the court's ruling was upheld by the federal appellate court, and NOAA Fisheries officials publicly acknowledged that the agency would not treat hatchery fish and wild fish differently, the pressure from the exclusionists still mounted pressure to exclude hatchery-spawned fish from annual fish counts. When only 30,000 wild Chinook salmon returned to the Klamath River in the fall 2004 – an exceptionally low number, but not inconsistent with some past years – NOAA Fisheries reverted to its former position that hatchery-spawned salmon would not be included in future counts. As a result of the one river's meager numbers of wild fish (there are many coastal rivers in Washington, Oregon, and northern California), the government eliminated more than half of the commercial trolling salmon season along major portions of the West Coast. Further, for the year 2005, the government eliminated all salmon fishing – commercial, sport, and individual – near the mouth of the Klamath River itself. This decision harmed many fishermen, including Thomas Harris of Harbor, Oregon. He described the NOAA Fisheries-caused crisis in a letter to Pacific Legal Foundation attorney, Russell Brooks. It stated, in part:

> *The problem we are facing ... is the virtual destruction of our industry by the National Marine Fisheries Service* [also called NOAA Fisheries] .... *We are a group of families and small business owners who venture out on the ocean to catch Chinook salmon using the hook and line method (no nets). Each trip lasts 1 to 4 days at which time we return to ports up and down the coast to sell our catch to receiving stations. This industry has gone on for close to a hundred years allowing us to make a living and support our families. In my case, I have been a commercial fisherman for 47 years and have watched the industry change but never as dramatically as it will this year.*
>
> *There are several thousand fishing vessels, each owned by a working family or small business owner that are permitted by each state to harvest salmon during the seasons set by the* [National Marine Fisheries Service, now NOAA Fisheries]. *Besides the owners of these boats, each one normally carries a crew of 1 or 2 hands who also support their families from this industry. As many as 8 to 10 thousand fishing families and small business owners are affected by what the N.M.F.S. does every year. Here are the problems:*
>
> *The N.M.F.S. regulates and dictates the times and areas we can fish, called "setting the season." The criteria used is based on computer models which the N.M.F.S. creates from data they say matters. The models are always based on the weakest river on the West Coast, and this is always the Klamath River .... The data ... is only based*

on the ... "wild fish." The hatchery spawned Chinook are totally dis-counted and not used at all in the models. N.M.F.S. says these fish are different and do not count. We disagree with N.M.F.S. Hatchery and naturally spawning fish are the same with no differences. I believe Judge Hogan [referring to the 2001 ruling cited above] *has already ruled on this issue in federal court.*

The rivers on the coast will be flooded with Chinook [hatchery] *salmon this fall* [2005]. *It is projected that 6 to 7 million adult Chinook will return, 200,000-plus hatchery fish in the Klamath River alone. 1.7 million are projected for the Sacramento River and millions more elsewhere. None of these fish go into the N.M.F.S. computer model.*

The N.M.F.S. will set our fishing season [for 2005] *on their projected model of 30,000 wild Chinook* [based on 2004], *"the real ones," returning to the Klamath River. With these numbers be-ing used, our season will be virtually non-existent.*

This puts 10,000 families either unemployed, bankrupt, or at-tempting more dangerous fisheries to pay the bills, for which they are not equipped. All because 6 million Chinook salmon are different and don't count to the N.M.F.S. ...

What was especially difficult for commercial and sports fishermen to understand was that, as Harris' letter pointed out, the projections for re-turning spring 2005 hatchery salmon indicated "the largest runs in the last 50 years," according to Rayburn Guerin, president of Oregon Trollers Association.[15] Nonetheless, NOAA Fisheries drastically shortened the commercial and sports fishing seasons based on the previous year's count of only the returning wild fish to one river. These reductions, which varied by coastal locations, led to one of the most devastating losses of liveli-hoods and jobs the West Coast fishing industry and related businesses ever experienced. Not only were 8,000 - 10,000 fishing families left with virtually no incomes to pay their bills for major portions of the year, but hundreds of proprietors and employees working in fish markets, seafood restaurants, canneries, smokehouses, ice houses, fishing gear stores, as well as boat sales, repair shops, and fuel dealers suffered severe economic losses and social dislocation as a result. Some estimates put the industry and personal damages at $100 million.

"Hundreds of fishermen and businesses face bankruptcy because the federal government [wouldn't] let people fish despite the fact the ocean is teeming with [hatchery] salmon," said PLF attorney, Russ Brooks, at the time. "It's not just a single fishing season that's at stake here, it's the future of thousands of hardworking American families and a way of life that has existed for over 100 years."[16] All of this because NOAA Fisheries continues to practice politicized science by selectively counting only so-called wild salmon, while disregarding their genetically identical hatchery-spawned cousins. "Worst of all," wrote Brooks, "this will happen for no good reason."[17]

THE FLY THAT SUPPRESSED RECOVERY OF AN ECONOMICALLY DEPRESSED REGION

The Delhi sands flower-loving fly is a 1.5-inch-long orange and black insect native to the Delhi dunes of southern California's San Bernardino and Riverside Counties. Spending most of its life in a larval state, below ground, it emerges for fewer than 10 days, during which it finds a mate and breeds. After the females lay their fertilized eggs under the sandy soil, the adult flies die. All 11 known populations of the fly occur within an eight-mile radius of one another.

The FWS listed the fly as endangered in 1993, when its entire population was estimated to number in the low hundreds. Because of the economic consequences the fly's listing would impose on the people of the area in future years, it is worth noting that FWS' 1996 Recovery Plan[18] acknowledged that "[t]he extinction of the Delhi sands flower-loving fly in the immediate future is a likely event," even with the protections of the ESA.

Located just east of Los Angeles County, San Bernardino and Riverside Counties, and their communities of Colton, Rialto, Fontana, Riverside, and Rubidoux, grew rapidly in the 1980s due to cheaper housing prices for those commuting to jobs in Los Angeles County. Yet, the region contained several economically depressed areas, with significant unemployment. In 1986, at the counties' request, the State of California designated a 10,000-acre site straddling both counties as the "Agua Mansa Enterprise Zone."[19] The counties envisioned numerous medium and heavy manufacturing companies locating their facilities within the enterprise zone, and providing some 20,000 jobs.

About the same time as the Agua Mansa Enterprise Zone was created, San Bernardino County began plans to build a $470 million earthquake-proof hospital to serve as the central emergency medical center for the County, as well as a primary burn care center and teaching facility. Located in City of Colton, not only would the modern 373-bed facility provide much-needed medical services to the region, it also would provide 2,500 skilled health-care and related jobs. Although the County completed its acquisition of the 68-acre hospital site prior to the fly's 1993 endangered listing, within hours before construction was to begin, the sighting of eight of the flies in the area triggered a FWS warning to the County that construction would likely "take" members of the species in violation of the ESA.

Upon receipt of the notice, the County went back to the drawing boards and modified its layout and design plan, moving the hospital 250 feet to avoid directly impacting the fly's likely habitat area. This change required acquisition of nearly 10 additional acres, which cost the County taxpayers an additional $3.5 million. The County agreed to dedicate the original 10-acres as a fly habitat preserve, to be protected by a County-constructed and maintained chain link fence. The County also provided an additional 100-foot-wide corridor to – theoretically – facilitate interbreeding between colonies in two separated habitat areas. In addition, FWS required the County to fund a five-year $480,000 study of the fly's behavior patterns. Altogether, the estimated costs of mitigation required to offset the hospital's potential impact on the fly totaled more than $4 million. After the County agreed to all of this, the FWS gave the green light for construction to commence.

In late 1995, with construction under way, the County informed the FWS that because growing traffic congestion at an intersection near the hospital's entry would cause serious delays for injury victims seeking emergency medical services once the hospital opened, it needed to redesign the intersection. It proposed utilizing part of the 100-foot-wide corridor linking the two fly colonies. FWS responded that because the County's plan would significantly reduce the size of the corridor intended to allow the two fly colonies to interbreed, if the County proceeded with its plan, FWS would file an ESA enforcement action.

At this point, a frustrated San Bernardino County, the Cities of Colton and Fontana, and the National Association of Home Builders, whose members' projects were being held up by FWS over to the fly, filed a pre-emptive lawsuit against FWS, seeking to have the ESA, as applied to the fly, declared unconstitutional. Because the Constitution provides Congress with only limited and specified powers (Article 1, Section 8), every act of Congress must have its basis in the Constitution. The Endangered Species Act of 1973 has its basis in the Commerce Clause, which allows Congress "[t]o regulate commerce ... among the several states."

In *National Association of Home Builders v. Bruce Babbitt* (Babbitt, as Secretary of the Department of Interior, oversees FWS), plaintiffs meri-toriously argued that the ESA was not intended to apply to a species such as the fly that did not move in "commerce" – meaning it neither had com-mercial value, nor moved across state lines (interstate commerce.)[20] In another expansion of federal power through the Commerce Clause, the federal trial court ruled that because two botanists had traveled across state lines to visit the fly's habitat, Secretary Babbitt had authority under the Commerce Clause to prevent a county hospital and other structures from being built in its habitat area.

In a 2-1 decision, the U.S. Court of Appeals (District of Columbia Circuit) stated: "Each time a species becomes extinct, the pool of wild species diminishes. This, in turn, has a substantial effect on interstate com-merce by diminishing a natural resource that could otherwise be used for present and future commercial purposes. ... [T]he 'taking' of endangered animals ... if permitted, would have a substantial effect on interstate com-merce by depriving commercial actors of access to an important natural resource – biodiversity."[21]

Thus, according to this example of exclusionist thinking, it doesn't matter that the particular species in question has no connection to com-merce whatsoever. If "biodiversity" is affected, commerce is presumed.

Unsuccessful in its lawsuit, the County put on hold its efforts to rede-sign the intersection. Only after the City of Colton, in which the hospital was located, agreed to set aside 160 acres as fly habitat (in return for also being allowed to develop 80 acres of prime commercial land) was the County allowed to modify the intersection to ease anticipated traffic congestion at the hospital's entry.

Finally, in 1999, with lengthy delays attributable solely to disputes over the fly, the Arrowhead Regional Medical Center opened for business. At no time during these delays was there any evidence that members of the two fly colonies actually traveled through the corridor to interbreed, or that they even were cognizant of the presence of the corridor.

At the same time, development of the 10,000-acre Agua Mansa Enterprise Zone, as well as numerous commercial and residential building projects in the cities, lay stymied by the fly. In the neighboring town of Fontana, for example, the fly-caused delay in construction of a 500-acre mixed residential and commercial development threatened the builders with default on $46 million in bonds they had floated to bring in sewer and water lines to the area. By 1997, some 11 years after the economic zone had been created, the FWS, with few exceptions, still was not allowing building in the zone; at the same time it was pushing to have hundreds of acres added as fly preserve. Even with the attractive special tax benefits, few companies were building in the zone because of the high costs of complying with regulations to protect the fly. Consequently, few of the 20,000 jobs that the zone was intended to provide had materialized.

As with other examples cited in this book, here again the chasm between the exclusionists' "species first – people-last" view and those who regard the needs and interests of people as primary, is glaringly apparent. Greg Ballmer, the University of California at Riverside entomology professor who had petitioned the FWS to list the Delhi sands flower-loving fly as endangered, defended the listing in the language of the old balance-of-nature philosophers:

> The ecosystem works so efficiently. Do we want to continue to tamper with that? And how much tampering can happen, before the entire system collapses. If you want to look at it spiritually, if a deity put all these creatures here to function as a community, should we be playing God and saying what shouldn't be here? How much should humans meddle? [22]

Balmer and the FWS, of course, also were tampering and playing God in a way that harmed many. John Travaglione, an elected member of the Riverside County Board of Supervisors at the time, who also sat on the board of the Agua Mansa Enterprise Zone, expressed his frustration:

> *This is one of the most ridiculous issues we've had to deal with in my 22 years on the Board of Supervisors .... Economic growth, in terms of jobs and tax revenue, is the life's blood of a city or county. Biologists who talk about saving habitat at the expense of jobs and economic growth don't have a clue what it takes to enhance and ensure the economic viability of an area .... I don't care what happens to the fly. I care about an economically viable area that means survival for humans.[23]*

Rudi Mattoni, the UCLA professor who helped draft the fly's preservation plan, explained:

> *To preserve condors and eagles has no meaning unless you preserve the entire habitat .... It's the habitat, stupid. The Delhi Sands dunes habitat is a national treasure. It has as much value as Yosemite or Yellowstone .... The fly vs. jobs controversy is all smoke and mirrors. This is about money. This is about profits for developers.[24]*

Julie Briggs, City Attorney for Colton, voiced the dispute this way:

> *I believe in preserving species. I believe in preserving habitat.* [But] *it's hard to throw your support behind a maggot ....* The Delhi Sands dunes habitat [that Professor Mattoni called a national treasure] *is a bunch of weeds and dirt. The 250 to 300 acres biologists have targeted as prime fly habitat — they call it 'ground zero' — is an area surrounded by a cement quarry, a sewage plant and some junk yards .... We'd be spending millions of dollars to recreate a habitat that's already been disturbed.[25]*

In 1999, biologists hired by FWS to count the flies in their prime habitat found very few of the insects. At the same time, FWS was seeking 2,000 additional acres of land for fly habitat. This angered city officials whose local residents would have to pay as much as $200 million in taxes or bonded indebtedness to acquire that much land. Still, multimillion dollar commercial and residential building projects in communities within the fly's habitat remained stalled.[26]

Three years later: September, 2002. Colton's planned $12 million sports complex named "Big League Dreams," an accompanying hotel and restaurant, together with the hundreds of jobs these projects would have provided, have all been shot down by FWS. As City Manager Daryl Parrish put it: "Instead there will be flies." Not only had the city indebted itself through the sale of bonds to fund the entertainment park, it also was losing $130,000 in escrow costs for purchase of property near Interstate 10 on which the park would have been built. A short distance away, the City of Fontana's proposed 218-acre office and industrial complex was getting the same treatment from FWS.[27]

A few days later, Mayor Deirdre Bennett of Colton addressed a press conference at a trash-strewn intersection of her city near Interstate 10. She wielded a giant fly-swatter. Because the larvae of the fly is burrowed under the city's sandy soil, the hauling of trash has been hampered. She and officials of Fontana, Rialto, and the County of San Bernardino were angered by FWS' mandate that trash along the freeway in their jurisdictions be picked up by hand, while forbidding the use of heavy machinery for that purpose.

> *To us and the majority of Americans with any common sense at all,* [Delhi sands flower-loving flies] *are pests, nothing more, nothing less — pests we have historically grown up swatting. The U.S Fish & Wildlife Service does not want us to disrupt this area as it may disturb the fly. Our national government encourages trash and debris to favor a fly. The American public surely must find this shocking.*[28]

Four years later, in May, 2006, the City of Colton has again been in negotiations with FWS over fly habitat. "We're currently at the table with them," said City Manager Daryl Parrish. "We're really going to demand results this time. For things to continue along as they have is unacceptable from our standpoint." That would include the failure of the FWS to restore 150 acres of fly habitat that Colton earlier dedicated for that purpose, and 35 more acres near the Arrowhead Regional Medical Center that FWS allowed to become a site for homeless camps and illegal dumping. "The big issue we keep hammering is, 'Stop the land grab,'" said Assistant City Manager Mark Nuaimi. "Stop acquiring more habitat and start focusing on restoring the habitat you already have ... let us develop our economy."

For Mayor Bennett, the federal government's unrelenting support of the fly had reached critical proportions. "Because of the economic situation of our city, if we don't get development on the west side, we won't be able to afford to provide police and fire services at the level our residents deserve," she said. Mayor Ken Eshelman of Fontana was more direct. He referred to FWS' costly preservation plan as "legalized extortion."

And what was FWS' response?

"We understand they are concerned," said FWS spokesman, Jane Hendron. "We're working to balance their need for economic development with the conservation needs of the species."[29] And the exclusionist mantra remained close at hand, as expressed by Greg Ballmer.

"If somebody gave you a shelf full of books, would you throw them out before reading them?" he asked. "There could be a fungus that cures cancer growing in the dirt here and we don't even know about it."[30]

NOTES:

1. *Range Magazine*, Fall 2004, p. 76, photos included, http://www.rangemagazine.com/archives/fall2004/contents.htm

2. 53 *Federal Register* 27130, July 18, 1988.

3. "War Over Water Strains Klamath," *The Sunday Oregonian*, May 6, 2001, p. A1.

4. "Water War Pits Farms Against Fish," *Los Angeles Times*, Sunday, May 6, 2001, p. A1.

5. Kimberly Strassel, "Rural Cleansing," *Wall Street Journal and Opinion.Journal.com.*, July 26, 2001.

6. *Scientific Evaluation of Biological Opinions on Endangered and Threatened Fishes in the Klamath River Basin*, Interim Report from the Committee on Endangered and Threatened Fishes in the Klamath River Basin, 2001-2002, National Research Council's National Academy of Science.

7. Bruce Pokarney, "Klamath Basin crisis: one year later," *Property Rights Research*, August 10, 2002; http://www.propertyrightsresearch.org/klamath_basin_crisis.htm

8. The Surf-Ocean Beach Commission's "Petition to Remove the Pacific Coast Population of the Western Snowy Plover from the Federal List of Threatened Species Pursuant to the Endangered

Species Act of 1973," filed with the FWS, July 29, 2002; also *Surf Ocean Beach Commission v. U.S. Department of Interior*, USDC, Eastern District of California, Case No. CIV.S-04-0242 FED RJM.

9. 60 *Federal Register* 11768, March 2, 1995.

10. *Coos County Commissioners v. Department of Interior*, USDC, Oregon, Case NO. 02-6128-HO; attorneys with the Pacific Legal Foundation brought this challenge on behalf of the plaintiffs.

11. Jeff Barnard, "Snowy plover costs projected to be huge," *Associated Press*, August 17, 2005.

12. Livingston Stone, *United States Commission of Fish and Fisheries. Part II. Report of the Commissioner for 1872 and 1873*. An Inquiry into the Decrease of the Food Fishes, The Propagation of Food-Fishes in the Waters of the United States. With Supplementary Papers. Washington: Government Printing Office, 1874, pp. 203 - 207.

13. James A. Lichatowich, *Salmon Without Rivers: A History of the Pacific Salmon Crisis,* Island Press: 1999, p. 131.

14. *Alsea Valley Alliance v. Evans*, 161 F. Supp. 2d 1154, 1163-64 (District of Oregon, 2001; this case was brought on behalf of the plaintiff by attorneys of Pacific Legal Foundation.

15. "Shortened season a blow to salmon fishermen," *The Register Guard* (Eugene, Oregon), April 16, 2005.

16. "PLF files lawsuit to block federal regulation slashing fishing season by more than half despite record numbers of salmon," June 3, 2005. http://www.pacificlegal.org/?mvcTask=pressReleases &id=322

17. "U.S. puts fish above families," Special to the *Sacramento Bee*, July 16, 2005.

18. Final Listing Rule, 58 *Federal Register* 49881, September 23, 1993.

19. An enterprise zone is an economically depressed area that is designed by the State of California to encourage and stimulate growth, development, and investment in the area. Taxpayers that conduct business activities within the boundaries of an enterprise zone receive special tax incentives, partially based on their hiring demographics.

20. In its brief, Pacific Legal Foundation attorneys challenged the federal government's ever-expanding reach through the Commerce Clause, arguing that unless firm limits are placed on increasing federal power under the Commerce Clause, there will eventually be nothing, no matter how small or local in nature, that the federal government does not control, and that is contrary to what the Framers of the Constitution intended.

21. *National Association of Home Builders v. Babbitt*, 130 F. 3d 1041 (D.C. Circuit 1997).

22. "Rare fly buzzes into debate on jobs," *Riverside Press Enterprise*, May 12, 1997.

23. *Ibid.*

24. *Ibid.*

25. *Ibid.*

26. "Insect hunt coming up empty: A survey has failed to net any evidence that the Delhi Sands flower-loving fly breeds on undeveloped property in Fontana," *Riverside Press Enterprise,* September 11, 1999.

27. "Fly project swats ballpark project," *Riverside Press Enterprise*, September 24, 2002.

28. "Cities hope to swat flies," *Riverside Press Enterprise*, September 26, 2002.

29. "Colton seeks fly accord," *San Bernardino Sun*, May 6, 2006.

30. "Unique compromise could end tiny fly's grip on SoCal town," *Associated Press* article appearing in *The San Jose Mercury News*, January 20, 2007.

CHAPTER 13

TRAMPLED PROPERTY RIGHTS

IT'S DIFFICULT TO decide what is worse: losing one's livelihood, as depicted in the previous chapter, or losing one's home, or the use of one's property. The home and property owners in the following stories are representative of numerous others around the country undergoing the same or similar treatment under the ESA.

THE SAGA OF MIGHTY MOUSE

As noted earlier, in 2004 Hurricane Ivan devastated Perdido Key, a barrier island off the Florida panhandle. The powerful storm destroyed or heavily damaged most of the homes and business structures on the island. Agencies empowered by the ESA prohibited victims from rebuilding their homes or business properties and returning their lives to normal.

In typical heavy-handed style, the FWS threatened to sue Escambia County if it granted any post-Ivan building permits for Perdido Key, and the County reluctantly imposed a building permit moratorium. It was all because of the Perdido Key beach mouse, listed as endangered in 1985. For many years, a full 60 percent of the island, on the public lands of federal and state parks, has been designated critical habitat for the mouse. The FWS exploited Ivan's structural devastation as an opportunity to expand the critical habitat to the now empty privately owned lots. Meanwhile, the lives of the people whose homes were destroyed on September 16, 2004, continue in a state of economic, social, and emotional disarray, damaged as much by the ESA's preference for the Perdido Key beach mouse as by the fury of Hurricane Ivan.

"U.S. Fish & Wildlife has stagnated our recovery and threatens to negatively impact our economic future indefinitely with their claim to jurisdiction over 'suitable habitat' for this species," lamented Beth Barrios of the property owner group, Perdido Property Rights, Inc.

Valerie Fernandez, managing attorney with Pacific Legal Foundation's Atlantic Center in Stuart, Florida, said: "What's especially outrageous is that federal officials targeted my clients' homesites as 'critical habitat' after their homes were destroyed by Ivan, even though there is no evidence of beach mouse presence there. So the government took advantage of a tragedy to essentially confiscate these people's property. I say 'confiscate,' because the homeowners can't rebuild as long as the feds say their land is needed for mice."[1]

More than three years after "Ivan the Terrible," wreaked havoc, Paul and Gail Fisher and others are not out of the woods. As of mid-November, 2007, many of the private parcels on Perdido Key that had hosted homes and businesses remain vacant. Nor have the owners received any compensation from the federal government for its taking of their property for the mouse.

THE BALD EAGLE FLIES OFF THE ESA LIST;
PROPERTY OWNERS REMAIN TETHERED

Ed Contoski owns 17 acres of unimproved land abutting the westerly shore of Sullivan Lake in Morrison County, Minnesota. He and his parents before him have paid taxes on the property since 1939. In January, 1930, some nine years before the Contoskis acquired the property on Sullivan Lake, the National Audubon Society testified before a congressional hearing in Washington, D.C., that the American bald eagle was on the verge of extinction.

As Dr. Gordon Edwards and others have pointed out, the bald eagle's great decline in the lower 48 states between the 1870s and the 1970s was due primarily to violent causes such as shooting, trapping, lead poisoning from eating carrion killed by lead buckshot, electrocutions by power lines, and collisions with solid structures.

Although Congress had enacted the Bald Eagle Protection Act in 1940 (renamed the Bald and Golden Eagle Protection Act in 1962) making it a federal crime to "take," that is, to kill, trap or otherwise harm bald eagles, because of lack of enforcement, eagles continued to be deliberately killed as described in Chapter 1. By 1963, the number of mated pairs in the lower 48 states was down to an estimated 417. When, in the early 1970s, the federal government finally got serious about enforcing the Bald and Golden Eagle Protection Act, the decimation stopped and the eagle's numbers began to rise. In addition, in more recent years much of the biological community has come to conclude that the recovery of the brown pelican and the raptors, including falcons, ospreys, and eagles, began to increase their numbers as a result of the banning of DDT in 1972. With the help of the media, this position also is generally accepted by the public.

Following the eagle's 1978 listing as endangered under the ESA, millions of dollars were spent on eagle recovery programs.[2] In addition, the efforts of federal and state agencies, tribes, universities, and many private grassroots organizations contributed to the eagle's resurgence. By 1995, the bald eagle populations in the lower 48 states had increased so significantly that the FWS downlisted the species to threatened. Four years later, with 5,800 breeding pairs in the lower 48 states, President Clinton announced that the FWS is formally proposing that the eagle be declared fully recovered, with final action (delisting) due in one year.[3]

In 2004, with retirement approaching, Ed Contoski decided to subdivide and sell his property. Although 10 of the 17 acres were wetlands and would remain unimproved, an appraisal placed the value of the remaining seven acres at $425,000, provided they could be developed. Contoski then engaged a surveyor to prepare a residential subdivision plan consisting of five lots on the seven acres.

Shortly before his subdivision application came before the Morrison County planning board for approval, Contoski received a notice from wildlife authorities that an active bald eagle nest had been spotted in a tree near the middle of his proposed subdivision. When he acknowledged that eagles had used the nest in past years, but none had occupied the nest in the current year, he was informed that under the ESA a nest was considered "active" until eagles were absent for five years. He was further informed that no cutting of trees or building of roads or cabins could occur within a 330-foot radius of that tree.

As a practical matter, this "no development" radius encompassed all or portions of his five proposed lots. Notwithstanding the President's 1999 press conference announcing the eagle's recovery, over five years later FWS still had not delisted the eagle. The longer the delisting was delayed, the longer Mr. Contoski's modest subdivision plan was stalled. Finally, in 2005, Ed Contoski filed suit in Minnesota federal court to compel FWS to delist the recovered bald eagle.[4]

"I'm not against eagles," he said, "but they're not endangered anymore."[5] Agreeing that the eagle was no longer in danger of extinction, the federal court ordered the FWS to officially delist the eagle pursuant to the ESA not later than June 29, 2007. There were then more than 9,700 breeding pairs in the lower 48 states. But the FWS was not merely dragging its feet during the years between the eagles announced recovery and the court-ordered delisting. It was developing a means to extend ESA-protections to a species no longer in danger of extinction, a dubious task considering the ESA only was intended to provide protection to a species while it is threatened or endangered.

In exclusionist thinking, based on the balance-of-nature cult, there is no such thing as a "recovered" species; all wild species are constantly in jeopardy from man's propensity to build. And in the exclusionist view, only harsh enforcement of strong laws can constrain the human propensity to build.

FWS biologist, Laura Ragan, of the Fort Snelling, Minnesota, regional office, explained that after the President announced the eagle recovered in 1999, FWS received thousands of comments expressing concern for the eagle's safety once it was no longer protected under the ESA. The FWS needed to analyze and address these concerns, she stated.[6] Reading

between the lines, that explanation suggests that the large exclusionist organizations orchestrated a deluge of comments to the FWS, urging per-
petual protection of the eagle and its habitat, including Mr. Contoski's five
lots, from development. And that is precisely what the FWS did.

In early June, 2007, less than a month before it delisted the American
bald eagle pursuant to the court order, the FWS attached new regulations
to the nearly 70-year old, seldom-used Bald and Golden Eagle Protection
Act. The FWS did this by simply lifting the ESA's 330-foot "no development" radius regulation and dropping it into the rejuvenated Bald and
Golden Eagle Protection Act. Thus, even though the eagle is no longer in
danger of extinction, and no longer entitled to the ESA's special protective
regime, the FWS will be deploying the same restrictive regime as under the
ESA. And it made this major grab of expanded jurisdiction without asking
Congress to amend the ESA. As a result, the FWS arguably has the authority to prohibit Mr. Contoski, and other property owners like him from
ever building on their land. With Minnesota now home to 1,312 breeding
pairs of eagles, and Wisconsin, 1,065,[7] there are numerous owners in those
states who may never be allowed to develop or actively use their land.

An ESA-Listed Snake Thwarts Property Owners Use of Their Land

The Alameda whipsnake is a slender, fast-moving, burrowing snake
native to California. In 1997, FWS listed the three-foot-long snake as a
threatened species. Although the ESA requires that FWS designate the
species' critical habitat at the time of listing, it allows FWS to opt out of
an early designation if it cannot readily determine the species habitat needs
and range at that time.

The ESA also imposes on FWS certain duties prior to its designation of critical habitat. One of those duties, the sole ESA provision that
takes people's interests into consideration, requires FWS to perform an
economic and social evaluation to determine how the designation will impact the people and communities in the affected region.

Since the ESA's enactment, exclusionist litigators such as the Center
for Biological Diversity (CBD) have become highly adept at using its species protection provisions to deny property owners the use of their land.

Many people believe that diminution of private property is more their mission than species protection. The case of the Alameda whipsnake provides a clear example of how such groups, often working in tandem with the government, abuse property owners.

In 1999, CBD sued the FWS for failure to designate critical habitat for the whipsnake. To no one's surprise, the FWS quickly settled the suit, agreeing to designate critical habitat "on an expedited basis." Within just months of its settlement with CBD, the FWS designated seven geographical areas encompassing 406,708 acres of mostly privately owned land within California's Alameda, Contra Costa, San Joaquin, and Santa Clara Counties as critical habitat for the whipsnake. There was just one problem: in no legitimate respect did the FWS perform the labor-intensive and time-consuming designation process in accordance with the ESA.

FWS openly acknowledged that its biologists did not possess adequate survey data to know what land the whipsnake actually occupied. Instead, all lands within the range of the snake that biologists *believed* might contain its habitat components were thrown into the designation. Numerous frustrated owners of affected land informed FWS of the designation's overreach. One rancher was representative, informing the FWS that after several months of conducting day and night observations and thorough field surveys looking for Alameda whipsnakes, not a single one was found on his ranch.

Yet, for property owners wanting to build personal homes on their land, and those planning to sell their land in preparation for retirement, the economic and social burdens, and the emotional strain imposed by the flawed and excessive designation were enormous. For commercial owners planning to build sorely needed homes in the vastly overpriced resale Bay-area market, the designation spelled disaster. Property values instantly dried up; no one in his right mind would purchase land that could not be used because it was critical habitat for an ESA-listed species. Although the property owners pleaded with FWS for six years to be relieved of the onerous effects of the designation, or at least for FWS to be more precise as to which land the snake occupied, FWS showed more accommodation to the CBD than it did the property owners.

Finally, in 1999, property owners and other interested parties filed suit in federal court challenging FWS' expansive and ill-founded designation of critical habitat for the whipsnake.[8] In a landmark opinion setting aside the designation, the trial court found that the FWS had failed to perform an adequate biological survey of the snake's actual whereabouts, stating: "the court has found that the Service failed to articulate any rational basis for including certain areas within the critical habitat, and therefore abused its discretion in doing so."[9] And in the courtroom a strange thing happened.

After six years of telling the affected property owners that the snake's critical habitat designation was not really having a negative economic or social impact on them, despite obvious evidence to the contrary, the FWS "concede[d] that [its] economic analysis in regard to the critical habitat designation for the snake was in error."[10] The trial court readily agreed, and ruled in favor of the petitioning property owners.

ENDANGERED FISH DENY A SMALL LANDOWNER THE USE OF HIS PROPERTY

Robert Morris owns a half-acre parcel in Philipsville, California. The only economic value of his property is five large trees. When he informally inquired of NOAA Fisheries Service about obtaining a permit to cut and sell the trees as timber, the Service balked. Cutting the trees would, in its biologist's opinion, violate the ESA by removing shade on, and causing soil erosion in, the stream running through his property that is critical habitat for endangered salmon. With anadromous fish species like salmon that spend their lives in both the ocean and coastal rivers or streams, NOAA Fisheries' critical habitat restrictions apply to all land situated on either side of such rivers and streams as the Service determines is necessary to preserve the fish.

Mr. Morris' only lawful option was to enter into a Habitat Conservation Plan with NOAA Fisheries that would legally bind him to either: replace in kind the shade and erosion-free soil that the five trees had provided the salmon for the few minutes it took them to swim through his property; or, pay the government the cost of acquiring property elsewhere that would provide the fish a stream with the same amount of shade and erosion-free soil that cutting down the trees on his property would eliminate. The first alternative was a physical impossibility on Mr. Morris' half-acre parcel. And because the cost of the second alternative far exceeded the value of his land and the trees, it was economically untenable. A frustrated Morris finally filed suit in federal court.[11]

His suit claimed that NOAA Fisheries' designation of his half-acre as critical habitat for the salmon amounted to a taking of his property's value for species preservation, a "public use," entitling him to "just compensation" under the Fifth Amendment ("nor shall private property be taken for public use, without just compensation"). The court rejected Mr. Morris' suit on the procedural ground that before he could sue in court on a takings claim, he would first have to go through NOAA Fisheries' formal permit application process and be turned down – a legal doctrine known as "exhaustion of administrative remedies." Of course, going through the formal permit process would cost Morris more than his property with the trees was worth. Besides, NOAA Fisheries had preliminarily indicated that it would not grant the permit.

The ESA may do a poor job at actually protecting species, as shown in Chapter 10, but excels at putting small property owners like Mr. Morris – who is hardly any kind of big developer – in these types of lose-lose situations. Without the threat of a takings claim as leverage, such small landowners may never be able to use their property for a viable purpose. The federal government has virtually declared their land a wildlife preserve for the benefit of the public, yet it pays them nothing for having taken their property.

RATS, WILDFIRES, AND LOST HOMES

As noted earlier, in 1988, the FWS listed the Stephens' kangaroo rat (k-rat) as an endangered species in parts of Riverside, San Bernardino, and San Diego Counties in southern California. According to FWS, the species was listed because of widespread habitat loss due to urban and agricultural developments.

The ESA provides that a listing is to be based on the best scientific data available at the time, but when the k-rat was listed, FWS had little current biological information about the species. Earlier studies indicated that although plowing disturbed k-rats living in the fields, those populations that survived along the natural edges of the fields "reinvaded after the fields had been left fallow." Such studies also showed that k-rats moved better and found food more easily on terrain that was mostly open or sparsely vegetated.[12] From these studies, the FWS concluded that private agricultural lands that had been previously plowed would provide good recovery habitat for the k-rats if further plowing of the land was prohibited.

As noted at the outset, Andy and Cindy Domenigoni owned a cattle ranch and grain farm outside the community of Winchester, in Riverside County, California. Five generations of the family worked the land since 1879. In 1990, without their knowledge or consent, more than 1,600 acres of the Domenigonis' ranch were placed in an ESA reserve "study area" as part of a Habitat Conservation Plan for the k-rat. One day, private biologists were discovered illegally trespassing in an 800-acre section that the Domenigonis had allowed to lie fallow for two years in order to rest and rejuvenate the soil. Asked to leave, they returned shortly thereafter with an FWS biologist and an armed law enforcement officer. These federal bureaucrats proceeded to inform the Domenigonis that their planned preparation of the 800-acre section for grain planting would constitute an illegal "take" of the k-rats that they had found inhabiting that section. Because k-rats prefer the open terrain the earlier plowing had created, the k-rats had taken up residency during the two years of lying fallow. [13]

The FWS agents further cautioned the Domenigonis that if they were later found to have disked 800-acres of fields in violation of the ESA, they could face a year in federal prison, a $50,000 fine for each and every "take" of a rat, substantial mitigation costs to restore the land, and impoundment of their farm equipment.[14]

"As a result of shutting down our ability to farm that property," Cindy Domenigoni testified before a House Resources Committee hearing in 1996, "we incurred over $75,000 in lost income for each of the three years that we were unable to grow grain there. We have also spent over $175,000 on legal fees, biological surveys, and other related costs. Our costs total over $400,000 in lost income and direct costs because of the impact of the Endangered Species Act. These costs do not include thousands of dollars in damages to our fences and equipment that occurred during the California Fire of October 1993."[15]

At the beginning of the dry season in the years preceding 1992, the county fire chief notified residents whose homes were in fire-vulnerable areas that they should take the precaution of disking a firebreak around their homes to cut off the fuel source that allows grass fires to reach the structures. Most residents had gladly complied. In 1992, however, the FWS also sent out a notice to all residents within the k-rats' habitat area, instructing that they should not disk the land around their homes, as the disk blades would cause a "take" of the k-rats, in violation of the ESA. Thus, receiving two notices – one from the local jurisdiction advising them to disk, and one from the federal government instructing them not to disk, most residents did nothing.

As the dry season approached in 1993, the Domenigonis' close neighbor, Michael Rowe, sent them two letters asking that they remove the vegetation and brush that had accumulated over the previous five years in the 800-acres next to his small farm and home. As Cindy Domenigoni testified, "[h]e legitimately feared that, should a fire come, he would be in great danger of losing his home from the amount of fuel that had built up so close to his property ... we had pleaded with the [FWS] to allow us to disk a fire break in order to protect the safety of our neighbor, Mr. Rowe .... They told us not to disk the fire break."[16] One FWS response to the Domenigonis' requests was the following: "Due to the presence of this federally endangered species, discing of the firebreak would harm this species. As this area is within a proposed Preserve for Stephens Kangaroo rats, incidental take under the current permit is not authorized."[17]

The "California Fire," as it became known, occurred between October 26 - 31, 1993. "I must remind you," Mrs. Domenigoni told the Resources Committee members, "that my husband and I were out during the height of the fire, herding our cattle out of its path, and into safer pastures. We were able to survive the fire burning all around us, as we huddled with our horses and our cattle in a tiny seven acre field that we had farmed that year. Had the entire 800 acres been farmed as well [which FWS had prohibited them from doing for the past three years], others might have been more fortunate with their own homes and property." She said that in the nearly 120 years the area had been farmed, there had never been as large or as damaging a fire as this one. "The fires in the past had always been contained to minimal acreage burned ... due to the patchwork landscape effect from our agricultural practices," she said.[18]

During the early morning hours, their neighbor, Michael Rowe, saw the fire approaching and decided to act, despite the federal government's threat of prosecution. With his tractor, he wildly drove around his home several times with the disk blades cutting through the five-year accumulation of highly flammable brush and vegetation. As a result of his quick action and ultimate disregard for the FWS' prosecution threats, Mr. Rowe was able to create a buffer-zone around his home, saving it from the oncoming fire.

In all, the California Fire burned 25,100 acres in Riverside County and destroyed 29 homes, including that of Anna Klimko. She had obeyed FWS' order not to disk a firebreak around her home because of the k-rat. She wound up digging through the ashes for whatever family keepsakes she could find. "For what?" she told the media. "A rat?" As it turned out, she and the 28 other homeowners did not lose their homes for a rat.

After the fire, the Domenigonis personally examined the 800-acre section FWS biologists had cited as occupied habitat of the k-rat the previous three years. Finding no evidence of k-rats, they asked FWS to reexamine the land and tell them if they could farm it again. In other words, a farmer had to ask the federal government for permission to farm his own farmland.

FWS biologist John Bradley came out and performed the survey. After finding no k-rats on the 800-acre section, he gave the Domenigonis a verbal green light to go forward with their farming activities. Not long thereafter, they were surprised to read in their local newspaper a highly revealing comment about the k-rat and their farmland by biologist Bradley. According to Mrs. Domenigoni, Bradley had told the reporter "that it was not the fire that had caused the destruction of the k-rats and their habitat. Rather, while we were under orders not to farm the land by the Service, the brush and weeds in the field had grown too thick for the k-rats' preference, and they had simply left the area, *long before the fire occurred.*"[19] (Emphasis added.)

So ultimately it wasn't for a rat at all. Rather, it was all a power play by government enforcers of the ESA. That came as little comfort to the fire victims. One additional point about the ESA and the Stephens' kangaroo rat deserves mention.

In May, 1995, the Riverside County Farm Bureau submitted to FWS a petition to delist the k-rat. The petition pointed out, among other things, that with the discovery of other substantial populations of k-rats at different locations within Riverside County in the seven years since its listing, the k-rat was not in danger of extinction and "the species was listed in error." Three months later FWS responded, stating that it was unable to review the delisting petition due to limited resources; furthermore, "that delisting petitions ranked as a low-priority."[20]

In February, 2002, seven years later, the Riverside County Farm Bureau submitted another petition to delist the k-rat, which contained most of the same information and the same grounds for delisting as its 1995 petition. Finally, in April, 2004, after reciting all the pertinent information that the Farm Bureau had submitted nearly ten years earlier, FWS issued a preliminary finding on the Farm Bureau's petition to remove the k-rat from the ESA. "We find that the petition presents substantial information and are initiating a status review to determine if delisting this species is warranted."[21] By July of 2007 it had been more than three years since FWS' preliminary finding, yet nothing further has been heard from the Service relative to the delisting of the Stephens' kangaroo rat.

When the Domenigonis disclosed plans to plow their 800-acres of fallowed fields in 1990, the FWS managed to get biologists out to survey for k-rats within a matter of hours. What followed were ill-founded land use regulations for the protection of the k-rat that impacted people's property usage in the extreme. Consider what happens when a legitimate request is made that the FWS take steps to delist a species, one that may have been listed in error to begin with, thereby removing onerous and unnecessary burdens from the backs of affected property owners. In such a case, the FWS can't manage to get the job done in 12 years.

It's no wonder the ESA is so despised by those on the receiving end of its abuse. As for exclusionist organizations, they compound the problem.

Exclusionist Denial

Consider, for example, this statement from the website of Defenders of Wildlife:

> *States-rights proponents, business factions, private-property organizations and lobbyists from natural-resource-user groups are bombarding*

the media with horror stories describing how the rigidity of the Act is robbing people of their right to develop private property. Though many of these anecdotes have achieved mythic proportions, little evidence exists to support them.[22]

In similar style, the National Environmental Trust's website states:

Over the past decade, a coordinated campaign has promoted a variety of misconceptions about the Endangered Species Act ... These falsehoods have been repeated often enough that, to many, they feel like familiar old truths .... Looking closely at most of the rhetoric about the Act, one sees a mix of claims, anecdotes, and bromides .... Looking more closely, one is hard pressed to find independent verification for most of the claims and stories about the law. There is no evidence to suggest, for example, that the brunt of the Endangered Species Act falls primarily on ordinary Americans and the owners of private property or that the Act harms economic growth.[23]

The two passages sound remarkably similar in their effort to minimize and undermine the substantial evidence of the ESA's harsh impact on the property rights, livelihood, and personal safety of ordinary people. This tells Anna Klimko that the loss of her house is anecdotal, and somehow illusory. It tells Paul and Gail Fisher that the government refusal to let them rebuild their destroyed house is simply part of a myth, therefore unworthy of attention. It tells the Domenigoni family that their financial losses are nothing more than a smear campaign of big business, in search of ever-higher profits. It tells the families of firefighters who perished that their losses are essentially worthless. That is to be expected from people who regard human beings, as Greenpeace veteran Patrick Moore noted, as "a cancer on the Earth."[24]

We should note again that such callousness and denial does not proceed from people who live in some pristine state of innocence. Rather, it proceeds from people who own or rent property, who drive automobiles and wear leather shoes and belts, who work in buildings that occupy land formerly inhabited by animals and plants, and who employ every possible modern convenience and consume the energy it takes to operate them. But then, exclusionists are hypocrites of the first order. Juxtapose Al Gore's

An Inconvenient Truth alongside his 10,000-square-foot, 20-room, 8-bath-room home in Nashville.[25]

Exclusionists are remarkably consistent in their opposition to electrical power generation. And although the U.S. demand for electricity will increase by more than 50 percent over the next 25 years, requiring the construction of some 1,200 new power plants producing 300 megawatts each, or 65 new plants every year,[26] with the exception of solar power, which experts predict will take 25 years to become a viable contributor to electrical power generation,[27] exclusionists are opposed to every source of energy utilized in the United States.

For a prime example consider Senator Edward Kennedy, who opposes the nation's first offshore wind farm, the Cape Wind Project, that would supply electricity to Cape Cod, Martha's Vineyard, and Nantucket in his home state of Massachusetts. He has introduced legislation to prohibit the placement of wind turbines within 1.5 nautical miles "of shipping and ferry lanes," a disguise to stop the construction of the 130 windmills that might affect the water view from his family's vacation home.[28]

Such contradictions by exclusionists add hypocrisy to injury, though on one level we should be grateful for the confession. With their well-hewn practice of blaming the victim, exclusionists illustrate the antihuman, anticivilization views that prompted Patrick Moore to leave an extremist movement for more positive concerns. The antipeople view has its origins in the prescientific ethos of fundamentalist pantheism. That ethos underlies and empowers the ESA, and is the primary reason it is "broken," As the adage has it, things broken need to be fixed.

NOTES:

1. "Feds are warned: Retract 'mouse habitat' that bars hurricane victims from rebuilding – or face lawsuit," Pacific Legal Foundation Press Release of July 19, 2007, on the filing of its "60-day notice" informing FWS of its intention to challenge the extended beach mouse critical habitat regulations in federal court. http://www.pacificlegal.org/?mvcTask=pressReleases&id=822

2. According to the FWS Bald Eagle Expenditure Report of July 25, 2007, federal funds expended for eagle recovery between 1989 and 2006 amounted to more than $230 million

3. "President Clinton and Vice President Gore: Celebrating the Return of the American Bald Eagle," The White House At Work, July 2, 1999.

4. *Contoski v. P. Lynn Scarlett, Acting Secretary of the Department of Interior, and FWS.*, Civil No. 05-2528, United States District Court, District of Minnesota; Mr. Contoski was represented by attorneys from the Pacific Legal Foundation.

5. "Minnesota nest could swing bald eagles' status," *Star Tribune* (Minneapolis-St. Paul), October 31, 2006.

6. *Ibid.*

7. Final Rule Removing the Bald Eagle in the Lower 48 States From ESA Listing. 72 *Federal Register* 37346, July 9, 2007.

8. *Home Builders Association of Northern California v U.S. Fish and Wildlife Service and Center for Biological Diversity,* United States District Court, Eastern District of California, CV F 01-5722 AWI SMS; the plaintiffs were represented by attorneys from Pacific Legal Foundation.

9. *HBANC v. FWS and CBD*, Memorandum Opinion Re Plaintiffs' Motion for Summary Judgment and Defendants' Cross Motion for Summary Judgment, May 9, 2003, .p. 51 - 52.

10. *Ibid.*

11. *Morris v. United States*, 392 F.3d 1372, 1374 (Fed. Cir. 2004); he was only able to challenge NOAA Fisheries because of representation by attorneys for Pacific Legal Foundation, who do not charge fees for their services.

12. Final Rule on Listing the Stephens kangaroo rat, 53 *Federal Register* 38465, September 30, 1988.

13.Testimony of Cindy Domenigoni, House Committee on Resources, May 20, 1996.

14. *Ibid.*

15. *Ibid.*

16. *Ibid.*

17. Letter of Richard Zembal, Deputy Field Supervisor, Fish and Wildlife Service, to Cindy Domenigoni, July 1, 1992.

18. Testimony of Cindy Domenigoni, *op. cit.*

19. *Ibid.*

20. 69 *Federal Register, 21567. April 21, 2004.*

21. *Ibid.*

22. Snape and Ferris, "Saving America's Wildlife: Renewing the Endangered Species Act," (2002), http://www.defenders.org/pubs/save02.html

23. National Environmental Trust, "Introduction," *The Assault on the Endangered Species Act*, 2005, p. 1.

24. Moore, "Environmentalism in the 21st Century," *op. cit.*

25. "Gore isn't quite as green as he's led the world to believe," *USA Today*, December 7, 2006, http://www.usatoday.com/news/opinion/editorials/20060809goregreen_x.htm

26. "Cleaner Environment," CARE (Coalition for Affordable and Reliable Energy), http://www.careenergy.com/cleaner_environment/clean-coal technology.asp

27. Bjorn Lomborg, *The Skeptical Environmentalist*, Cambridge University Press, p. 134.

28. "Senator Kennedy says no to windmills in his back yard," *Washington Times*, National Weekly Edition, March 6-12, 2006, p. 1; "Wind Power - Yellow Light For A Green Energy Source," *Christian Science Monitor*, March 2, 2006, p. 15.

HOW TO FIX
A BROKEN ESA

As THESE ACCOUNTS and many others confirm, the Endangered Species Act commits a "taking" on a massive scale. In the hands of government and exclusionist enforcers, the ESA takes away the rights of Americans to the reasonable use of their homes and property, to their right to a livelihood, and even takes away their right to protect their lives from wildfires and floods.

These ESA takings stand at odds with normal human behavior, are incompatible with the Constitution of the United States, and are an abuse of fundamental human rights. Such takings also violate the American philanthropic tradition, which rushes to help those in need rather than denying victims the help they need, or even worse, slapping them with fines and jail time. These ESA takings also are destructive of common sense in achieving the kind of species conservation the vast majority of Americans hold dear and practice in their lives.

The ESA is philosophically flawed, scientifically askew, prodigiously expensive – beyond the point of calculation – harmful to human beings, based on perverse incentives, and a failure at its appointed task of protecting endangered species. Taken together, if this is not a case that the ESA is "broken," as Assistant Interior Secretary Craig Manson said, it is hard to imagine what a broken statute would look like.

Five species recovered in 35 years does not spell success to any but the reactionary and willfully blind. Suppose a federal education program for high-risk students enrolled 1,355 children over the course of 35 years, but had graduated only five, at a cost of tens of billions of dollars?[1] Would it take more than three decades for the media to investigate and expose such a wasteful and ineffective program? Would it take 35 years for members of Congress to pressure the federal education bureaucracy to make the program successful or see it terminated, or for the taxpayers to protest such a boondoggle? Such a dysfunctional program would have been either reformed or eliminated long before. The ESA has avoided reform, and that needs to change. This does not mean, however, that actual protection of species needs to change.

Following the tragic events of September 11, 2001, Congress enacted the U.S.A. Patriot Act, giving the government broad powers to protect national security. Initially, Americans generally accepted it as a necessary tool in detecting foreign terrorists planning to harm our homeland. However, while the overwhelming majority of citizens stood little chance of being targeted for Patriot Act electronic surveillance by the government, once it was reported that the Act's eavesdropping and email message interceptions had been extended to domestic targets, a public backlash began. Concerns that the government was overreaching and intruding on individual privacy were widely heard.

My colleague at the Pacific Legal Foundation, attorney M. Reed Hopper, raised a key question this situation presented. Does the concern for individual privacy mean the American people don't care about national security? "Of course not," Hopper says, "But it does suggest that many, if not most are unwilling to trade their privacy and liberty for a greater degree of safety." As Hopper wisely recognizes, "we live in a world of competing social values and no single value … trumps all other social values." He adds, "The overriding problem with the Endangered Species Act is that it does not balance the goal of species protection with other social values."[2] Instead the ESA pits people against species, urban centers against rural communities, and an axis of exclusionist and government enforcers against property owners. It also contributes heavily to the increasing growth, cost, and wasteful inefficiency of the federal government.

The goal of protecting and preserving endangered species is a worthy one, but the ESA will remain ineffective in achieving that worthy goal so long as landowners fear being penalized tomorrow for accommodating species today. For the ESA to become a successful agent for species preservation, it must in its substance, implementation, and enforcement "[engage] property owners in the effort to protect species." In so doing, says Randy Simmons, "we will also follow [naturalist Aldo] Leopold's admonition that 'conservation will ultimately boil down to rewarding the private landowner who conserves the public interest.'"[3]

Rewarding private landowners is better and more positive than the 35-year approach of punishing them. Policy makers could take a cue from Greenpeace founder Patrick Moore, who after 15 years of negative activism said, "I decided I'd like to be in favor of something for a change."[4]

In the wake of the continuous barrage of lawsuits over the Act, Professor Patrick Parenteau, an ESA expert at the Vermont Law School, said the "real fault" is "with the administration and Congress. They should change ESA requirements if they don't believe them to be truly justified."[5]

This author agrees that the requirements should be changed, and in a positive spirit offers the following recommendations:

(1) The ESA should elevate the status of human beings to a position at least equal with that of the species. The overriding deficiency of the ESA is that, for the most part, it disregards and disrespects humans, which effectively places man in a subsidiary position. With the ESA now 35 years old, Congress needs to update the Act's intent, purpose, and policy statement to recognize at all stages of the species protection, restoration, and preservation process that man's economic and social needs, endeavors, and interests are to be considered and balanced along with the needs of the species.

(2) The ESA should define "species" and "subspecies" in conformity with requirements of the International Code of Zoological Nomenclature, and remove "distinct population segment" from the definition of "species." The ESA's redefining and replacement of the seminal scientific

concept of species with a definition designed to achieve a political objective has rudely thrown the noble goal of conservation into the rough and tumble world of politics and ceaseless controversy. The affixing of the deliberately undefined term "distinct population segment" to the definition of species enables the government to list and set aside critical habitat for arbitrarily and subjectively chosen plants and wildlife with vague local names that have no meaningful connection to biological nomenclature. Thus, of the many so-called species listed under the ESA, relatively few have received any meaningful benefits from the Act – largely the result of the politicization of the term "species."

(3) The ESA should require that private land not be included in a species' "critical habitat" if public lands are sufficient for the conservation of the species.

Even when public lands alone will provide sufficient habitat to conserve a threatened or endangered species, the government designates vast amounts of private property as "critical habitat" – primarily because it has little incentive not to. The Alameda whipsnake is a perfect example. When the whipsnake was listed as a threatened species, the FWS reported that only 20 percent of the snake's known habitat was on private land and that this land was not essential to the conservation of the species. However, when it designated critical habitat, pursuant to court order, the Service included not only occupied habitat but "potential" habitat that did not contain the physical or biological features essential to the conservation of the species. This resulted in the inclusion of 248,270 acres of private land, or 61 percent of the total critical habitat area of 406,598 acres.

The western snowy plover, the California red-legged frog, the California coastal gnatcatcher, and various species of fairy shrimp are other species where overly broad critical habitat was designated on private land. The practice of regulating private property that is not essential to the conservation of the species imposes unfair and unnecessary regulatory burdens on private citizens.

(4) The ESA should provide that where a listed species' critical habitat must extend to private land in order to provide for the conservation of the species, the government shall either secure the species' use of that land through cooperative, voluntary arrangements with the landowner, enter into lease or easement agreements with the landowner and pay reasonable

compensation for the public use of the land, or purchase all or so much of the private land as is needed as critical habitat, with just compensation.

(5) The ESA should require that where protection of a listed species pursuant to the Act interferes with an existing federal contract, *e.g.*, the Klamath Basin farmers in Chapter 12, who sustained major economic losses when the government shut off their contract irrigation water, the government should either compensate the property owners for their economic losses, or find a way to meet its contractual obligation.

(6) The ESA should provide a streamlined "incidental take permit" process, especially for small projects unlikely to have any significant impact on the listed species. The ESA allows the "taking" of a listed species, by permit, if it is merely incidental to, and not for the purpose of, carrying out an otherwise lawful activity. However, the cost of applying for a permit is high and often prohibitive for small landowners. For example, a permit application under Section 10 of the Act requires the applicant to submit a conservation plan. Even the smallest conservation plan can exceed $50,000 in cost. This sum would far exceed the value of many projects that are likely to have no significant impacts on protected species. Consider the family in Humboldt County, California, that owns a small ranch in marbled murrelet territory. The family would like to cut a few trees on its property to augment its modest income. Although the protected birds do not nest in those trees, the family must first obtain an "incidental take permit" from the FWS just in case one were passing through their property and killed by a falling tree. But the cost of the application is beyond the family's means and many times more than the value of the trees.

Thus, the Act places heavy burdens on the regulated community without providing any meaningful protection to listed species. And although the FWS or NOAA Fisheries may provide some relief for small projects through their own regulations or practices, the Act itself makes no distinction between the level of detail required for an insignificant project like laying bricks for a backyard patio or a major project like the development of an entire subdivision. Therefore, the Act should provide a streamlined process, especially for small projects unlikely to have any significant impact on the listed species.

(7) The ESA should define the term "reasonable and prudent alternatives or measures" to mean ones "economically feasible" for the permit

applicant. The ESA currently allows a property owner to "take" a listed species if he takes "reasonable and prudent alternatives or measures" to mitigate the impact of his proposed use. However, because those terms are not defined in the Act, federal agencies often impose "alternatives or measures" not economically feasible for the property owner, thus nullifying his proposed use without rejecting it outright as the ESA requires.

By requiring Robert Morris to purchase other land with shade trees over a stream through which fish passed in order to mitigate for the five trees on his land he wished to cut for timber, NOAA Fisheries imposed an economically unfeasible "alternative" that forced him to abandon the proposed use. As a result of NOAA Fisheries not officially rejecting his proposed use, it also prevented him from gaining "standing" to file a Fifth Amendment "takings" claim. It is unfair to property owners for the government to have it both ways.

(8) The ESA should require the listing of species, and the designation of critical habitat, based only on "substantial" evidence in the administrative record as a whole. The Act currently requires the listing of threatened or endangered species, and the designation of critical habitat, based only on the "best available" scientific evidence. However, both the implementing agencies and the courts have interpreted "best available" to mean any evidence whatsoever. This has resulted in unnecessary listings and overly broad critical habitat designations.

Over the past 35 years, the most common reason for a species to be removed from the ESA-list has been "original data in error." Although each of the species delisted had been originally listed on the basis of the "best available" scientific evidence, that evidence in time was found to be wrong. Likewise, when FWS adopted its final rule designating critical habitat for the Alameda whipsnake the Service admitted it included non-essential habitat in the designation because of a lack of better, but easily obtainable scientific data:

"We recognize that not all parcels within the proposed critical habitat designation will contain the primary constituent elements needed by the whipsnake [which the ESA requires]. Given the short period of time in which we were required to complete this proposed rule, and the lack of fine scale mapping data, we were unable to map critical habitat in sufficient detail to exclude such areas." 65 *Federal Register* at 58,944. Therefore, to avoid data errors that result in unnecessary listings and overly broad critical habitat designations, such determinations should be based only on *substantial* evidence in the record as a whole. A reasonable definition of "substantial evidence in the record as a whole" would require, at a minimum, that the evidence be peer reviewed and include more than merely some evidence that supports the decision. It would, instead, require the agency to take into account whatever in the record fairly detracts from the weight of the evidence including any contradictory evidence or evidence from which conflicting inferences could be drawn.

(9) The ESA should require specific findings that areas designated as critical habitat are "essential" – that is, absolutely necessary – for the conservation of the species. The Act defines "critical habitat" to include *only* those areas actually occupied by the species that are *essential* to the conservation of the species as well as those areas that are unoccupied by the species, at the time of listing, that the Secretary determines are *essential* for the conservation of the species. However, the FWS and the NOAA Fisheries have virtually never made such a finding. Rather, they tend to rely on the species' historical range and routinely include potential or merely possible habitat areas in the critical habitat designation. In effect, they take the term "essential" to mean nothing more than "desirable," as was demonstrated in the designations for the Alameda whipsnake, the California red-legged frog, the California coastal gnatcatcher, and the various populations of Pacific salmon. This failure of the agencies to follow the statutory criteria undermines the intent of the Act to limit the scope of critical habitat, and imposes unnecessary burdens on the regulated community. Therefore, the Act should require specific findings that areas designated as critical habitat are "essential," that is, absolutely necessary, for the conservation of the species.

(10) The ESA should require the designation of critical habitat only after a recovery plan has been developed. As is, the ESA creates a dilemma for federal regulators and an unnecessary problem for landowners. Although the government is supposed to designate critical habitat at the time of listing a species as threatened or endangered, the problem is that at the time of listing, the government has not yet ascertained what is necessary or essential for its recovery. Further, creation of a "recovery plan" requires extensive and time-consuming research – research that is

not available at the time of listing. To "hedge its bets," the government invariably overstates critical habitat to include not only "essential," but also "potential" or even "possible" habitat. This subjects an undue amount of private land to federal control prematurely and is contrary to the intent of Congress. Therefore, the ESA should require the designation of critical habitat only after a recovery plan has been developed.

(11) The ESA should require formal, independent "peer review" of scientific and economic information regarding a species, and the result of such review should be made a part of the public record. In the case of the 2001 Klamath Basin irrigation water shutoff described in Chapter 12, the Biological Opinion which FWS accepted without peer review was subsequently found faulty by an independent panel of scientists, but not until after 1,400 farm families suffered enormous economic losses as a result of the Biological Opinions' flawed findings.

(12) The ESA should define "adverse modification" to include only those changes to a species' critical habitat that are likely to result in actual, imminent harm to the species. The designation of critical habitat has major repercussions for private landowners, the states, and the nation. By way of example, critical habitat has been designated for only 10 percent of California's more than 290 federally listed threatened and endangered species, but that 10 percent habitat designation includes nearly 40 percent of the area of the State. By the time critical habitat is designated for all these species, the State of California will have been blanketed many times over. Critical habitat for a single species, such as the California red-legged frog, have included millions of acres.

Under Section 7 of the ESA, federal agencies must ensure that any activities they authorize, fund, or carry out are not likely to "result in the destruction or adverse modification" of critical habitat. The term "adverse modification" is not defined by the Act and subject to varying interpretations. Although federal regulations require such modification to be "substantial," even small changes have been successfully challenged by preservationist litigants. As a result, the use of land, public or private, that is designated critical habitat can be severely limited, or prohibited altogether without affording significant protections to listed species.

Congress tried to avoid the onerous impacts of critical habitat when it amended the ESA in 1978 by limiting the scope of the designation to "essential" habitat areas. However, federal regulators continue to designate overbroad critical habitat areas while exclusionist litigants argue that "adverse modification" should preclude even minor changes to the land. Therefore, the ESA should define "adverse modification" to include only those changes which are likely to result in actual, imminent harm to a listed species.

(13) The ESA should require that the economic impact analysis currently employed as part of the designation of critical habitat be employed as well with the listing of the species. Although under the ESA the designation of critical habitat is based on a balancing between the best scientific data available and its economic impact on people's land use in the area, the listing of the species is based solely on the best scientific data available. Thus, the listing process contains no balancing between the science that supports the listing and the economic impact on people's use of their land. The only means of achieving balance between the conservation of the species and people's use of their land is to extend to the listing process the same economic impact analysis now required prior to critical habitat designation.

(14) The ESA should define "harm" to require proof that an activity will actually kill or injure a listed species. Section 9 of the ESA prohibits the "taking" of any endangered or threatened species. 16 U.S.C. § 1538(a)(1)(B). However, the Act allows such "taking," when authorized, if such taking is incidental to, and not the purpose of, carrying out an otherwise lawful activity. *See* 16 U.S.C. § 1539(a)(1)(B). The term "take" means to "harass, harm, pursue, hunt, shoot, wound, kill, trap, capture, or collect, or to attempt to engage in any such conduct." 16 U.S.C. § 1532(19).

The term "harm" was interpreted by regulation to mean: an act which *actually* kills or injures wildlife, and may include significant habitat modification or degradation where it *actually* kills or injures wildlife by significantly impairing essential behavioral patterns, including breeding, feeding, or sheltering. 50 C.F.R. § 17.3 (emphasis added). This interpretation was upheld by the U.S. Supreme Court in *Babbitt v. Sweet Home Chapter of Communities for a Great Oregon*, 515 U.S. 687 (1995.)

However, the FWS ignores the requirement of *actual* injury in its day-to-day implementation of the Act. For example, in *Arizona Cattle Growers Association v. U.S. Fish and Wildlife Service*, 273 F.3d 1229 (9th Cir Dec 2001), the Service argued that it could prohibit grazing on federal land without any proof of harm to any species. Although this argument was rejected by the Court, the Service has not embraced the court decision. Therefore, the Act should define "harm" to require proof that an activity actually will kill or injure a listed species.

(15) The ESA should provide that in crisis or emergency situations that reasonably pose a threat to human life, health, or safety, such as impending wildfires, hurricanes, floods, and other disasters, the "take" of endangered or threatened species by private or government actions to prevent, prepare for, diminish, defend against, or respond to such events shall not be deemed a violation of the ESA, as a matter of law.

Such reforms are reasonable, practical, and will require little or nothing in the way of new costs. Indeed, they are likely to both save money and help the public hold the government accountable. More important, these reforms will in no way impede the ability of officials to protect species and conserve plants and wildlife, a worthy goal supported by this author and most Americans.

These long overdue reforms simply recognize that government policy based on flawed principles and bad science endangers the rights of human beings. These reforms will enable policy makers to "restore" those rights and maintain a reasonable balance between conservation and human progress.

NOTES:

1. This analogy, but with 1998 data, was originally offered by H. Sterling Burnett. Ph.D., of the National Center for Policy Analysis, in the Center's *Brief Analysis* No. 276, "The Endangered Species Act: First Step toward Fixing a Costly Failure," August 6, 1998, http://www.ncpa.org/ba/ba276.html

2. M. Reed Hopper, "Habitat Conservation and Property Rights: Irreconcilable Differences or Just Growing Pains?" *ABA Trends* (a publication of the American Bar Association), May/June 2007.

3. Randy T. Simmons, "Nature Undisturbed - The Myth Behind the Endangered Species Act," *PERC Reports*, Property and Environmental Research Center, March 2005, Vol. 23, No. 1, p. 5; citing Aldo Leopold, *The River of the Mother of God and Other Essays*, ed. Susan L Flader and J. Baird Callicott. Madison: University of Wisconsin Press, 1991, p. 201.

4. Moore, "Environmentalism in the 21st Century." *op. cit.*

5. Mark Clayton, "Politics Undercut Species Act, Suit says," *Christian Science Monitor*, November 20, 2007, http://www.csmonitor.com/2007/1120/p03s01-usgn.htm

About the Author

Dave Stirling joined Pacific Legal Foundation as Vice President in 1999, following two decades of public service in California state government. After 10 years of private law practice in Southern California, Mr. Stirling was elected to the California State Assembly for three terms. After choosing not to seek a fourth term, Governor George Deukmejian appointed him as General Counsel of the state's controversial Agricultural Labor Relations Board, where, after six contentious years, he succeeded in changing a blatantly biased, yet taxpayer funded, public agency into one that was more fair and balanced in the performance of its neutral responsibilities within California's vital agricultural industry.

He was appointed by the Governor to a judgeship on the Sacramento County Superior Court, where he handled the most difficult and emotional cases involving family law matters. Judge Stirling resigned from the bench in 1990, to serve as Chief Deputy Attorney General.

In this capacity, he functioned as second-in-command to the Attorney General at the California Department of Justice, the second largest civil and criminal justice agency in the country after the U.S. Department of Justice. Among other responsibilities, Chief Deputy Stirling provided general oversight supervision for the Department's 4,500 employees, including 1,000 deputy attorneys general handling an ongoing civil and criminal justice caseload of some 55,000 court cases and 6,000 administrative proceedings. He served eight years in this capacity.

Mr. Stirling was the Republican candidate for state Attorney General in the November, 1998, general election.

Mr. Stirling is a sought-after speaker on behalf of the Foundation, and a prolific writer, with articles published in newspapers, online publications, and magazines around the country. He was a Visiting Fellow at the Hoover Institution at Stanford University during the research and early writing of this book. He is a graduate of Principia College and received his Juris Doctor degree from the Tulane University Law School. He and his wife and daughter reside in the Sacramento River Delta community of Walnut Grove, California. Mr. Stirling also has two adult sons.